Pre-Columbian Art of Mexico and Central America

LIFT COLORPLATE

Pre-Columbian Art of Mexico and Central America

Text and notes by *HASSO VON WINNING*

Selection of plates by *ALFRED STENDAHL*

HARRY N. ABRAMS, INC. *Publishers* NEW YORK

Library of Congress Catalog Card Number: 68-13065

All rights reserved. No part of the contents of this book may be

reproduced without the written permission of the publishers

Harry N. Abrams, Incorporated, New York

Printed and bound in Japan

Contents

List of Maps

vii

PERIODS		Date	CENTRAL MEXICO (GREATER VALLEY OF MEXICO)	HUASTECA	WESTERN MEXICO	CENTRAL VERACRUZ AND TABASCO
POSTCLASSIC	LATE	1500	*Conquest*			
		1400	AZTEC III–IV	*Aztec Empire*	*Tarascan Empire*	
		1300	CHALCO			
		1200	TEXCOCO	PÁNUCO		
	EARLY	1100	AZTEC II			
		1000	TULA–MAZAPAN (AZTEC I)		TARASCAN	
		900		LAS FLORES		TAJÍN III
CLASSIC	LATE	800	COYOTLATELCO			
		700	TEOTIHUACÁN IV			
		600				YOKES PALMAS HACHAS
	EARLY	500	TEOTIHUACÁN III			NOPILOA
		400				UPPER REMOJADAS II
		300				
FORMATIVE	TERMINAL	200	TEOTIHUACÁN II (MICCAOTLI)			
		100	TEOTIHUACÁN I (TZACUALLI)			
		A.D. 0 B.C.				TAJÍN I
	LATE	100	PROTO-TEOTIHUACÁN		LATE CHUPÍCUARO	
		200			Morrett Site	UPPER REMOJADAS I
		300				
		400	CUICUILCO–TICOMAN		EARLY CHUPÍCUARO	LOWER REMOJADAS
		500				
	MIDDLE	600	TLAPACOYA			
		700				
		800	TLATILCO (OLMEC)			LA VENTA (OLMEC)
		900				
		1000				
		1100				
		1200				
	EARLY	1300				
		1400	EARLY TLATILCO	PAVON		EARLY LA VENTA
		1500	EARLY ZACATENCO EL ARBOLILLO I			
		1600				
		1700				
INCIPIENT AGRICULTURAL		1800				
		1900				
		2000				
		3000				
		4000				
		5000				
PALEO-INDIAN		6000				
		7000				
		8000				
		9000				
		10,000				

(Vertical labels in WESTERN MEXICO column: COLIMA–NAYARIT–JALISCO EFFIGIES; MEZCALA)

Left Table

OAXACA	MAYA LOWLANDS	
	YUCATAN CAMPECHE	SOUTH (PETEN)
MONTE ALBÁN V (MIXTEC)	*Mexican Absorption*	
	MAYAPÁN	
MONTE ALBÁN IV	TOLTEC	*Petén abandoned*
	JAINA	
MONTE ALBÁN III-B		TEPEU
MONTE ALBÁN III-A	EARLY PERIOD	TZAKOL
MONTE ALBÁN II		
		CHICANEL
MONTE ALBÁN I (OLMEC)		
		MAMOM

Adapted from G. R. Willey, R. Piña Chan, I. Bernal, and others.

Right Table

PERIODS		LOWER CENTRAL AMERICA	
		COSTA RICA	PANAMA
1500			PLAIN RED AND UNPAINTED ALLIGATOR WARE ("CLASSIC" CHIRIQUÍ)
1400	PERIOD VI	LATE POLYCHROME (LUNA WARE)	
1300			
1200			
1100			LATE COCLÉ
1000			
900		MIDDLE POLYCHROME (NICOYA POLYCHROME)	TRANSITIONAL COCLÉ
800			
700	PERIOD V		EARLY COCLÉ
600		EARLY POLYCHROME	
500			
400	PERIOD IV		DEVELOPMENTAL POLYCHROME
300			
200			
100			
A.D. 0	PERIOD III		
B.C. 100			
200			
300			
400			
500	PERIOD I–II		
600			
700			
800			
900			
1000			
1100			
1200			
1300			
1400			
1500			

Publisher's Preface

THE IDEA FOR THIS PUBLICATION originated in the monumental exhibition of Pre-Columbian art which Earl Stendahl was asked to organize in 1956. Opening in the Haus der Kunst, Munich, in 1958, it traveled to other major European cities for more than three years, and was a significant factor in the upsurge of interest, among both scholars and the public, in ancient Mexican and Central American art.

The material was borrowed from museums and private collectors in Europe and the United States, as well as from Mr. Stendahl's own collection, and provided a synopsis ranging from the middle of the first millennium B.C. to the Spanish Conquest in A.D. 1521. Since that time the selection has been substantially expanded and edited. South America was excluded from both the exhibition and the book, thus allowing more comprehensive coverage of the regions treated. The sculptural art of Western Mexico and Veracruz, which comprises a wide variety of ceramic figures, has been given particular emphasis, since comparatively few publications adequately cover this field.

The compilation and organization of the material in this book was placed in the hands of Alfred Stendahl, who is also responsible for most of the photography. Hasso von Winning, a specialist in Mexican archaeology and associate of the Southwest Museum in Los Angeles, has summarized the history and culture of the regions and civilizations involved, and has prepared the charts, maps, and documentation.

Most of the pieces have not been previously published, but a number have been commented upon in widely dispersed monographs and illustrated in museum catalogues and other scholarly publications. The author provides such information in his notes.

In the descriptions of the individual pieces, special emphasis has been placed on those characteristics that are particularly noteworthy but that may not be immediately apparent, thus guiding the viewer to a deeper understanding.

This volume is dedicated to the memory of Earl Stendahl (1888–1966), who by his zest for adventure, both in the pusuit of knowledge and the object of art itself, gave so much impetus to the appreciation of this ancient American art.

The publishers wish to thank the many collectors and lending institutions for their co-operation, and Dr. Thomas S. Barthel for valuable advice; Dr. Gordon F. Ekholm for reading the text and making valuable suggestions; Dr. Tatiana Proskouriakoff for information regarding a large Maya sculpture; Dr. Linton Satterthwaite for the dating of Maya stone carvings; and Dr. J. Eric S. Thompson for his interpretation of glyphic inscriptions on Maya stone carvings.

Introduction

THE ARTISTIC MANIFESTATIONS which accompanied the cultural evolution of Mexico and Central America during the long time span between the middle of the second millennium B.C. and the Spanish Conquest in 1521 should be appreciated not solely in terms of our own art ideals, but with consideration for the religious motifs embodied, for from the early beginnings religion pervaded practically every aspect of daily life of the individual, the village, and the state. Pre-Columbian art was therefore primarily inspired by religious thoughts and practices. The great splendor of the colorful temple compounds, the monumental stone carvings, the delicate ceremonial pottery vessels and finely modeled clay figurines, and particularly the intricate symbolism in ornamentation and hieroglyphics, convey to us the prolific endeavors of the ancient inhabitants to propitiate the gods, the purveyors of daily sustenance, whose power could destroy as well as create. The dependence on rain for the growing of maize, the basic staple on which the New World civilizations thrived, was one of the greatest concerns, evident in the very early emergence of a rain-god, accompanied later by a growing number of fertility-gods.

The religious mainspring in sculptural and pictorial art accounts for much that is symbolic and abstract in Pre-Columbian art. Thus certain forms of ornamentation seem to us obscure or meaningless when the relationship with the religious context is not easily recognizable. Yet to the ancient craftsman every detail had a function, and, though he—or she, if they were ceramists—certainly did not lack creative ability, he was bound by tradition to adhere rather closely to time-honored canons. Stylistic patterns and shapes therefore changed but slowly within geographical regions. New art styles introduced by trade or, perhaps, by traveling artists, sometimes over considerable distances, were accepted selectively unless imposed by invading forces, and even then they were blended into existing patterns.

EARLY HUNTERS
AND THE BEGINNINGS OF AGRICULTURE

The physiographic configuration of Mexico and Central America, which includes vast mountain chains, highland plateaus, lowlands with dense tropical forests, and swampy as well as semiarid regions, greatly influenced the cultural development. Toward the end of the Pleistocene period (about 7000 B.C.), climatic changes caused the drying up of extensive grasslands, bringing about the extinction of abundant herds of elephants, mastodons, and other large fauna. Consequently, the widely scattered hunters, who in small groups had ranged over the continents pursuing these animals, were forced to rely more on other means of subsistence, such as collecting wild food plants and trapping small animals. Evidence of successful adaptation to this mode of life has recently been discovered in caves in northeastern Mexico (Tamaulipas) and in the south-central highlands (the Valley of Tehuacán), where organic remains, including wild corn, are remarkably well preserved. By a fortunate combination of circumstances the early gardeners of the Tehuacán valley succeeded, between 5000 and 4000 B.C., in domesticating corn, which gradually spread over most of North and South America. Other food plants, particularly pumpkin, squash, beans, and chili peppers, were domesticated for the first time in one or the other of these regions, with considerable time intervals. The millenniums during which agriculture emerged in the various regions and gradually took hold over the entire Mesoamerican area is known as the Archaic stage (7000–1700 B.C.). It was an era of very slow but steady population growth and of very slow cultural advance.

THE MESOAMERICAN CULTURAL AREA

An understanding of the cultural development that took place during so many centuries in a territory of such huge dimensions, which embraces most of Mexico and much of Central America, is not possible without the aid of convenient spatial and temporal divisions.

In the north of Mexico semiarid conditions were not conducive to sedentary agricultural village life, and up to the sixteenth century after Christ the area, known as the Gran Chichimeca, was inhabited by nomadic gatherers and hunters. The boundary which at that time delimited the sharply contrasting high cultures to the south followed approximately the courses of the Pánuco, Lerma, and Sinaloa rivers. The southern limit of these high cultures can be drawn from the mouth of the Motagua River along Lake Nicaragua to the Gulf of Nicoya. The land within these borders, which shifted somewhat during the preceding stages, has been defined as Mesoamerica by Kirchhoff. In this vast culture area different ethnic groups on various rather advanced culture levels share certain significant traits which are not found among the peoples outside the area.

Inside Mesoamerica seven separate subareas are recognized, each distinguished by various cultural patterns and by their particular art styles. The boundaries of these subareas are defined in broad terms only. The first subarea, the northern highland region, was a frontier land that witnessed frequent invasions by nomadic tribes. On the Pacific coast, the cultures of western Mexico (Nayarit, Colima, and Jalisco) pertain fully to Mesoamerica only after the onset of the Classic period, when the border expanded northward to include the coastal region as far north as Guasave in Sinaloa. A third subarea is the central highland harboring the greater Valley of Mexico. The Gulf coast subarea includes the states of Veracruz and Tabasco. To the south, Oaxaca and parts of Chiapas make up a fifth subarea. Finally, the lowland Maya and the highland Maya subareas include the Yucatan Peninsula, most of Chiapas, Guatemala, British Honduras, western Honduras, and El Salvador.

In addition to this geographical subdivision it is necessary to divide the archaeological history of Mesoamerica into time blocks, each of which characterizes a temporal continuity of particular cultural traits. For the Mesoamerican area the following sequence is generally recognized: the Formative period, with three subdivisions (Early, Middle, and Late), from 1700 B.C. to A.D. 300 (lately the time span between A.D. 150 and 300 has been recognized by some students as a Terminal Formative phase); the Classic period, divided into Early and Late, from 100 B.C. to A.D. 900; and the Postclassic period, divided into Early and Late or Historic, from A.D. 900 to the Spanish Conquest in 1521. It should be borne in mind that the duration of these broad time units is not uniform throughout all of the various subareas.

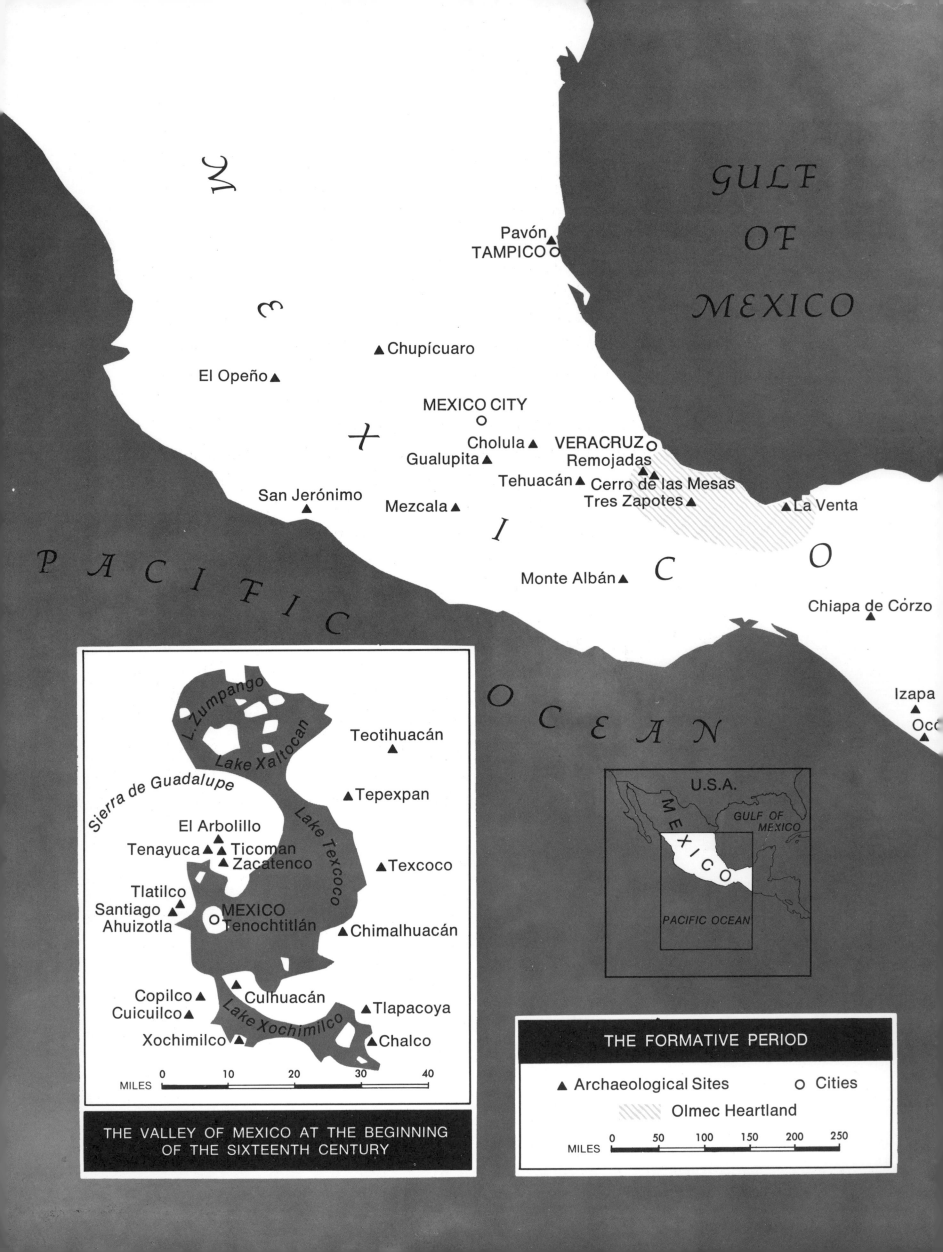

GULF
OF
MEXICO

Pavón ▲
TAMPICO ○

▲ Chupícuaro

El Opeño ▲

MEXICO CITY
○

Cholula ▲   VERACRUZ ○
Gualupita ▲   Remojadas
Tehuacán ▲ Cerro de las Mesas
San Jerónimo ▲   Tres Zapotes ▲   ▲ La Venta
Mezcala ▲

Monte Albán ▲

Chiapa de Córzo ▲

PACIFIC   OCEAN

Izapa ▲
Oco ▲

THE VALLEY OF MEXICO AT THE BEGINNING OF THE SIXTEENTH CENTURY

L. Zumpango
Lake Xaltocan
Teotihuacán ▲

Sierra de Guadalupe

▲ Tepexpan

El Arbolillo ▲
Tenayuca ▲ ▲ Ticoman
▲ Zacatenco
Lake Texcoco

▲ Texcoco

Tlatilco ▲
Santiago ▲
Ahuizotla
MEXICO ○
Tenochtitlán
▲ Chimalhuacán

Copilco ▲   Culhuacán ▲
Cuicuilco ▲   Lake Xochimilco   ▲ Tlapacoya
Xochimilco ▲   ▲ Chalco

MILES 0   10   20   30   40

U.S.A.
MEXICO
GULF OF
MEXICO
MEXICO
PACIFIC OCEAN

THE FORMATIVE PERIOD

▲ Archaeological Sites   ○ Cities
Olmec Heartland

MILES 0   50   100   150   200   250

I

THE FORMATIVE PERIOD

IN MEXICO

The Formative Period in Mexico

EARLY FORMATIVE

ONCE AGRICULTURE BECAME GENERALLY ESTABLISHED and man had better control over his food supply, great cultural changes took place, beginning about 1700 B.C. In the Valley of Mexico the farmers were settled in little hamlets on the shores of the lakes, where they planted corn, beans, and squash, and supplemented their diet by fishing and hunting. Their technology was simple but adequate, and changed little during the following five centuries. Stone artifacts included mortars and pestles for crushing seeds, metates (stone slabs) for grinding corn, and stone scrapers. Bone awls were used for working skins into garments. Projectile points shaped like laurel leaves were used for hunting. The round-bottomed domestic pottery, for cooking and storage, was mainly plain or burnished red. Decorated pottery, with incised lines forming geometric patterns, was also made.

Small clay figurines were made in large numbers, depicting women to the almost entire exclusion of males, which seems to suggest a fertility cult based on the mother earth concept. The earliest ceramics are technically perfect, and it is indeed puzzling to see the emergence of a full-blown ceramic technology without any apparent antecedents. The question whether the manufacture of pottery was invented in the Americas or introduced from Asia remains unsolved, although the evidence for transpacific sources is impressive. Distinctive vessel shapes and methods of decoration occur in coastal Ecuador as early as 3000 B.C., and show striking similarities with contemporaneous Jōmon pottery of southern Japan.

In the New World the manufacture of pottery appears to have taken place earlier in South America than in Mesoamerica. Recent discoveries in the Tehuacán valley (Mexico) include an evolutionary series of stone vessels which, in time, were confined to three vessel forms that are identical with the earliest ceramic forms in Mesoamerica. The possibility has been suggested that these stone vessels were occasionally paralleled by clay bowls and that eventually the latter took the place of the stone vessels completely. At any rate, the development of ceramics must have been a long process of trial and error until technical perfection was achieved, and was probably not confined to one region in particular.

The Early Formative stage development is not restricted to the Valley of Mexico, with its type sites at El Arbolillo, Zacatenco, and Tlatilco, but is also well documented on the Gulf coast (La Venta, Pavon), in the Chiapas highlands (Chiapa de Corzo), in the Guatemala highlands (Kaminaljuyú), and on the Pacific coast (Ocós, on the Chiapas-Guatemala border). The wide dispersion of these sites, which nevertheless are linked by similar general technological and aesthetic qualities, suggests that the Early Formative cultures were spread evenly over the entire Mesoamerican area.

MIDDLE FORMATIVE

The fairly uniform development in Mexico and Central America became diversified during the following stages. Toward the end of the second millennium before Christ a steady increase in population gave rise to numerous new settlements. In the Valley of Mexico, in addition to the earlier sites, Xalostoc and Tlapacoyan were expanded to the size of villages. Subsistence depended not only on corn, beans, and squash, but also on intensive hunting, which is suggested by pottery effigies of ducks, fish, and turtles.

The sudden increase in villages in the Valley and elsewhere is attributed to the successful development of new and better varieties of maize, resulting in a more plentiful food supply. The improved highland varieties were probably diffused into the southern Veracruz lowlands, where they thrived in the alluvial soils, benefiting from a longer growing season than is possible in the highlands (M. D. Coe, 1963, p. 32). Subsequently, the utilization of the abundant food sources gave rise to the first civilization of Mesoamerica, the Olmec, between 1000 and 200 B.C.—probably beginning somewhat earlier and reaching a florescence at La Venta about 800 to 400 B.C. That Olmec influences reached the central highlands early in the Middle Formative period is demonstrated at Tlatilco, a center known for its burial complex, which since the 1940's has yielded exceptionally well-made figurines and pottery vessels in considerable quantities.

When Olmec invaders settled in Tlatilco and dominated the long-established native population, which had not progressed beyond the Zacatenco rural stage, they brought with them a host of traditions so far unknown in the Valley of Mexico. Tlatilco is situated in the western part of the Valley and its archaeological deposits correspond to the Early and Middle Formative periods. The Early Formative ceramics are similar to those of other contemporaneous sites. With the incursion of peoples from the Olmec group of the Gulf coast, new decorative techniques such as rocker stamping, excising, and zoned or paneled ornamentation were introduced. The early figurines give way to figures with oblique eyes and complicated hair arrangements, the so-called "pretty lady" type (Vaillant's Types D-1 and D-2; Vaillant, 1962, p. 40).

The numerous innovations ascribed to the Olmec had a momentous impact on future developments of Mesoamerican culture as a whole. The Olmec, therefore, justifiably have been considered the bearers of a mother culture from which stem the inspirations that during the Classic period led to an unsurpassed flowering. In the Early Formative period the farmers and hunters, like most primitive peoples, adorned themselves by painting their faces and bodies, but they wore no clothes except for turbans and sandals. During the Middle Formative period, trade with the Gulf coast and southern regions supplied the peoples of the Valley with cotton, supplementing the fibers from the yucca and maguey plants which were used chiefly for cordage and netting. The figurines show that women dressed in skirts, wore mantles, and, quite naturally, continued to paint their faces with red and yellow pigments. Male figurines began to be added to the formerly exclusive female group, a trait attributed to Olmec incursions. Represented are acrobats, ballplayers with one hand gloved, dwarfs, bearded men, and individuals whose garments, masks, and hats seem to distinguish them as sorcerers, probably the forerunners of a priestly class.

Increased dependence on agriculture, linked with the threat of adverse natural phenomena such as droughts and floods, necessitated the function of intermediaries between man and the supernatural. The significance and purpose of these figurines have been the subject of much speculation. They were kept in the huts and accompanied the dead in their graves. Very likely they were images of deified supernatural forces, which were given human form and hence human dress and ornaments.

In this period belong also the first recognizable representations of gods. Jaguarlike motifs, consisting of claws, jaguar mouths with prominent fangs, and broad noses, occur on pottery and figurines of clay and stone and are the hallmark of Olmec art. These characteristics stress the tropical origin of the Olmec, who worshiped a feline deity connected with rain or water, which later developed into the cult of the rain-god Tlaloc.

Irrigation and terracing, the latter for better use of the moisture in the soil, supported a large population in the Valley of Mexico during the Late Formative period (300 B.C. to A.D. 300). Many new villages were founded.

Political power was now probably consolidated in one chief with priestly functions. At Cerro del Tepalcate the oldest temple mound, so far as we know, was erected, made of adobe and crudely cut stone, which supported a temple built of wattle and daub, with a red-painted floor. This temple was destroyed and rebuilt at various intervals, with the platform enlarged at every building stage. At Cuicuilco an oval-shaped structure with terraced platforms was erected, faced by two ramps that gave access to the altars on top, built of rough unworked stone. It was later partially buried under the lava flow from the eruption of the Xitle volcano. This phenomenon caused a large part of the population to migrate to the southeastern part of the basin, where it concentrated in the Teotihuacán area.

Although the Late Formative period evidenced a specialization of trades and the emergence of a priestly class, it nevertheless reflected a cultural impoverishment brought about by a new social order. The artistic refinement noticeable in the earlier Olmec pottery is no longer prevalent. New styles and decorative patterns emerge, with predominantly polychrome and negative-painted wares. Some of these, as well as figurine types, were introduced from Chupícuaro (Guanajuato), which had attained a higher level of culture than that of the Valley of Mexico.

The abundant grave furniture from Chupícuaro, a site no longer open to archaeological research since its flooding by an artificial lake in 1950, has been described and classified by Muriel Porter (1956). Characteristic are the small flat figurines with eyes, nose, hair, and jewelry modeled by filleting and incising. In the Early Phase eyes are slanted and noses long, and the figurines resemble a type well known in the Valley of Mexico and ascribed to the Ticoman Phase (Vaillant's Type H-4). Because of their great abundance in Chupícuaro it seems likely that they originated there.

Figures of larger size occur less frequently. They are hollow and are decorated in geometric patterns in red, black, and buff, with a lustrous surface. Eyes are usually diamond-shaped, and a groove on top of the head indicates that the hair is parted in the center, as is also customary in the small figurines.

The pottery of Chupícuaro is equally attractive and is either black to brown or painted in red and white on buff, with very long "spider leg" or mammiform supports.

Indications are that Chupícuaro developed an elaborate burial cult with a ceramic style of its own, and maintained exterior relations chiefly with the Valley of Mexico, but also with the west coast area. The Early Chupícuaro Phase, which is contemporary with Middle to Late Formative Ticoman, merged without abrupt changes into a Late Chupícuaro Phase terminating with the onset of the Classic period.

A yardstick for the artistic achievements during the three Formative periods can be seen in the quality of the grave offerings. In the Early Formative the dead were buried with only a few pieces of utilitarian pottery and some, often fragmented, figurines. In the Middle Formative, offerings consisted of fine kaolin pottery, bottle-shaped jars, effigy bowls, masks of clay, hematite mirrors, elaborate figurines, and pectorals of shell imported from the Gulf coast. In the Late Formative, shell artifacts persisted and polychrome pottery was added, but figurines show less refinement.

In broad terms, the development during the Formative evidences little stylistic differentiation, although there existed regional variations within a broad, basically uniform pattern. Toward the end of this era the Maya area and the rest of Mexico began to assume characteristics of their own and developed clearly differentiated art styles.

Olmec Civilization

Since the La Venta Olmec were the originators of the first major ceremonial center and of the first great art style, it has been suggested that civilization in Mesoamerica originated in the lowlands, where milpa agriculture (small plots cleared and farmed) was practiced in association with an elaborate rain and fertility cult. Another school of thought favors the semiarid highlands as the center of development, exemplified by Teotihuacán as the first and largest true city of Mesoamerica. A strong case is made for the effectiveness of irrigation agriculture at Teotihuacán as the only means to support its large concentrated population, estimated in the tens of thousands. Moreover, the earliest development of maize cultivation at Tehuacán favors the highlands as the center of origin of village agriculture.

As a plausible compromise of both viewpoints, it has recently been suggested that between 900 and 200 B.C. Mesoamerica pursued its development along two distinct lines. In the lowlands, under milpa or slash-and-burn (jungle cleared for a season) agriculture, ceremonial centers evolved under a priestly hierarchy. In the highlands, on the other hand, irrigation agriculture gave rise to secular cities like Teotihuacán and the settlements in the Tehuacán valley, among others.

The heartland of Olmec civilization is located on the alluvial plains of the southern coast of Veracruz, and over the border into Tabasco. There the most important ceremonial center, La Venta in Tabasco, was built on an island surrounded by mangrove swamps, featuring temple mounds of earth and large stone sculptures, some with hieroglyphic inscriptions. It was a large, carefully planned center, which must have been under the control of a powerful group of priest-rulers. The weight of some of the colossal heads is estimated at up to twenty tons; no stone is available in the vicinity of La Venta, so the material had to be brought to the site by water transport, probably from the volcanic Tuxtla mountains some fifty air miles to the west. Since agricultural methods of the period would support only a very limited population residing at the site, it has been estimated that the very considerable labor force required to transport and erect the heavy monuments and build the earth structures was recruited from the area westward, between the Tonalá and Coatzacoalcos rivers. La Venta was not a market center but the seat of a priestly hierarchy dedicated to the worship of fertility-gods.

The characteristics of Olmec sculpture are best summarized by Covarrubias, one of the foremost students and collectors of Olmec art. The small sculptures, usually made of jadeite, serpentine, or other hard stone, depict plump or very slender men, rarely women, with short noses and perforated septa. Necks are often thick. The lower part of the faces is broad, with heavy jowls and thick chins. Eyes are clearly Mongoloid, sometimes almond-shaped or merely narrow slits between heavy eyelids. A hallmark is the large trapezoid mouth, known as the "Olmec" or jaguar mouth, with corners drawn downward and a thick flaring upper lip suggesting the fierce expression of a snarling jaguar. Arms and legs are short and well made, with small hands and feet. The figures are usually naked and sexless, or clad in a simple loincloth or short skirt. Olmec-style figures are recognizable by their strong feline appearance combined with infantile faces, a mixture of jaguar and baby features (Covarrubias, p. 56).

The Olmec developed ingenious techniques for the carving not only of colossal sculptures but of small figurines of semiprecious hard stone, using mostly serpentine and jadeite. Aside from jaguarlike figures, they portrayed human beings with large, heavy-jawed faces and slightly slanted eyes set between heavy eyelids. Diagnostic is a large trapezoid mouth with thick, curving lips, sometimes showing broad teeth, and a V-shaped incision in the forehead. The occurrence of these traits outside the heartland of southern Veracruz—at Tlatilco, in many parts of Guerrero, Morelos, and to the southeast as far as El Salvador—underscores the vigor with which the Olmec disseminated their religious ideals into distant areas.

The Formative Period in Mexico

Captions and Notes

PLATES 1–56

1. GROUP OF FIVE FEMALE FIGURINES. / Tlatilco, Mexico D.F. Middle Formative period. Solid buff clay with traces of red, cream, and yellow paint. Height, 3 1/2 to 6 1/2″. Collection Mr. and Mrs. Vincent Price, Los Angeles.

    The various hair arrangements, headdresses, and skirts are of ethnographic significance. The figures to left and right on the bottom row are probably dancers. The figure between them has a design incised on one leg.

2. WOMAN. / Tlatilco, Mexico D.F. Middle Formative period. Type D–2. Solid buff clay with red and cream paint. Height, 5 1/2″. Private collection.

3. WOMAN. / Tlatilco, Mexico D.F. Middle Formative period. Solid brown clay. Height, 2 1/4″. Collection Stendahl.

    The headdress and tasseled hair arrangement are Olmec traits. The modeling of arms and hands is typical for western Mexico figures.

4. WOMAN. / Tlatilco, Mexico D.F. Middle Formative period. Type D–2. Solid buff clay with red and cream paint. Height, 4 1/2″. Collection Jay C. Leff, Uniontown, Penn.

    Pantaloons suggest that the figure is a dancer.

5/6. WOMAN WITH TWIN HEADS SHOWING THREE EYES. / Tlatilco, Mexico D.F. Middle Formative period. Solid buff clay with red, white, and yellow paint. Height, 3 1/4″. Collection Proctor Stafford, Los Angeles.

7. WOMAN. / Tlatilco, Mexico D.F. Middle to Late Formative period. Burnished red on buff clay. Height, 17″. Collection Tatsuzo Shimaoka, Japan.

    The navel is perforated to provide a firing vent.

8. CHILD TIED TO CRADLE. / Tlatilco, Mexico D.F. Middle Formative period. Solid buff clay. Height, 3 3/8″. Collection Stendahl.

    The weight on the forehead induces cranial deformation (*see* plate 11).

9. MASK. / Tlatilco, Mexico D.F. Middle Formative period. Brown clay with red and yellow paint. Height, 4 1/2″. Collection Proctor Stafford, Los Angeles.

10. MASK. / Tlatilco, Mexico D.F. Middle Formative period. Brown clay with red and yellow paint. Height, 5 1/4″. The Museum of Primitive Art, New York.

11. SEATED MOTHER HOLDING BABY TIED TO CRADLE. / Tlatilco, Mexico D.F. Middle Formative period. Solid brown clay with red, white, and yellow paint. Height, 3 3/4″. Collection Proctor Stafford, Los Angeles.

    A pad or weight is tied in place on the forehead to achieve cranial deformation.

12. DANCER. / Tlatilco, Mexico D.F. Middle Formative period. Solid buff clay with red, cream, and yellow paint. Height, 3 3/4″. Collection Mr. and Mrs. Vincent Price, Los Angeles.

13. ACROBAT WITH LEFT FOOT ON HEAD. / Tlatilco, Mexico D.F. Middle Formative period. Burnished reddish-brown clay. Height, 15 1/2″. Collection Proctor Stafford, Los Angeles.

    There are openings in the mouth and right foot. Illustrated in *Präkolumbische Kunst*, item 7, pl. 24. A similar piece is in the Covarrubias collection (Covarrubias, pl. 6).

14/15. SEATED FIGURE (*two views*). / Central Mexico. Middle to Late Formative period. Burnished cream clay. Height, 12 1/2″. Thomas Gilcrease Institute of American History and Art, Tulsa, Okla.

16. TORSO. / Central Mexico. Middle to Late Formative period. Burnished brown clay. Height, 9 1/2″. Collection Mr. and Mrs. Vincent Price, Los Angeles.

17. CYLINDRICAL HOLLOW STAMP DEPICTING WALKING FELINE (*with drawing*). / Tlatilco, Mexico D.F. Middle Formative period. Brown polished clay, deeply carved. Height, 3 3/8″ diameter, 3 5/8″. Museum of the American Indian, Heye Foundation, New York.

The impression is also illustrated, but upside-down, in Covarrubias, fig. 13.

18. FIGURINES WITHOUT EYES. / Valley of Mexico. Late Formative period. Vaillant's Type H–1. Solid burnished cream clay. Height: 3″ and 2 1/2″. Collection Stendahl.

Failure to indicate the eyes by incisions was deliberate, for numerous specimens of this type are known from the Late Formative period at Ticoman, Tetelpan, and other Valley of Mexico sites (Vaillant, 1931, p. 256, pl. 61).

19. SEATED MAN; SEATED WOMAN; KNEELING WOMAN GIVING BIRTH. / Cuanalan, Valley of Mexico. Late Formative period. Solid buff clay with traces of red paint. Height: 3 7/8″, 2 7/8″, 3 1/4″ respectively. Collection Stendahl.

The figures correspond to Vaillant's Type H–4. The man is wearing a headdress held in place by a chin strap. The women have elaborate hair arrangements. Features and ornaments are indicated by filleting.

20. FLAT-BOTTOMED BOWL WITH BIRD DESIGN. / San Baltasar Temaxcalac, Puebla. Middle Formative period. Black clay with red and white paint. Height, 4 1/2″; diameter, 6″. The Museum of Primitive Art, New York.

The flat-bottomed bowl appears to be an Olmec innovation, whereas the rounded base is the predominant form in Early and Middle Formative period pottery. The cylindrical vessel offers a good surface for a decorative style which gained great popularity in Early Classic Teotihuacán plano-relief pottery, achieving its effect through contrast between rough and smooth surfaces.

21. WOMAN. / Morelos. Middle Formative period. Buff clay with red and cream paint. Height, 10″. Collection Mr. and Mrs. Martin R. Needleman, Los Angeles.

The figure shows Olmecoid elements. The perforated navel is a firing vent.

22. SEATED FIGURE. / Central Mexico. Middle Formative period. Buff clay. Height, 14 1/2″. Collection Mr. and Mrs. Millard Sheets, Claremont, Calif.

The headdress is indicated by incised lines and perforations in the back. The mouth and eyes are also perforated, for use as firing vents.

23. MAN. / Matamoros, Puebla. Middle to Late Formative period. Solid burnished cream clay with traces of red paint. Height, 4 1/8″. Collection Mr. and Mrs. Martin R. Needleman, Los Angeles.

24. BOTTLE WITH CONSTRICTED BODY. / Santa Cruz, Morelos. Middle Formative period. Burnished red clay. Height, 12″; diameter, 7 5/8″. Collection Mr. and Mrs. Millard Sheets, Claremont, Calif.

25. WOMAN. / San Antonio Tomeyucan, Morelos. Middle to Late Formative period. Brownish red clay. Height, 18″. Collection Mr. and Mrs. Francis V. Crane, Marathon, Fla.

The headdress is indicated by incised geometric motifs which supplement the rich filleting of the earlier D–1 and D–2 types. The body decoration, which covers only one half of the torso, is comparable to the blanket or mantle worn similarly by Colima, Jalisco, and Nayarit figures.

26. WOMAN. / Santa Cruz, Morelos. Middle to Late Formative period. Burnished tan clay with red paint. Height, 21 1/2″. Collection Dr. and Mrs. George C. Kennedy, Los Angeles.

The figure corresponds to Vaillant's Type D–3, which developed out of Type D–1, the "pretty ladies." The navel is perforated to provide a vent. Illustrated in *Präkolumbische Kunst*, item 1, pl. 25.

27. WOMAN. / Chupícuaro, Guanajuato. Late Formative period. Buff clay with red and white paint. Height, 3 7/8″. Collection Natalie Wood, on loan to the University of California at Los Angeles.

The figure is naked except for her jewelry, which consists of ear disks and a multiple-strand necklace with pendant. The long nose and slanted eyes are a characteristic of the early Chupícuaro phase. Large-breasted figures from Chupícuaro were reported by Porter, pl. 16 p, q; 17 d, h.

28. WOMAN. / Chupícuaro, Guanajuato. Late Formative period. Buff clay with traces of white paint. Height, 2 1/2″. Collection Stendahl.

29. WOMAN. / Chupícuaro, Guanajuato. Late Formative period. Buff clay with red, white, and black paint. Height, 10 7/8″. Collection Natalie Wood, on loan to the University of California at Los Angeles.

30. DETAIL OF PLATE 31.

31/32. TWO KNEELING FIGURES, EACH HOLDING DOG. / Chupícuaro, Guanajuato. Late Formative period. Buff clay with red and white paint. Height: 7″ and 6⅝″ respectively. Collection Natalie Wood, on loan to the University of California at Los Angeles.

Decorative pellets applied to the shoulders are rarely seen in Chupícuaro figures, but occur frequently on Colima and Jalisco ones. A kneeling figure showing the same treatment of the lower part of the body and of the hands is illustrated in Porter, fig. 16 n.

33. THREE FIGURES. / Chupícuaro, Guanajuato. Late Formative period. Buff clay with white and red paint. Height: 3⅛″, 4⅜″, 3⅛″ respectively. Collection Natalie Wood, on loan to the University of California at Los Angeles.

The central figure is playing a flute.

34. EFFIGY VESSEL REPRESENTING A HUMAN LEG. / Chupícuaro, Guanajuato. Late Formative period. Burnished brown clay. Height, 9″. Collection Natalie Wood, on loan to the University of California at Los Angeles.

35. MOTHER HOLDING CHILD; WOMAN WITH FLOWER; PERSON CARRYING CHILD. / Chupícuaro, Guanajuato. Late Formative period. Buff clay with red and white paint. Height: 2⅜″, 3¼″, 2¾″ respectively. Collection Natalie Wood, on loan to the University of California at Los Angeles.

36. PAIR OF RECUMBENT FIGURES. / Chupícuaro, Guanajuato. Late Formative period. Buff clay with white and red paint. Height, 1¼″. Collection Natalie Wood, on loan to the University of California at Los Angeles.

The rudimentary modeling of the legs and feet, with their projecting heels and toes and concave soles, occurs occasionally at Chupícuaro in the Early Phase (cf. Porter, fig. 16 u, x), but more frequently in Jalisco (cf. Kelly, fig. 82 b) and Nayarit.

37. DOG EFFIGY VESSEL WITH THREE LEGS. / Chupícuaro, Guanajuato. Late Formative period. Burnished dark-brown clay. Height, 9½″. Collection Natalie Wood, on loan to the University of California at Los Angeles.

38. PREGNANT WOMAN; MOTHER AND CHILD; WOMAN. / Chupícuaro, Guanajuato. Late Formative period. Buff clay with red and white paint. Height: 3½″, 4⅞″, 4⅝″ respectively. Collection Natalie Wood, on loan to the University of California at Los Angeles.

39. PREGNANT WOMAN; WOMAN. / Chupícuaro, Guanajuato. Late Formative period. Burnished buff clay with red and black paint. Height: left, 9½″; right, 14⅛″. Collection Natalie Wood, on loan to the University of California at Los Angeles.

40. *Profile view of plate 39*, PREGNANT WOMAN.

41. ANTHROPOMORPHIC JAGUAR. / Cuautla, Morelos. Middle Formative period. Mottled brownish-green stone. Height, 5⅞″. Collection William P. Palmer.

The V-shaped indenture in the forehead of this "baby face" type figure is an Olmec trait.

42/43. COLOSSAL HEAD. / San Lorenzo Tenochtitlán, Veracruz. Middle Formative period. Basalt. Height, 9′. Museo de Antropología, Jalapa, Veracruz.

The back of the head (above) is very well preserved. The decoration consists of a net held by a broad band and tied in a knot at the back.

44. MALE FIGURE WITH ONE ARM MISSING. / Central Mexico. Middle Formative period. Mottled green jade. Height, 5½″. American Museum of Natural History, New York.

45. HEAD WITH JAGUAR MOUTH AND NOSE. / Southern Veracruz. Middle Formative period. Lava. Height, 27″. Collection Stendahl.

46. FIGURE WITH JAGUAR ATTIRE; TWO HOLLOW BEADS DEPICTING DEATH'S-HEADS; EIGHT HOLLOW CARVED BEADS USED AS RATTLES. / Figure from Veracruz; beads from Rio Balsas, Guerrero. Figure, Middle Formative period; beads, probably Classic period. Collection Stendahl.

The male figure has the typical Olmec face and wears a cap with jaguar ears and an upright curved jaguar tail in the back. The beads are carved in the same pattern. The top has a circular perforation. The front has a smaller circular perforation which contains a polished disk of pyrite, surrounded by a raised edge with radially carved notches giving the impression of an eye with black pupil and red iris. The back of the bead is flat and undecorated. The remaining surfaces are carved with scrolls and diagonal lines in similar motifs. Each bead has two lateral suspension holes placed near the upper back side. Finally, a cut was sawed from the base toward the suspension holes, so that the bead shows a slot at the base. One bead contains a small corrugated shell with a perforation at the end and traces of red pigment. The death's-heads are similarly perforated and the eyes were inlaid with pyrite, of which one piece is still in place.

47. FIGURE WITH INFANTILE ("BABY FACE") EXPRESSION. / Guerrero (?). Middle Formative period. Green jade. Height, 2 1/4". Collection Stendahl.

48. WOMAN. / Central Mexico. Middle Formative period. Green stone with traces of red paint. Height, 3 3/4". Private collection.

49. BEARDED MAN. / Puebla (?). Middle Formative period (?). Dark-green steatite. Height, 11 1/2". Collection Jay C. Leff, Uniontown, Penn.

50. FIGURE WITH ARM MISSING. / Guerrero (?). Black serpentine. Height, 3 1/4". Collection Proctor Stafford, Los Angeles.

This figure is typical of the Olmecoid style found in Guerrero.

51. FIGURE WITH INFANTILE ("BABY FACE") EXPRESSION. / Veracruz. Middle Formative period. Dark-green serpentine. Height, 4 1/4". Private collection.

52. SEATED FIGURE WITH JAGUAR HEAD. / Central Mexico. Middle Formative period. Mottled green-and-brown serpentine. Height, 11". Collection Bruno Adriani, Carmel, Calif.

53. FIGURE HOLDING SMALLER FIGURE. / Southern Mexico. Middle Formative period. Green jade. Height, 8 5/8". Mr. and Mrs. A. B. Martin, Guennol Collection, Brooklyn Museum, New York.

54. WINGED FIGURE. / Guanacaste, Costa Rica. Middle Formative period. Bluish-green jade. Height, 2 1/4". Mr. and Mrs. A. B. Martin, Guennol Collection, Brooklyn Museum, New York.

This Olmecoid figure undoubtedly originated in Mexico. It perhaps represents a bat-god. Described and illustrated by Lines, pp. 119–20 and fig. 1.

55. EAGLE PENDANT. / Guerrero. Green diopside jadeite. Height, 2". Thomas Gilcrease Institute of American History and Art, Tulsa, Okla.

A similar pendant is illustrated in *Indigenous Art of the Americas*, p. 75, no. 41.

56. CROUCHING JAGUAR (*two views*). / Southern Veracruz. Middle Formative period. Basalt. Height, 20". The Museum of Primitive Art, New York.

1. Group of five female figurines.
Tlatilco, Mexico D.F. Middle Formative period. Solid buff clay with traces of red, cream, and yellow paint. Height, 3 1/2 to 6 1/2".

The 'Modern' Art of Ancient Mexico

GILLETT G. GRIFFIN

For most people Pre-Columbian art means "primitive" art and "primitive" is something exotic and rather ugly, like the objects used as interior decoration at Trader Vic's. Kalua ads and tourist souvenirs have further warped our point of view about Pre-Columbian art and we tend to pass it off as something vaguely barbaric. Actually, the ancient art of Mexico and Peru can be universally moving if one searches out the finest examples. I recall that Pál Kelemen, the first European art historian to examine Pre-Columbian art, remarked to his wife that in his long lifetime association with art history he had never seen a piece of ancient American art which wasn't inventive or even one which was vulgar.

Pre-Columbian means literally *before Columbus*—or pre-1492. It does not present a simple picture. There is no one culture, such as Aztec, to hang various styles on, but rather a bewildering number of cultures with names often difficult to our ears, such as Zapotec, Totonac, Huastec or Teotihuacán. Dates span more than 3,000 years and include many culture horizons. To confuse things further, little is known about most of them and experts often disagree about major as-

Gillett G. Griffin, B.F.A. Yale, is Curator of Pre-Columbian and Primitive Art at The Art Museum, Princeton. Former Curator of Graphic Arts in the Princeton University Library, a designer and illustrator as well as collector, he has done illustrations for many publications including UNIVERSITY. He has visited Mexico often, and reported his discovery—with Carlo T. E. Gay—of ancient Olmec paintings in "Cave Trip Discloses Earliest American Art," UNIVERSITY, Fall 1967.

"Picasso-type" fertility figurine from Tlatilco Valley, circa 1000 B.C., one of the "pretty ladies" referred to in text.

pects such as placement in time or interrelationships. There is much speculation. Nevertheless the art speaks for itself.

The Princeton Art Museum displays an unusual concentration of fine pieces of Pre-Columbian art. It has avoided large architectural monuments, concentrating instead on smaller pieces of exceptional quality. It has attempted to give a rounded picture of Pre-Columbian civilizations, emphasizing the highest cultures of Mesoamerica, especially Pre-Classic works from many cultures, and Maya ceramics.

The earliest great culture of Mexico was the Olmec. The first Olmec piece to be published was a colossal stone

head discovered in Tres Zapotes in 1862 and reported in 1869. It was not until the late 1920s that the Olmec style was recognized as a separate culture and only in the 1940s did people begin to accept it as an extraordinarily ancient one. Some Olmec material has more recently been dated to the second millennium B.C.

The large Olmec monuments of stone, like the colossal heads, have been found in the states of Veracruz and Tabasco, and that is where scholars believe that the Olmecs originated. A recent exhibition at the Princeton Art Museum has set forth a new thesis: that the Olmec had their cultural genesis in the rocky and mountainous state of Guerrero. Near the provincial town of Xochipala, a number of small clay figures and stone bowls have begun to appear. Their style is reminiscent of other figures which can be dated to before the Olmecs of the great Veracruz sites. But these Xochipala figures are living, vital portraits. Their vitality and naturalism is astounding. Outstanding among these early portraits is the ritual group shown on page 23.

The Xochipala exhibition not only brought together for the first time a number of pieces from a new site, it also attempted to suggest a chronology of styles and an interrelation with Olmec and Pre-Classic styles elsewhere. For the first time one could trace styles which seem to commence naturalistically at Xochipala and become increasingly stylized until one arrives at the highly refined little fertility figures from the Valley of Mexico which archaeologists have dubbed were at work identifying funds for following summers. Incidentally, that church eventually committed $12,000 over three years, creating the unusual situation of a local religious body giving funds to a university. By the third year, the local school system was getting support from Title III of the Elementary and Secondary School Act of 1965 (project to advance creativity in education); funds from that source, paid directly to the school system, permitted relatively large numbers of University undergraduates to receive pay for working in the schools during the academic year; also, a number of high school teachers were paid from these funds to work in University engineering labs with their pupils during the summer segment of the now-year-round expanded program called *Engineering and Secondary School Education.* Part of the costs are gradually to be absorbed by the school system itself as it becomes convinced of the program's value. Meanwhile the program, having strengthened Princeton University's program in teacher education, has entered the catalogue of the engineering school. Participating in this program is a major step in an engineering student's earning New Jersey teacher's certification.

As for the University-Community College collaboration, we knew before planning began that the National Endowment for the Humanities wanted both to help community colleges and to relate the humanities to technology. Previously the Endowment had funded a program at Princeton for connecting civil engineering education more closely with the humanities, especially art, architecture, and history, so that we would look at the cultural, political and social values implicit in the engineering of public works. Indeed, it was the Endowment that funded the conference at which Mayor Gibson issued his call.

That call is, as yet, unanswered because the resources are not in hand, but we are confident that they will be when the program structure is sufficiently well designed to assure some success—because what administrators of funding agencies ask is just what research engineers ask of their experiments—that they be so planned that success is almost assured.

Indeed, central to "the engineer's

Badged and authorized, students spent a day in RCA's Princeton labs. They also visited Franklin Institute, Philadelphia, worked at Princeton's Computer Center.

approach" to university-community relationships which I have been describing is the engineer's definition of the word "experiment." At Princeton, "Design of Engineering Experiments" is a semester course for graduate students in engineering; and, throughout the University, experimenters put a great premium on the well-posed problem and the well-designed experiment. Engineers take the view that a real experiment is so much more costly than its design that it should be carried out only after such careful initial planning that the experiment's results are essentially predictable. There is a common confusion about experiments; people often think that the outcome of an experimental program needs to be uncertain. The layman has confused the technical use of the word "experimental" with a common meaning such as "unthought out." The fact is, if an experimenter does not know precisely where his experiment is leading, and usually just what results are expected, it is almost certain that he will fail. The analogy between engineering experiments and social experiments, while not complete, is nevertheless immensely suggestive because it forces program designers to think each operation through to the outcome and to

raise the most serious difficulties before planning goes very far.

Given all this emphasis on the certainty of results, well designed experiments frequently produce surprises—and these are often the most significant results. Still, surprises are very different from experimental mistakes.

If a concrete bridge is to be securely built and is to satisfy a need economically, then the designer must be certain that the materials have been carefully tested and the construction procedure itself designed against failure. It would be silly to argue against the extra cost of this control on the ground that the artist's rendering of the bridge is so beautiful and the people's traffic needs are so great that construction ought to proceed without waiting for well worked out designs. The same principles apply to the building of university-community bridges, however much those principles may seem to complicate and even to compromise the pure ideals of university public service.

The first and ancient requirement of a bridge, after all, is to remain standing. But the second and modern imperative is that a standing bridge must also serve rather than disrupt the two communities it connects. □

"pretty ladies," such as the intriguing "Picasso-type" on the first page of this article.

Archaeologists have broken down time periods in Mesoamerican art into three categories: (1) the Pre-Classic period, which includes the earliest farmers, the Olmec—the first great civilization—and a number of other formative cultures; (2) the Classic period, commencing about the beginnings of the Christian era and terminating about 900 A.D., a time of the highest reaches of civilization in various parts of Mexico and the Maya world; (3) the Post-Classic period, from 900 A.D. to the Spanish conquest of Mexico in 1521 A.D., a time of warring states and militarism, terminating with the Aztec empire. Each of these periods produced individually splendid styles of art in a number of regions.

The most inventive period was the Pre-Classic. The Olmec worked jade and other hard stones into masterpieces such as the mask from Guerrero on page 25. Early Xochipala clay portrait figures gave way to Olmec stylization, and at the same time local "peasant" styles appeared all over Mexico in confusing profusion, the most famous of these being the "pretty ladies" of Tlatilco, referred to earlier.

Life-size Aztec mask of finely finished wood with traces of stucco, gold leaf, and pigment, circa 15th century A.D. It is the only known surviving Aztec mask of wood in pure Aztec style.

But the tiny, elegant Huastec figures from Pánuco, shown on page 24, though less well known as a culture, are in their way as monumental as the great early dynastic sculptures of Egypt.

In the west of Mexico, other cultures created large, hollow figures of humans, animals and birds and a variety of ceramic shapes, such as the drinking vessel from Colima shown on page 24.

THE Classic period curtailed the number of types of vessels and refined their shapes. The artists re-discovered the portrait and were capable of making life-size hollow clay sculptures which, in Veracruz for instance, show penetrating observation in depicting types. We may see two splendid examples—the portrait of a smiling old man and of *Huehueteotl*, the Old Fire God, shown on page 25. The smiling figures of Classic Veracruz may be the earliest true smiles in art history.

In Oaxaca the Zapotecs favored an ideal facial type on their funeral urns —the most important aspect of the Zapotec urn being the head-dress and vestment, symbolizing the deity or

"Ritual group" from Xochipala, circa 1500 B.C., possibly the earliest ceramic sculptures from Mexico. Enigmatic—is it a shaman and his apprentice, father and son, mother and daughter, husband and wife?—it is curiously sexless but is a distinctive portrait of an aged person communicating with an idealized youthful person. There is an electric rapport between them. The group transcends regional art styles or even Mexican art—it is universal. Some 2000 years later this vitality appears in Maya ceramic art.

Drinking vessel from Colima (about half actual size), circa 100 B.C. When filled with liquid, it represents a pond with four houses around it and a canal or stream as a spout to drink or pour from—an ingenious concept.

combination of deities pertinent to the deceased. The Zapotecs created extraordinarily rich plastic surface modeling on their urns. But for Classic refinement the Maya produced some of the most compelling small ceramic sculptures in the world. These are the delicate little figures found in burials on the island of Jaina, off the coast of Campeche in Yucatan. Because Jaina is a small island and only part of it a cemetery there can be only a limited number of these figures. Their meaning and use is uncertain. Some are whistles, some rattles, others are elegant portraits of priests, ballplayers, captives, women and dwarfs. Their presence is immediate and compelling. Most are mold-made, many of these hand-finished with fine extra touches added to costume or hair style. These molded figurines are often rattles or whistles. A smaller number are solid, completely hand-modeled figures of outstanding delicacy and refinement; in Mexico these are called *pastillaje*. Princeton is fortunate to be able to display an extraordinary group of these Jaina figures, four of which are shown on pages 26 and 27.

WE find that less art was produced during the Post-Classic period,

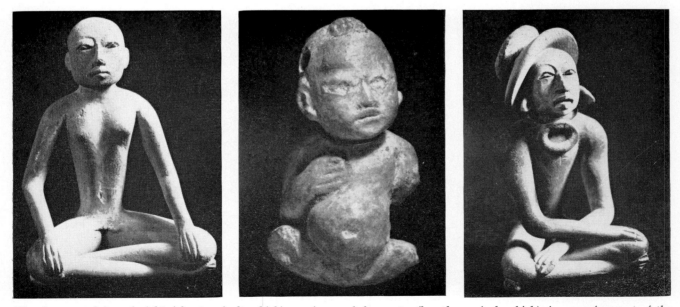

The figures at left and right (about 3 inches high) are from Pánuco, near Tampico, circa 400 B.C. These tiny figures have all the monumentality of early dynastic Egyptian sculpture. The baby, center (less than 2 inches high), is a rare fragment of the Olmec influence on the earliest Zapotec art. Circa 800 B.C., it shows a sweetness and natural motion astonishing in Zapotec art.

Olmec stone mask from Guerrero, circa 1000 B.C., is stylized into a series of curves and triangles. It bespeaks aloof remoteness of earliest Mexican civilizations.

Elegant attendant figure from a Zapotec tomb, circa 700 A.D. Dignified and sculpted with great plastic feeling, it was used as an incense burner.

Fragment of a life-size hollow sculpture from Veracruz, circa 500 A.D. A delightful portrait of a smiling old man who brings us a pleasant sense of joy.

probably due to the restless and troubled times. The art itself is often hard and unyielding, reflecting the material concerns of its period. An Aztec sculpture of a seated youth with bent head is eloquent and expresses more than usual empathy in Aztec sculpture, but the most unusual piece in the Pre-Columbian section of the Art Museum is a wood mask in pure

Aztec style, the only surviving pure Aztec wood mask we know of. The Aztecs, who were late-comers to the highlands of Central Mexico, often turned to the Mixtecs, their neighbors to the southeast, for goldwork, fine ceramics, and decorated books. The Mixtecs were experts in the manufacture of mosaic inlaid objects of wood. Most of the masks and knife-handles

carried off by the Spaniards to Europe as curiosities were of Mixtec manufacture. This one surviving Aztec piece displays a sensitivity usually lacking in Mixtec work.

THE more one explores pre-Columbian art, the more one realizes how little is actually known. It is a field which still offers new horizons

Remarkable portrait of the Old Fire God, Huehueteotl, circa 100 A.D. Huehueteotl is generally depicted as an ancient stooped man sitting cross-legged, bearing on his head a large dish in which fire *was kept. This fragment, slightly smaller than life-size, is as vivid as a Roman portrait and probably dates to about the same period. The Art Museum has several similar portraits of the same deity.*

and unexplored territories. The picture changes dramatically with each new find. But authorities disagree widely on many aspects of the field. The debate is reminiscent of those in Europe in the 18th century as to which was earlier, Greece or Rome. In the early 19th century Egyptian hieroglyphs had not been deciphered and a huge and primal civilization lay locked in mystery. Today only some of the Maya glyphs are deciphered and most remain enigmatic, a challenge to epigraphers. Whereas certain cultures have been investigated, others which produced works of art of great merit remain virtually unexplored.

The cultures of West Mexico, for instance, left few architectural remains and the tombs (the best sources of materials of pre-historic cultures) have been looted. The only officially excavated West Mexican tomb was dug a number of years ago but has never been published. We have a few Carbon-14 dates establishing that some materials date to the turn of this millennium, but styles indicate that there may be a wider range of time.

The whole "Olmec problem" is only 40 years old and no two people agree completely on the complicated aspects of it. In fact our knowledge is so thin and the sites actually penetrated so few in comparison to those in existence that one must say the field is a new one. Whereas the Mediterranean

Like others on this and the facing page, this figure was found on the island of Jaina. All are circa 7th or 8th century A.D. The one above (nearly actual size) is of a gesturing priest or nobleman wearing a heavy collar of jade beads and an elaborate removable headgear. In life the headgear must have been made of some light material, possibly feathers and papier mâché.

This vigorous little sculpture is a whistle (about two-thirds actual size) in the form of a bearded dwarf.

world is picked over to the point that one can no longer expect to discover sites which could rewrite history—only add to it or back it up—Mexican archaeology is at a point of primacy which implies that whole cultures can still be uncovered.

It is a great misfortune that no archaeological work has ever been undertaken at Xochipala. The state of Guerrero is known for its wildness and possibly archaeologists have preferred not to risk excavation in that region. In a country as rich in archaeological sites as Mexico, the low earthen mounds of Guerrero may have appeared drab and provincial in comparison to the dramatic ceremonial centers and complexes of other regions.

Obviously it would be impossible to encompass all of the areas of Pre-Columbian art in one short article or to do much justice to any one part of it. The Princeton holdings in Pre-Columbian and Primitive art in the past few years has grown remarkably from a handful of pieces acquired randomly to an esthetically important collection. Exhibitions and frequent changes of objects have rendered it a fine teaching and missionary vehicle. Generous donors have chosen wisely and with great discrimination. It may be said that though the collection is relatively small it takes its place solidly beside the other great collections of the world. □

Splendid statuette of the Old Moon Goddess, Ixchel, shield in one hand, the other hand clenched as if to carry a bone scepter. Her face bears traces of a brilliant turquoise pigment known as Maya Blue, a color apparently sacred to the Maya. The hag-like caricature of her face suggests that she was in her descendancy as a deity when this sculpture was made.

Hollow, mold-made figurine (about half actual size) of a young woman weaving. Of exceptional sensitivity and elegance.

(*Continued from p. 5*)

that seemed not to have its feet on the ground financially.

"Right! Yes. Very definitely," he said. "The only reason I didn't cite that one is that it *has* been solved. And we *are* feeling the benefits. No one can seriously question Princeton's fiscal good faith or good sense today, thanks to our having faced some hard truths and dealt with them."

He added that "helping to bring Princeton's expenditures into balance with resources was not the only action of the Priorities Committee that has helped in fund raising. Under Bowen's guidance the committee worked out new methods of making long-term projections of University needs which have made it possible for us to talk with potential donors about the long-term approach to supporting Princeton—as an investment, a continuing commitment, not a one-shot thing. So, now that we are planning forward on a routine and regular basis —a program basis—we can go to individuals and agencies and say, 'We have our house in order. We're able to look ahead. This permits *you* to look ahead, too, and correlate your resources with our long-range needs.'"

And did donors always go along with that?

Bessire laughed and said, "Well, universities in relation to donors are a little like foreign aid in relation to Congress. The question of accountability comes up. Everybody understands that you could do a better job of planning if you had financial commitments over a longer period, but some who give money don't want administrators, whether of foreign aid or universities, to feel too relaxed and independent. They sometimes take the view that 'If I give too far ahead they won't come back to me.' Or, 'It's good for them to have to hustle every year.' Well, that's O.K. if it doesn't downgrade what the hustling is for. But the faculty and officers and trustees of a university can be forced to spend an inordinate amount of time on fund raising, to the neglect of such vital matters as curriculum development and the provision of new and varied social opportunities on campus, unless major donors express faith in the institution by taking a long-term approach."

N ow, what about the specific things the Development Office was doing to help Princeton solve the problems he had enumerated at our first session? (Bessire is a dark-haired, compact man with a reputation for taking meals seriously. We had asked him earlier whether talking about money problems during mealtime would spoil his appetite, and he had told us, "Any development officer who can't eat and talk about money at the same time starves.")

"I see our effort as falling into five categories," he said, and ticked them off: "Communication, Information, Collaboration, Imagination, Conservation." But, he said, "communication is so much the most important of these that all the others could be subsumed under that one heading. W*e have to communicate the University's needs to potential donors.* That, in the end, is all we can do—though we can do it effectively or ineffectively.

"If we are asking for larger sums

than ever before, we have to make it absolutely clear *why.* If we are competing with other good causes, we have to make it known exactly how good our cause is. If some people are turned off higher education in general, as some are in this country today, we have to do our share to get them turned on again. If some don't appreciate the unique contribution that private colleges and universities make to the nation, we have to help straighten them out. If some of our alumni don't understand why the University deals with certain problems the way it does, we have to do our level best to make them want to understand, and then help them to do so. And so on. All matters of communication."

He cited one specific problem that called for a strong communication effort. "Princeton believes that a significant transfusion of federal aid to higher education should be 'tied to the student;' that is, that needy students should be able to select the college or graduate school they wish to attend and be provided with federal assistance which would in turn bring an accompanying cost-of-instruction allowance to the institution. This, then, would join federal aid to institutions with federal support for needy students. Also, we think this would promote a healthy kind of competition among colleges and universities to attract students. We are opposed to a form of federal support which would grant funds to institutions based solely or primarily on the number of students attending them.

"It is part of the job of University officers and our Development Office to make people in Congress and elsewhere in Washington understand why we favor the student-connected aid, and why in the long run it will be most beneficial to the nation. And we have to let our own friends know how much we need their help in this."

W E allowed him a brief eating pause and then reminded him that he had listed "Information" as the second category of responses—or the first sub-category under "Communication."

"Right. If our message to potential donors is to be convincing and effective, we in development work have to be deeply informed about the overall purposes and policies of our universities, and about each specific program or project we're seeking support for. That's crucial. And, on the other side, we have to be deeply informed about our potential sources, too—the individuals, foundations, corporations and government agencies we're seeking support *from.* What are *their* needs, policies, attitudes, resources? Because essentially what we're trying to work out is a match-up between our need to have and their need to give.

"I should have added, under Communication, that this is not a one-way thing. Development officers have to serve as a line of communication from donors back to the university, as well as vice versa. This is a sensitive matter, but it needs to be understood. When an institution is dependent on donors, it needs to be aware of the attitudes that are forming among those donors, preferably before they are formed.

"If a negative feeling toward higher education is building up among certain constituencies, a university needs to know about it—not, God forbid, so it can trim and adjust its policies

2. Woman.
*Tlatilco, Mexico D.F. Middle Formative period.
Type D–2. Solid buff clay with red and cream
paint. Height, 5 1/2".*

3. Woman.
*Tlatilco, Mexico D.F. Middle Formative period.
Solid brown clay. Height, 2 1/4".*

4. Woman.
*Tlatilco, Mexico D.F. Middle Formative period.
Type D–2. Solid buff clay with red and cream
paint. Height, 4 1/2".*

5/6. Woman with twin heads showing three eyes (detail below). *Tlatilco, Mexico D.F. Middle Formative period. Solid buff clay with red, white, and yellow paint. Height, 3 1/4".*

9. Mask.
*Tlatilco, Mexico D.F. Middle Formative period.
Brown clay with red and yellow paint. Height,
4 1/2".*

7. Woman.
*Tlatilco, Mexico D.F. Middle to Late Formative
period. Burnished red on buff clay. Height, 17".*

8. Child tied to cradle.
*Tlatilco, Mexico D.F. Middle Formative period.
Solid buff clay. Height, 3 3/8".*

10. Mask.
*Tlatilco, Mexico D.F. Middle Formative period.
Brown clay with red and yellow paint. Height,
5 1/4".*

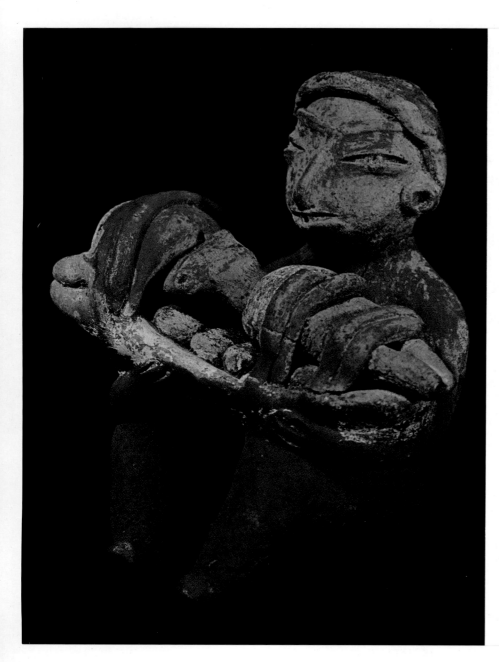

11. Seated mother holding baby tied to cradle. *Tlatilco, Mexico D.F. Middle Formative period. Solid brown clay with red, white, and yellow paint. Height, 3 3/4".*

12. Dancer.
Tlatilco, Mexico D.F. Middle Formative period. Solid buff clay with red, cream, and yellow paint. Height, 3 3/4".

13. Acrobat with left foot on head.
Tlatilco, Mexico D.F. Middle Formative period. Burnished reddish-brown clay. Height, 15 1/2".

14/15. Seated figure (two views).
Central Mexico. Middle to Late Formative period.
Burnished cream clay. Height, 12 1/2".

16. Torso.
Central Mexico. Middle to Late Formative period.
Burnished brown clay. Height, 9 1/2".

17. Cylindrical hollow stamp depicting
walking feline (with drawing). *Tlatilco,*
Mexico D.F. Middle Formative period. Brown
polished clay, deeply carved. Height, 3 3/8" ;
diameter, 3 5/8".

18. Figurines without eyes.
*Valley of Mexico. Late Formative period. Vaillant's
Type H–1. Solid burnished cream clay. Height: 3"
and 2 1/2".*

19. Seated man; seated woman; kneeling
woman giving birth. *Cuanalan, Valley of Mexico.
Late Formative period. Solid buff clay with traces
of red paint. Height: 3 7/8", 2 7/8", 3 1/4"
respectively.*

20. Flat-bottomed bowl with bird design.
*San Baltasar Temaxcalac, Puebla. Middle
Formative period. Black clay with red and white
paint. Height, 4 1/2"; diameter, 6".*

21. Woman.
*Morelos. Middle Formative period. Buff clay with
red and cream paint. Height, 10".*

22. Seated figure.
Central Mexico. Middle Formative period.
Buff clay. Height, 14 1/2".

23. Man.
Matamoros, Puebla. Middle to Late Formative period. Solid burnished cream clay with traces of red paint. Height, 4 1/8".

24. Bottle with constricted body.
Santa Cruz, Morelos. Middle Formative period. Burnished red clay. Height, 12"; diameter, 7 5/8".

25. Woman.
San Antonio Tomeyucan, Morelos. Middle to Late Formative period. Brownish-red clay. Height, 18".

26. Woman.
Santa Cruz, Morelos. Middle to Late Formative period. Burnished tan clay with red paint. Height, 21 1/2".

43

27. Woman.
Chupícuaro, Guanajuato. Late Formative period.
Buff clay with red and white paint. Height, 3 7/8″.

28. Woman.
Chupícuaro, Guanajuato. Late Formative period.
Buff clay with traces of white paint. Height, 2 1/2″.

29. Woman.
Chupícuaro, Guanajuato. Late Formative period.
Buff clay with red, white, and black paint. Height, 10 7/8″.

30. Detail of plate 31.

31/32. Two kneeling figures, each holding dog. *Chupícuaro, Guanajuato. Late Formative period. Buff clay with red and white paint. Height: 7″ and 6 5/8″ respectively.*

33. Three figures.
Chupícuaro, Guanajuato. Late Formative period. Buff clay with white and red paint. Height: 3 1/8″, 4 3/8″, 3 1/8″ respectively.

34. Effigy vessel representing a human leg.
Chupícuaro, Guanajuato. Late Formative period.
Burnished brown clay. Height, 9".

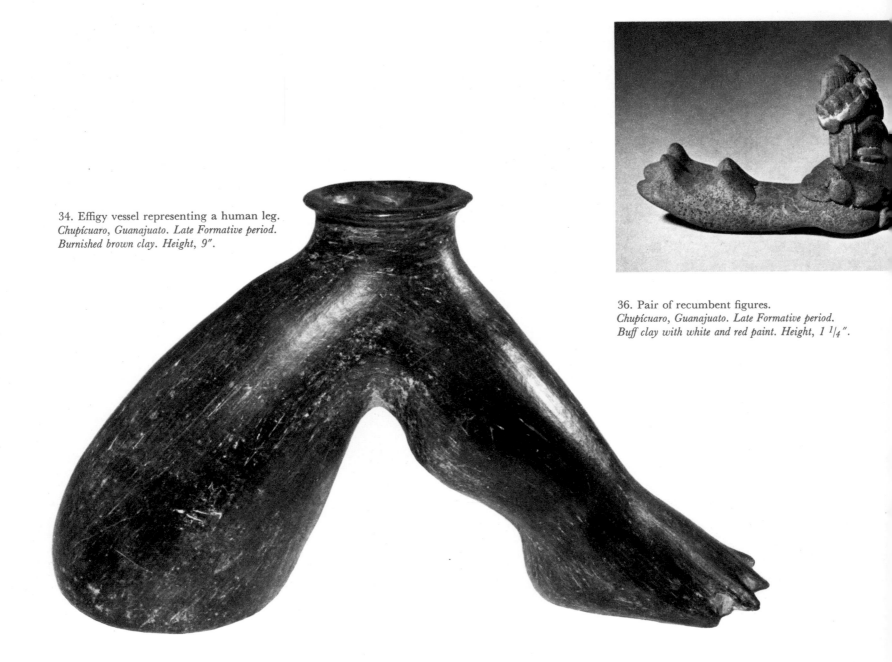

36. Pair of recumbent figures.
Chupícuaro, Guanajuato. Late Formative period.
Buff clay with white and red paint. Height, 1 1/4".

35. Mother holding child; woman with
flower; person carrying child. *Chupícuaro,*
Guanajuato. Late Formative period. Buff clay with
red and white paint. Height: 2 3/8", 3 1/4", 2 3/4"
respectively.

37. Dog effigy vessel with three legs.
*Chupícuaro, Guanajuato. Late Formative period.
Burnished dark-brown clay. Height, 9 $^1/_2$".*

38. Pregnant woman; mother and child;
woman. *Chupícuaro, Guanajuato. Late Formative
period. Buff clay with red and white paint. Height:
3 $^1/_2$", 4 $^7/_8$", 4 $^5/_8$" respectively.*

49

39. Pregnant woman; woman.
Chupícuaro, Guanajuato. Late Formative period.
Burnished buff clay with red and black paint.
Height: left, 9 1/2″; right, 14 1/8″.

41. Anthropomorphic jaguar.
Cuautla, Morelos. Middle Formative period.
Mottled brownish-green stone. Height, 5 ⁷/₈″.

40. Profile view of plate 39. Pregnant woman.

42/43. Colossal head.
San Lorenzo Tenochtitlán, Veracruz. Middle
Formative period. Basalt. Height, 9'.

44. Male figure with one arm missing.
Central Mexico. Middle Formative period. Mottled
green jade. Height, 5 1/2".

45. Head with jaguar mouth and nose.
Southern Veracruz. Middle Formative period. Lava.
Height, 27".

46. Figure with jaguar attire; two hollow
beads depicting death's-heads; eight hollow
carved beads used as rattles. *Figure from
Veracruz; beads from Rio Balsas, Guerrero.
Figure, Middle Formative period; beads, probably
Classic period.*

47. Figure with infantile ("baby face")
expression. *Guerrero(?). Middle Formative
period. Green jade. Height, 2 1/4".*

48. Woman.
*Central Mexico. Middle Formative period. Green
stone with traces of red paint. Height, 3 3/4".*

50. Figure with arm missing.
Guerrero(?). Black serpentine. Height, 3 1/4".

49. Bearded man.
Puebla(?). Middle Formative period(?).
Dark-green steatite. Height, 11 1/2".

51. Figure with infantile ("baby face")
expression. *Veracruz. Middle Formative period.
Dark-green serpentine. Height, 4 1/4".*

52. Seated figure with jaguar head.
*Central Mexico. Middle Formative period. Mottled
green-and-brown serpentine. Height, 11".*

53. Figure holding smaller figure.
*Southern Mexico. Middle Formative period. Green
jade. Height, 8 5/8".*

54. Winged figure.
*Guanacaste, Costa Rica. Middle Formative period.
Bluish-green jade. Height, 2 1/4".*

55. Eagle pendant.
Guerrero. Green diopside jadeite. Height, 2".

56. Crouching jaguar (two views).
*Southern Veracruz. Middle Formative period.
Basalt. Height, 20".*

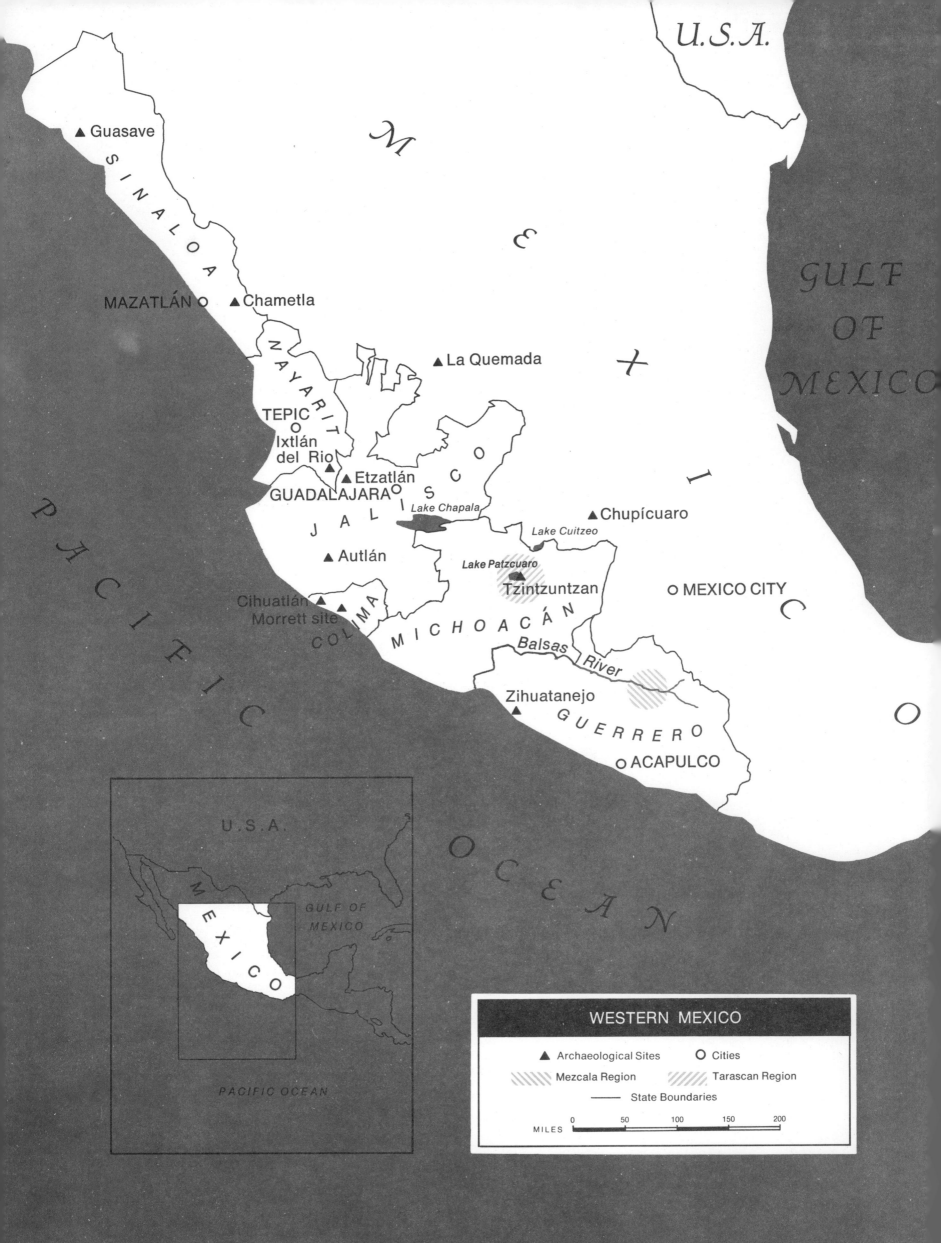

U.S.A.

M E X I C O

GULF OF MEXICO

PACIFIC OCEAN

▲ Guasave

S I N A L O A

MAZATLÁN ○   ▲ Chametla

N A Y A R I T

▲ La Quemada

TEPIC
○
Ixtlán
del Rio   ▲
▲ Etzatlán
GUADALAJARA ○

J A L I S C O

Lake Chapala

▲ Chupícuaro

Lake Cuitzeo

▲ Autlán

Lake Patzcuaro

Cihuatlán ▲ ▲
Morrett site

C O L I M A

M I C H O A C Á N

▲ Tzintzuntzan

○ MEXICO CITY

Balsas   River

Zihuatanejo
▲

G U E R R E R O

○ ACAPULCO

U.S.A.

M E X I C O

GULF OF MEXICO

PACIFIC OCEAN

WESTERN MEXICO	
▲ Archaeological Sites	○ Cities
▨ Mezcala Region	▨ Tarascan Region
— State Boundaries	

MILES 0   50   100   150   200

I I

ART OF WESTERN MEXICO

Art of Western Mexico

·THE ART OF WESTERN MEXICO is best known from large hollow clay figurines and vessels found in the states of Colima, Nayarit, and Jalisco, as well as specimens from Michoacán and Guerrero. These ceramics used to be erroneously considered to be products of the Tarascán culture, regardless of their geographical provenance or stylistic qualities. Tarascán-speaking peoples had no part in the much earlier development of the spectacular art styles in the regions just mentioned.

The Tarascán culture centered on the lake region of central Jalisco and Michoacán, and during the fourteenth and fifteenth centuries extended its political and cultural influences in various directions. At the time of the Conquest, the Tarascán empire reached to the Pacific. Expansion to the south was contained, not only by the steep mountain ranges which blocked the entry into the fertile Valley of Toluca and the Valley of Mexico, but also by the Aztecs' resistance to continued violation of their territory. The origin of the Tarascáns is not known. They retained certain culture traits associated with the Chichimec hunters. During Aztec times the Tarascáns excelled in the art of metalworking, carved ornaments of jade and obsidian, and made fine polychrome pottery with negative-painted motifs resembling those of the antecedent Late Formative Chupícuaro pottery of Guanajuato.

Thus Tarascán supremacy was a late phenomenon in the culture sequence and it is probable that, had the Spanish Conquest taken place at some later time, the Tarascáns would have succeeded in dominating all of their weaker neighbors and eventually the entire western part of Mexico.

COLIMA, NAYARIT, AND JALISCO

The early figurine complex of Colima, Nayarit, and Jalisco, with its large-size effigies, appears to be confined to the area between the Rio Grande de Santiago in the north and the Colima-Michoacán border in the south, and at one time included Michoacán, reaching as far as Chupícuaro (Guanajuato). The complex shares many of the Late Formative characteristics of Mesoamerica, but also developed individual traits that blended into a unique macrostyle. Regional ethnic differences characterize various substyles.

For archaeological purposes the coastal region from northern Sinaloa to Colima has been subdivided into fourteen ceramic provinces, but due to scant controlled excavations the area is still insufficiently known. Southern Nayarit and Colima are among the main provinces of commercialized excavations in Mexico. The figurines from the vicinity of Ixtlán del Rio are particularly popular and abundant and can be seen in widely dispersed museums and private collections. Archaeologically the Nayarit hinterland is of great importance, for it occupies the corridor through which southern influences may have spread to the coast farther north. Previous to the penetration of culture traits from central Mexico, Nayarit and Jalisco lay outside the northern limits of the Mesoamerican culture area.

On the basis of vaguely defined stylistic differences the hollow figurines are usually attributed to one of the three modern states—Colima, Nayarit, or Jalisco, each supposedly representing one substyle. Yet in collections without scientific antecedents the provenance may be uncertain. Some Colima figures, for instance, probably originated in Jalisco, because purported diagnostic traits are shared by both regions.

Due to the paucity of archaeological excavations the chronological sequence of the famous large figures is still uncertain. The majority of the clay sculptures has been found in tombs. A tenuous link for dating the remains of Colima tombs, which contained large, finely modeled figures of polished red ware as well as dog effigies, is provided by their local association with a restorable Teotihuacán vessel of a thin-walled orange ware. Although the association is not entirely secure, there is a reasonable probability that the remains of this tomb pertain to the Early Classic period. The dating of the hollow dog effigies of Colima within the Early Classic seems to be supported also by the occurrence of contemporaneous hollow dog effigies of thin orange ware at Teotihuacán.

The first clear-cut chronological evidence of a Late Formative or Early Classic occupation on the western coast by peoples of advanced Mesoamerican culture was recently established at the Morrett site, on the Colima-Jalisco border, by a radio-carbon date of about 150 B.C.

Throughout the Classic period the figurines retain the characteristics of the Formative stage (hand modeling, use of fillets and appliqués, nakedness except for turbans, disproportionate body features), yet certain substyles are marked by a high degree of perfection and inventiveness.

The advent of Toltec influences put an end to the large-figure complex, and mold-made types of smaller size, in the Tula-Mazapan tradition, were introduced.

A most comprehensive study of the characteristics of the large-figure complex, by Kirchhoff (pp. 49–69), established three categories which are believed to represent ethnic groups among the ancient population. The distinction is made on the basis of conspicuous details in dress, ornaments, and paraphernalia rather than on ceramic analysis or method of manufacture and decoration. Kirchhoff's classification was not intended for the chronological ordering of traits to determine their sequential development. Nevertheless, it is a useful and admirable approach by the ethnologist toward the reconstruction of the culture history of western Mexico. A typological classification by traits of the multiple elements inherent in the figurine complex should be attempted when more archaeological data are available. At present a mere tabulation of features could easily become unwieldy and thus meaningless. We shall therefore follow Kirchhoff's interpretations, inasmuch as they are applicable to the present collection.

The first category includes figures without dress, which are denominated the "Naked Group" in lieu of their unknown tribal name. The second category is characterized by polychrome designs simulating cotton garments woven in various colors; hence it is called the "Polychrome Group." These two groups of people were located in southern Nayarit and adjacent Jalisco, where they co-existed peacefully. A third category, or "Loincloth Group," is characterized by various forms of breechclouts, either modeled or painted. This group was located in Colima and adjacent parts of Jalisco and Michoacán and represents a culturally more advanced population.

It is interesting to note that the Polychrome Group and the Loincloth Group seem to be confined to territories which coincide geographically with two important kingdoms to the west of the Tarascan empire encountered later by the Spaniards—the kingdoms of Jalisco and Colima.

The Naked Group originally occupied the entire area, extending into Michoacán, and constituted the earliest population. In Nayarit they formed the bulk of the population, whereas in Colima they were subjected to inferior social status. A residual group of this early population survived in the coastal region south of Colima, where the Spaniards came into contact with a tribe whose men did not wear any clothes. For these reasons Kirchhoff is convinced that the Naked Group figures portray an ethnic entity and that the lack of clothes is a tribal custom and not confined to the performance of some ritual.

There are further characteristics noticeable in the Naked Group. Considerable care is given to the hair arrangement, particularly among the males. Men and women painted or tattooed their faces with motifs that are also seen on negative-painted pottery. Occasionally the mouth was excessively disfigured to make the lips protrude. Scarification on shoulders and arms, forming clusters of circular spots, was a common adornment of this group. Some figures are seated on low, four-legged stools, which are unknown in other parts of Mesoamerica but which occur in South America, where they were used by persons of rank. The lower social status of the Naked Group in Colima is indicated by the fact that they were modeled in smaller size, appearing in the role of litter bearers or water carriers, as warriors and musicians, suggesting that they were the servants of the Loincloth Group, who had achieved a more sophisticated culture level.

The Polychrome Group displays a great variety of characteristics and is confined to a minor region in southern Nayarit. The male garment consisted of a shirt and a very broad loincloth. The shirt was short-sleeved and reached to the navel. In some cases a longer shirt was worn, which inadequately covered the genitals; the loincloth was then omitted. Outside of southern Nayarit this long shirt was only used among the Tarascans of Michoacán. However, it was widely used among the tribes of western South America. In place of the shirt, some Nayarit figures are clad with a short blanket which covers the back or one side of the body, being suspended with strings attached to the corners of the blanket and tied on the opposite shoulder. This mode of wearing a blanket was not practiced in other parts of Mexico, where it was customary to tie the ends of the blanket into a knot. The loincloth, which was unusually broad, was sometimes decorated with a shell, or, more frequently, with a long concave object (gourd?) attached in front.

Most of the female figures of the Polychrome Group wear skirts, and sometimes the characteristic blanket on the side. Occasionally females are seen in short trousers. The hair is covered by bands or conical hats of Huastec type. Both the bands and the hats are painted with motifs that match the other garments.

A variety of objects appear in the hands of figures in this group, such as clubs and axes, bowls or jars, fans, shells, and musical rasps.

Associated with the Polychrome Group of figurines are the so-called house groups, which are restricted to southern Nayarit. They are particularly interesting insofar as they portray many aspects of communal life. These assemblages are made of coarse-grained clay and painted in white, red, and buff. The houses are covered with high-peaked four-sided roofs. Some houses are two-storied, with exterior staircases and several large doors. Significant is the often crowded arrangement of numerous persons inside and around the buildings.

The human figurines are small and crudely fashioned. Their headdresses and ornaments are modeled with fillets, but eyes and mouth are painted. Noses are usually excessively protruding. Men wear loincloths, women are dressed in skirts, but sexless individuals also occur. Their musical instruments include rasps, rattles, flutes, and drums. Short clubs, lances, and shields serve as weapons. Religious symbolism and images of deities are almost entirely lacking. The scenes express the commonplace, the daily chores and amusements of the villagers, and sometimes include some rather whimsical features. Children asleep, pairs of lovers, women with food platters, men carrying water jars, singing and dancing, all are shown with a naturalness that makes these clay assemblages informative source material for ancient village life. As far as subject matter is concerned they can be compared with Bruegel's portrayal of Flemish village life in the seventeenth century.

Within the Nayarit region the Naked and the Polychrome Groups have certain traits in common. Both groups wear rings in the nose and around the earlobes, a custom not found elsewhere in Mexico, but which occurs in Colombia. Facial scars, mouth deformation, and certain weapons are also shared by both groups.

The third category, the Loincloth Group, is centered in Colima. The variations in depicting the breechclout—from simple to elaborate forms—indicate that this exclusively male garment, as well as the sumptuous headdresses, served as a distinction of rank. Ear ornaments are usually in the shape of disks, and nose rings are exceptional. The dress of the women is much simpler than it is in the Polychrome Group.

Technically the Colima figures are of superior workmanship to those of the other regions. They are well fired and polished, body features are well proportioned. Eyes are usually large and the nails of hands and toes are carefully modeled.

The great realism achieved in clay sculpture of human figures is seen also in the superb artistry with which various animals are represented. Dogs, parrots, ducks, armadillos, turtles, and snakes are favorite subjects and were sometimes made in pairs. Their characteristic features are masterfully enhanced with a minimum of detail. The animals are modeled in the form of vessels and provided with a spout which is often cleverly adapted to form a handle. The utilitarian function of the zoomorphic effigies was perhaps not entirely secondary in importance, since these vessels, serving as grave offerings, could have been filled with water or some liquid food to accompany the dead.

Colima and Jalisco excelled also in the manufacture of smaller figurines. The Colima types show a considerable variety of attitudes and activities. They represent musicians with turtle-shell rattles, drum players, acrobats, hunchbacks, and warriors.

Noteworthy among the figurines of western Mexico is the lack of representation of deities. The clay sculptures depict individuals as they appear in activities of everyday life. Thus it is not surprising that skin diseases, deformities, and pathetically emaciated persons were portrayed with great realism. If deities or their priests were represented at all they cannot be recognized as such, because they lack the religious paraphernalia and symbolism which are typical of Mesoamerican iconography.

THE MEZCALA CULTURE OF GUERRERO

The state of Guerrero is archaeologically still terra incognita, although it is rich in cultural remains. Best known are the so-called Mezcala figures from the north-central region of the state, straddling the Balsas River. The chronological position of the Mezcala style is uncertain. Covarrubias (p. 76), a foremost authority on this subject, stresses the importance of this area as the one where Olmec culture had its origin, spreading toward the Gulf coast. On present evidence, however, it seems more likely that Olmec culture originated on the Gulf coast and spread inland (M. D. Coe, 1963, p. 33).

The Formative period is represented in Guerrero in accordance with the general pattern of the Valley of Mexico. Olmec traits are prevalent in certain regions. A Teotihuacanoid style took hold during the Classic period. There also existed several isolated local cultures of uncertain age and duration, among them the Mezcala culture. During the Postclassic period the area was under Puebla-Mixteca influence.

The Mezcala artifacts are typified by the use of very hard stone, in green, gray, or brown, sculpted into small human or animal figures, stone masks, and objects generally identified as temple models. The technique is well developed, the forms are conventionalized with a tendency toward the abstract. Features are rendered by straight grooves, often with sharp edges and a minimum of detail. Surfaces are carefully polished. From collections in the Berlin Museum and the National Museum in Mexico it is evident that Mezcala-type figures were traded to the north as far as La Quemada in Zacatecas and into adjacent Morelos. Since the former site is a Toltec-period fortification, the occurrence of Mezcala figures could imply a Postclassic flourishing. The concurrence of Olmec and Teotihuacanoid characteristics points out the complexity of the Mezcala style and the difficulty in determining its placement in a chronological sequence. It seems hazardous, therefore, as Eisleb (1961, p. 232) has pointed out, to attempt to explain cultural influences in this region solely on the strength of stylistic details.

Art of Western Mexico

Captions and Notes

PLATES 57–209

57. **MAN SEATED ON FOUR-LEGGED STOOL.** / Colima. Burnished red and ocher clay with traces of black paint. Height, 20″. Collection Mr. and Mrs. Robert A. Rowan, Pasadena, Calif.

   The opening on top of the head is shaped like the rim of a jar. Knobs on shoulders indicate scarifications. Being seated on a stool was an indication of superior rank.

58. **MAN AND WOMAN.** / Colima. Solid light-brown clay with traces of black paint. Height: 14³/₄″ and 12¹/₂″. Collection Stendahl.

   Features and decorations are indicated by fillets and incisions. Short, stublike arms are typical. Hands and feet are given little attention.

59. **ACROBAT.** / Colima. Solid buff clay. Height, 3³/₄″. Collection Stendahl.

   In both plates 59 and 60, the head is a whistle, with the mouthpiece on top of the headdress.

60. **ACROBAT.** / Colima. Solid buff clay with black spattering. Height, 3³/₄″. Collection Stendahl.

61. **WOMAN.** / Colima. Solid burnished cream clay. Height, 9⁷/₈″. The Elsa Lanchester Laughton Collection, Hollywood, Calif.

62. **DANCER WITH BIRD MASK AND GOURD RATTLES.** / Colima. Solid ocher clay. Height, 6¹/₂″. Collection Stendahl.

   The leg decorations are similar to those of Middle Formative period dancers from Tlatilco. Illustrated in *Präkolumbische Kunst*, item 899, pl. 72.

63. **DANCING FIGURE.** / Colima. Solid buff clay. Height, 9¹/₂″. Collection Morton D. May, St. Louis, Mo.

   The elaborate headdress consists of a bundle of reedlike objects and a jaguar mouth. A tubular nose rod is tied with a band around the figure's head. He wears a double row of beads around his neck, and a double string of beads across his chest supports a large tubular object. His skirt has four flaps. On his legs are rings below the knee and above the ankle. Beads adorn his slipperlike footgear. Both hands are modeled so that a rod or string can be inserted to support ornaments (bells?) or symbols. An almost identical piece in the Diego Rivera collection, holding a string from which pend two conical objects, is illustrated in *Arte precolombino de México*, fig. 75.

64. **DANCER WITH ANIMAL MASK.** / Colima. Solid buff clay with black patination and hollow head. Height, 6¹/₄″. Collection Stendahl.

   The mask combines feline features (ears and large incisors) with those of a bird (eyes and beak). The wings attached to the arms underscore the bird characteristics, but the projing stiff breast cover suspended from the neck is known from highland Mexico and reminds one of the long tunic, reaching from the neck to below the knees, on certain Teotihuacán figurines (cf. von Winning, 1960, figs. 2, 3).

65. **GROUP OF FOUR SMALL FIGURINE-WHISTLES.** / Colima. Reddish-brown clay with black patination. Height, 7 to 8³/₈″. Collection Stendahl.

   Left to right: the figures are playing a musical "rasp," blowing a flute, holding a dish (left hand missing), and holding a rattle and what may be a stick. They wear headdresses held on by chin straps, "cutaway" loincloths, and anklets. All the figures have a whistle mouthpiece in the back of the head.

66. **DANCE GROUP, WITH TWO MUSICIANS WITH RATTLES AND DRUM IN CENTER, CIRCLED BY NINE DANCERS WITH ARMS ON EACH OTHERS' SHOULDERS.** / Colima. Solid buff clay with traces of black paint. Height, 7″; diameter, 9¹/₂″. Collection William P. Palmer.

   The figures are affixed to a solid platform and all are adorned with headdresses, necklaces, and breechcloths. Seven of the figures have whistle heads and bindings around their chests.

67. MOTHER WITH TEN CHILDREN. / Colima. Solid burnished cream clay. Height, 5 1/4″. Collection Mr. and Mrs. Irwin Hersey, New York.

The rudimentary features and careless modeling of details suggest a Formative period date. The composition has a dynamic quality reminiscent of the anecdotal Nayarit village scenes.

68. WARRIOR WITH SHIELD AND WEAPON. / Colima. Buff clay with traces of black paint. Height, 5″. Collection Stendahl.

The helmet is held on by chin straps and a dog is perched on top. The head is a whistle. Rectangular, curved shields are confined to West Mexico.

69. MAN HOLDING A BOOMERANG-SHAPED OBJECT. / Colima. Burnished red clay with traces of cream and black paint. Height, 13 3/4″. Collection Proctor Stafford, Los Angeles.

The figure wears a helmet with chin strap and a large (shell?) pectoral.

70. MUSICIAN AND DANCER. / Colima. Brown-red burnished clay with residue of black paint. Height, 18 1/4″. Collection Mr. and Mrs. Robert Neuhaus, Orinda, Calif.

The helmeted figure wears a double chain of tubular stone beads, flaring cuffs, and knee ornaments. His broad loincloth is decorated with a device which has been interpreted as a shell penis-cover or as an object made from a plant. In his right hand he holds a rattle, in the left a gourd.

71. MAN HOLDING A BOWL IN HIS HANDS. / Colima. Burnished red and brown clay, with traces of black paint. Incised. Height, 16 1/2″. Collection Dr. and Mrs. William Greenspon, New York.

On either side hangs a trophy head suspended from shoulder straps. The custom of wearing trophy heads is rarely depicted in Mesoamerica, with the exception of clay figurines from Classic Monte Albán in Oaxaca (Leigh, 1961), on a clay figurine reportedly from Lubaantún in southern British Honduras, on display at the British Museum, and on stone figures from Costa Rica (Stone, 1961).

72. MAN. / Colima. Burnished reddish-brown clay with traces of black paint. Height, 12″. Private collection.

Figures depicting a wide range of ailments are not uncommon in West Mexico and also occur in highland Mexico and the Maya area, though with less frequency. This figure is of a man suffering from a knife-edged deformation of the shank bones known as "saber shin," which is associated with congenital syphilis, malnutrition, and aspects of dwarfism (see also plate 239). The opening is in the top of the head.

73. ACROBAT IN BACK-BEND. / Colima. Burnished dark-red clay with traces of black negative painting. Height, 12 1/2″. Collection Dr. and Mrs. George C. Kennedy, Los Angeles.

Shell breast pendant and loincloth in the form of a face mask. The rim of the vase is on top of the stomach.

74. WARRIORS WITH SLING AND STONE MISSILE. / Colima. Burnished red and tan clay with traces of black paint. Height, 11 1/2″. Collection Stendahl.

This pair of figures was found together in one tomb. Both are clad in padded cotton armor and have a shieldlike device attached to their backs. One figure has an animal head attached to his headdress.

75. FIGURE HOLDING A BOWL. / Colima. Burnished red and orange-red clay. Incised. Height, 13 1/4″. Collection Proctor Stafford, Los Angeles.

The figure wears a chin-strapped headdress and the characteristic mantle covering only one side, front, and back of the body.

76. SEATED FIGURE WEARING MANTLE WHICH COVERS FRONT OF BODY AND IS TIED AT BACK OF NECK. / Colima, Mexico. Brownish-red burnished clay. Height, 13 1/2″. Collection Mr. and Mrs. Alan E. Schwartz, Detroit, Mich.

77. MAN HOLDING A LARGE BOWL. / Colima. Burnished red clay with incising. Height, 18 1/2″. Collection Mr. and Mrs. Robert Schwarz, Jr., Tenafly, N.J.

This is illustrated in *Präkolumbische Kunst*, item 911, pl. 75.

78. MAN WITH A LOAD ON HIS BACK SUPPORTED WITH A TUMPLINE. / Colima. Burnished black and brown clay. Height, 12 3/8″. Collection Mr. and Mrs. Ellsworth La Boyteaux, Orinda, Calif.

Figurines of men or women with water jars usually carry these on one shoulder, a custom confined to the west coast. In other parts of Mesoamerica, and on the west coast as well, jugs were also carried on the head, and heavy loads were carried by supporting the weight on the back and securing them by a tumpline (*mecapal*) passed across the forehead. The *mecapal* is still widely used in Mexico and Guatemala.

79. MAN PLAYING A DRUM. / Colima. Burnished brownish-red clay with residues of white chalky paint. Height, 16″. Collection Stendahl.

The figure beats his drum with a bone fragment. Illustrated in *Präkolumbische Kunst*, item 910, pl. 77.

80. WATER CARRIER. / Colima. Burnished red and brown clay with traces of black paint. Height, 14″. Collection Mr. and Mrs. Robert Neuhaus, Orinda, Calif.

81. MAN. / Colima. Red and tan burnished clay with black paint. Height, 11 3/4″. Collection William P. Palmer.

The figure wears a helmet and neckpiece. An opening in the left hand serves as a firing vent and could also serve to hold some object.

82. WOMAN. / Colima. Burnished red clay with traces of black paint. Height, 13 1/4″. Collection Stendahl.

The opening on top of the head is shaped like a jar lip. Ear spools, necklace, bracelets, and scarification on shoulders provide decoration.

83. HELMETED HEAD. / Colima. Brownish-red clay with traces of black paint. Height, 10″. The Elsa Lanchester Laughton Collection, Hollywood, Calif.

84. HEAD. / Colima. Red clay with cream and black paint. Height, 9 1/2″. Collection Stendahl.

The opening on top of the head does not suggest its use as a jug. It is possible that the hollow clay portrait heads of Colima, varying in size from that of a fist to that of a normal head, were meant to represent trophy heads, as seen in plate 71. They are encountered in Costa Rica, where they were executed singly in stone, shown held by men, or affixed as part of the costume.

85. TWO MEN. / Colima. Burnished red and tan clay. Height: left, 16 1/2″; right, 15 1/4″. Collection Dr. and Mrs. George C. Kennedy, Los Angeles.

Both figures wear helmetlike headdresses, shell necklaces, and garments indicated by modeling and incising.

86/87. HUNCHBACK (*front and back view*). / Colima. Burnished brownish-red clay with calcareous deposit. Height, 13 3/4″. Collection Stendahl.

From early Spanish reports it is known that hunchbacks were among the jesters, musicians, and dancers at Moctezuma's court, where they held a position comparable to that of the jesters of medieval Europe. It is very likely that hunchbacks were believed to be endowed with magic powers as bearers of good or bad luck (*see* Linné, 1943, pp. 161–86).

88. HUNCHBACK. / Colima. Burnished red clay. Height, 12 3/4″. Galerie Israel, Tel-Aviv.

There is a juglike opening on top of the head and the eyes are perforated.

89. HUNCHBACK. / Colima. Burnished red and tan clay with traces of black and incising. Height, 13 3/4″. Collection Stendahl.

The headdress is held on by a chin strap and the firing vent in the top of the head is finished like a vase lip.

90. HUNCHBACK. / Colima. Burnished brownish-red clay with traces of black paint. Incised. Height, 13 1/4″. Private collection.

Eyes and mouth are perforated. This piece is illustrated in *Präkolumbische Kunst*, item 904, pl. 81.

91. IGUANA. / Colima. Black and cream on burnished red clay with calcareous deposit. Height, 6″. Collection Stendahl.

The position of the legs realistically portrays the slow-moving—when not endangered—giant lizards.

92. DANCING ANIMALS. / Colima. Burnished red clay with calcareous deposits. Height, 15″. Collection William P. Palmer.

The two animals are joined by a platform support at the feet and by the front paws. One pair of joined paws serves as the firing vent opening.

93. DOG SCRATCHING ITSELF. / Colima. Brownish-red clay with traces of black paint. Height, 11 3/4″. Collection Mr. and Mrs. Michel Meyer, Zurich-Kilchberg, Switzerland.

94. DOG EFFIGY. / Colima. Burnished red clay. Height, 20″. Collection Dr. and Mrs. William F. Kaiser, Berkeley, Calif.

The dog shows a wrinkled skin and protruding vertebrae and rib cage. Dogs are usually portrayed well rounded, since they were fattened deliberately and considered a delicacy to supplement the diet. From documentary sources it is known that the Aztecs, Tarascans, and Mayas enjoyed the meat of dogs and that certain species were raised solely as food. The custom may well have also prevailed among the ancient inhabitants of Colima. These effigies probably served a double purpose: to supply the dead master with a companion on his voyage to the underworld, and to provide him with nourishment (cf. Wright, 1960).

95. LOBSTER. / Colima. Burnished red clay with calcareous deposit. Height, 7 5/8″. Collection Mr. and Mrs. Arthur Barth, Los Angeles.

The firing vent on the back is shaped like a pot opening.

96. BIRD OF PREY HOLDING SNAKE IN BEAK. / Colima. Burnished cream clay with black and red paint. Height, 9 1/2″. Collection William P. Palmer.

97. PARROT. / Colima. Red and buff burnished clay. Height, 9 1/2″. Collection Proctor Stafford, Los Angeles.

98. DOUBLE DUCKS. / Colima. Burnished red and tan clay with traces of black. Height, 7 1/2″. Collection Stendahl.

The spout in back is a firing vent.

99. CRAB. / Colima. Burnished red clay. Height, 2 1/4″; diameter, 4″. Collection Stendahl.

100. COILED SNAKE. / Colima. Burnished dark-red clay. Height, 5 1/2"; diameter, 10 1/2". Collection Stendahl.

Rattles and diamond design incised. The firing vent is shaped like the spout of a jug.

101. YOUNG BIRD. / Colima. Burnished brownish-red clay with traces of black. Height, 7". Collection Dr. and Mrs. William F. Kaiser, Berkeley, Calif.

102. BIRD IN FLIGHT. / Colima. Brownish-red clay with traces of black. Height, 5 1/2". Collection Stendahl.

103. GLOBULAR JAR WITH THREE KNEELING-FIGURE SUPPORTS. / Colima. Burnished red clay with traces of black paint. Height, 9"; diameter, 10". Collection Mr. and Mrs. Francis V. Crane, Marathon, Fla.

104. JAR. / Colima. Burnished brown clay with black deposits. Height, 9 1/4"; diameter, 11 1/4". Collection Stendahl.

The potter here depicted a plate, decorated with incised geometric motifs, holding four cacti which form the body of the jar.

105. U-SHAPED JAR. / Colima. Brown-black mottled burnished clay. Height, 9 5/8". Collection Stendahl.

106. STEPPED CYLINDER JAR. / Colima. Burnished red clay with calcareous deposit. Height, 9 1/4"; diameter, 9 1/2". The Museum of Primitive Art, New York.

107. JUG. / Colima. Burnished red and tan clay. Height, 10 3/4". Collection Dr. and Mrs. George C. Kennedy, Los Angeles.

A number of such jugs, designed along more utilitarian lines, have occurred, usually with no spout but with the opening on top and a crossbar or bridged connection on top that would allow it to be carried suspended by a strap. Most of the utilitarian types of objects found in West Mexican tombs do not show signs of wear, and were probably refined examples of items in daily use.

108. CYLINDRICAL VASE WITH RELIEF DECORATIONS. / Colima. Burnished brown clay. Height, 8 3/4"; diameter, 7 1/4". Collection Morton D. May, St. Louis, Mo.

The design, repeated four times, represents a person surrounded by a double-headed serpent which is also seen in the headdress. In Huichol mythology it was believed that such a serpent encircled the world, and that the sun must pass between the arches of its body at sunset. The two-headed serpent is also a frequent motif in Huichol textiles. This tribe is located in the mountains on the border between Nayarit and Zacatecas (Lumholtz, pp. 306–7).

109. GLOBULAR GADROONED JAR WITH THREE PARROT-SHAPED FEET. / Colima. Burnished red clay with white paint. Height, 10"; diameter, 13 1/2". Collection Stendahl.

This jar represents an exaggerated seed pod.

110. JAR. / Colima. Burnished red clay. Height, 9 1/2"; diameter, 13". Collection Stendahl.

This jar is in the shape of a plate piled with fruit.

111. SPIKED BOWL WITH LID. / Colima. Brownish clay with traces of white paint. Height, 12". Collection Mr. and Mrs. James Grant, San Francisco.

Bird effigies used as lid handles are a common device. They occur also on Classic Teotihuacán pottery. The spikes on bowl and lid are a characteristic of incense burners. Two short chimneys flank the bird handle.

112. JAR. / Colima. Burnished brownish-red clay with calcareous deposit. Height, 8"; diameter, 11". Collection Josef Müller, Solothurn, Switzerland.

The shape reproduces a plate piled with fruit. Illustrated in Präkolumbische Kunst, item 921, pl. 83.

113. JAR WITH EIGHT HUMAN HEADS. / Colima. Burnished red and tan clay with traces of black paint. Height, 8"; diameter, 12". Collection Dr. and Mrs. George C. Kennedy, Los Angeles.

114. JAR WITH THREE IGUANA SUPPORTS. / Colima. Burnished red and tan clay. Height, 14"; diameter, 10 1/2". Collection Morton D. May, St. Louis, Mo.

115. MASK. / Colima. Brown clay. Height, 9 1/2". American Museum of Natural History, New York.

The use of masks was widespread, and originated in the Middle Formative period if not earlier. Some Teotihuacán figurines show that masks were used as pectorals, and played an important role in burial ceremonies.

116/117. INCENSE BURNER WITH LOOP HANDLE AND TWO JOINED FIGURES RIDING A JAGUAR (two views). / Colima. Red on buff clay with traces of black paint. Height, 19 1/4". Collection Dr. and Mrs. Melvin Silverman, Beverly Hills, Calif.

There is no indication of sex on either of the figures, which sit back to back and have four legs and two arms. Their shared body broadens in the center to form a conical bowl. Attached to this are the heads of the figures. A large loop handle is modeled like a serpent's body and intersected by additional entwined serpents, their heads protruding through the headdress. Such vessels were apparently incense burners.

118/119. INCENSE BURNER WITH REMOVABLE BASIN. / Colima. Reddish-brown clay with calcareous deposits. Height, 13″. Collection Mr. and Mrs. E.V. Staude, Los Angeles.

The bowl or basin has a concave shallow floor and a convex bottom with a short vertical tube ($2^3/4$″ in diameter) which can be slipped over another tube, smaller in diameter, which projects from the shoulders of the figure. Each tube is open only at the outer end. The nude male wears a band around his head and the large ear disks characteristic of Colima figures; he represents the Old God (called Huehueteotl by the Aztecs) or the fire-god (Xiuhtecutli), who are synonymous. Many representations of this god are known from Teotihuacán stone sculptures, which portray an old male, sitting cross-legged, with a large basin decorated with fire symbols on his head. The posture of the Colima figure, its broad face, and the position of the basin strongly suggest that the piece was fashioned after a Teotihuacán stone *incensario* that may have reached Colima by trade. For a detailed description, see von Winning, 1958, pp. 40–42. This piece is illustrated in *Präkolumbische Kunst*, item 906, pl. 78.

120. MODEL OF A WOODEN DRUM (*Teponaztli*). / Colima. Burnished red clay with calcareous deposit. Height, 3″. Collection Stendahl.

This model represents a drum, carved from a hollowed log, which can render two tones. The drum is supported on four legs and has a curious human-head effigy on the side.

121. TUBULAR EFFIGY INCENSE BURNER WITH APPLIQUED AND INCISED DECORATION. / Colima. Early Postclassic period. Reddish-brown clay with residues of white pigment. Height, $22^1/4$″; diameter, $13^1/2$″. Collection Mr. and Mrs. Paul Jones, Altadena, Calif.

On the inside, below the flaring neck, are several thornlike protrusions which support a slightly convex removable plate (diameter, $9^1/2$″; thickness, $5/8$″). The mouth is crescent-shaped and open. The eyes are represented by bowl-shaped sockets. A dog's head appears above the root of the nose. Numerous S-shaped appliqués are attached to the ear flaps, eyelids and sockets, nose, and on the sides of the cylinder. These ornaments are reminiscent of the undulating serpent bodies in the hands of Tlaloc figures, and represent the lightning that accompanies rain. The tip of the nose is reconstructed.

122. FIGURE. / Colima. Carved bone. Height, 2″. Collection Stendahl.

123. WOMAN. / Vicinity of Autlán, Jalisco. Solid buff clay with traces of white paint. Height, $9^1/2$″. Collection Dr. and Mrs. William F. Kaiser, Berkeley, Calif.

The decorated skirt represents a rectangular piece of cotton wrapped around the body, a custom still in use among Indians in Mexico today.

124. MAN. / Vicinity of Autlán, Jalisco. Solid buff clay with traces of white paint. Height, 10″. Collection Dr. and Mrs. William F. Kaiser, Berkeley, Calif.

The figure's dress consists of a helmet held on by a chin strap, a necklace of long tubular beads, arm bands, and a loincloth.

125. WOMAN. / Vicinity of Autlán, Jalisco. Solid pinkish clay with traces of white paint. Height, $8^7/8$″. Collection Mr. and Mrs. William H. Wright, Los Angeles.

The figure wears a wraparound skirt and ornaments.

126. WOMAN. / Michoacán. Buff clay with traces of white paint. Height, $8^3/4$″. Collection Mr. and Mrs. Peter M. Jenkyn, Austin, Texas.

The ornamentation is appliquéd.

127. SEATED HUNCHBACK. / Etzatlán region, Jalisco. Tan and dark-red clay. Height, 10″. Private collection, Italy.

The headpiece is held on by a chin strap; the figure's vertebrae protrude along the ridge of his hump.

128. SEATED MAN HOLDING BOWL. / Etzatlán region, Jalisco. Cream and red clay. Height, $8^3/4$″. Collection Mr. and Mrs. Thomas E. Krayenbuehl, Thalwil, Switzerland.

129/130. MAN; WOMAN. / Vicinity of Ameca, Jalisco. Burnished tan clay with red, black, brown, and red paint. Height of man, $16^3/4$″; of woman, $15^1/2$″. Collection Morton D. May, St. Louis, Mo.

The man wears trunks and the woman wears a skirt and carries a bowl of food on her shoulder.

131. FIGURE HOLDING SMALL CLUB OR STONE KNIFE. / Vicinity of Etzatlán, Jalisco. Burnished tan clay with black paint. Height, $24^1/2$″. Collection Mr. and Mrs. Robert A. Rowan, Pasadena, Calif.

132. MAN CARRYING A BALL HE IS READY TO THROW. / Vicinity of Ameca, Jalisco. Burnished cream clay with red paint. Height, 17″. Private collection.

From ball court scenes modeled on clay slabs it has been ascertained that the ceremonial ball game was played in masonry structures. The man, however, does not wear the protective garments customarily seen on ballplayers, nor is the ball propelled by the hands. He may represent a warrior with a missile to be thrown by hand or by sling.

133. WARRIOR HOLDING ROUND MISSILE. / Vicinity of Etzatlán, Jalisco. Burnished tan clay with black paint. Height, $10^3/4$″. Collection Dr. and Mrs. William F. Kaiser, Berkeley, Calif.

The figure wears a cape on his back and short trunks.

134. Two Women. / Vicinity of Ameca, Jalisco. Burnished cream and red clay with traces of black paint. Height: left, 10 1/4"; right, 8 5/8". Collection Mr. and Mrs. Martin R. Needleman, Los Angeles.

135. Pair of Joined Female Figures. / Vicinity of Etzatlán, Jalisco. Buff clay with traces of red, black, and cream paint. Height, 19". Collection Dr. Carrol C. Mendenhall, Gardena, Calif.

Ornamentation depicts headbands and scarification. This piece is illustrated in *Präkolumbische Kunst*, item 939, pl. 89.

136. Woman with Young Girl on Her Lap. / Vicinity of Etzatlán, Jalisco. Burnished tan clay with red and black paint. Height, 8 1/8". Collection Stendahl.

Both figures wear identical arm rings. These and the protruding chin suggest that these characteristics may indicate distinctions of rank or occupation.

137. Obese Woman. / Vicinity of Ameca, Jalisco. Burnished red and tan clay with traces of black paint. Height, 20 1/4". The May Department Stores Company, St. Louis, Mo.

The figure's dress and ornamentations are indicated by modeling.

138. Woman. / Vicinity of Etzatlán, Jalisco. Burnished brown and red clay with black and cream paint. Height, 19". Collection Dr. and Mrs. William F. Kaiser, Berkeley, Calif.

The short arms and stunted hands are stylistically related to features of small solid figurines of the Ortices phase (Early Classic) from the Tuxcacuesco region in Jalisco (Kelly, p. 116, fig. 79K). She wears a short apronlike skirt. The elongated head with the high flat forehead is a mark of beauty induced by cranial deformation during infancy.

139. Woman Holding Small Bowl. / Etzatlán region, Jalisco. White on red clay with traces of black. Height, 29". Private collection.

This figure is a mate to the one in plate 140. Her hair is hidden by a fringed cap. Necklace, arm rings, and belt are indicated with white paint.

140. Warrior Holding Cudgel. / Etzatlán region, Jalisco. Black and cream on red clay. Height, 28 1/2". Private collection.

He wears a short cape on one shoulder and short trousers.

141. Three Warriors. / Vicinity of Ameca, Jalisco. Buff clay with red paint. Height of tallest, 18". Collection William P. Palmer.

The warriors are protected by stiff armor and helmets, and hold short spears.

142. Animal Effigy (probably of a dog). / Vicinity of Guadalajara, Jalisco. Burnished cream clay. Length, 10 1/4". The Elsa Lanchester Laughton Collection, Hollywood, Calif.

143/144. Village Scene with Four Houses (*two views*). / Ixtlán del Rio region, Nayarit. Reddish-brown clay with black, red, white, and buff paint. Height, 12 1/2"; diameter, 17". Collection Mr. and Mrs. Alan E. Schwartz, Detroit, Mich.

This complex assemblage consists of four houses, a circular terraced structure in the center which probably served as an altar, twenty-three male and twenty-five female figures, and three dogs, all attached to a circular clay base supported by five cylindrical feet. The figures outside the buildings form four distinct clusters. None of the individuals are turning toward or facing the central altar, which apparently had only secondary importance in this village scene. Differences in dress and ornaments clearly denote social stratification. Various activities are portrayed which, by their casualness, convey the impression that the assemblage represents the everyday activities in a village rather than a ceremony. Figures of water carriers, musicians, women with plates of food, a love scene, a chieftain addressing a group of people, a man stealing food, and a sleeping child are portrayed. For a detailed description of this village group, see von Winning, 1959 ("Eine Keramische Dorfgruppe . . ."), pp. 138–43 and figs. 1–7.

145. Four Figures in a Dance Line. / Ixtlán del Rio region, Nayarit. Solid clay with traces of white, red, and black paint. Height, 3 3/4". Collection Stendahl.

146. Village Scene with Three Houses and a Marriage Ceremony. / Ixtlán del Rio region, Nayarit. Brown clay with black, white, and red paint. Height, 7"; diameter, 13". Collection Dr. and Mrs. George C. Kennedy, Los Angeles.

Three houses, a circular central platform, and sixty-one individuals (male and female, adults and children) are attached to a triangular base. All the houses have differently painted roof decoration. One house is open toward the outside, with two females looking out. The circular structure has three terraces. On the top are four male musicians, two women, and a child. Most of the figures grouped around the platform face toward the center, where two couples, among other figures, are seated, covered with a blanket reaching to their faces. Apparently this is an indication of a marriage ceremony (cf. *Codex Mendosa* 61). The onlookers on the periphery carry smaller figures on their shoulders.

147. Dance Group. / Ixtlán del Rio region, Nayarit. Solid clay with traces of black, white, and red paint. Height, 7". Collection Morton D. May, St. Louis, Mo.

The scene, mounted on a low platform, depicts a circle of ten dancers with a musician and a drummer in the center and two houses on one side.

148. TWO-STORY HOUSE OR SHELTER WITH EIGHT OC-CUPANTS. / Nayarit. Solid clay with traces of black and cream paint. Height, 9 1/4". Collection Stendahl.

149. TWO-STORY HOUSE WITH MULTIPLE-ROOF COMPLEX AND NINE OCCUPANTS. / Ixtlán del Rio region, Nayarit. Clay with traces of red, yellow, white, and black paint. Height, 6 1/4". Collection Stendahl.

The structure is divided into several separate rooms both upstairs and down, with two stairways leading to the upper floor from the outside. There are several piles of food in the rooms.

150. HOUSE COMPLEX WITH THREE ROOFS AND TWELVE OCCUPANTS. / Ixtlán del Rio region, Nayarit. Clay with traces of black and cream paint. Height, 7 1/4". Collection William P. Palmer.

The seated figures all have a blanketlike garment drawn around them. On the other side of the structure there are openings for two rooms under the main floor structure.

151. PERSON RECLINING ON PALLET WITH ATTENDANT. / Ixtlán del Rio region, Nayarit. Brown clay with yellow, red, and black paint. Height, 3 1/2". Collection William P. Palmer.

Two protrusions on the pallet restrain the head movement. It has been suggested that figurines of this type represent sick people. They are not uncommon, but are rarely shown with an attendant. Sometimes little dogs are seen lying near the person's legs.

152. HOUSE ON PLATFORM WITH RECLINING PERSON INSIDE. / Ixtlán del Rio region, Nayarit. Reddish-brown clay with black, white, and orange paint. Height, 7". Collection Stendahl.

Twelve figures comprise the scene. The reclining figure is wrapped in a blanket with his head resting against the shoulders and arms of a woman.

153. GROUP OF SIX WARRIORS WITH LANCES. / Ixtlán del Rio region, Nayarit. Reddish-brown clay with red, black, and white paint. Height, 4". Collection Stendahl.

The figures appear to be engaged in a tilting contest. Each man wears a two-pointed cap. The pinched triangular faces show few details, except for the prominent noses with nose rings below the septa. The warriors are seated with legs drawn up to support their lances. Capes cover shoulders and arms. The right hand rests near the end of the pole, which is guided by the knee and left hand. The poles or lances are decorated with red, white, and black rings.

154. BATTLE SCENE ON HILL. / Ixtlán del Rio region, Nayarit. Brown clay with red, white, yellow, and black paint. Height, 10". Collection Dr. and Mrs. George C. Kennedy, Los Angeles.

Twenty participants in various attitudes of combat using clubs, rocks, and slings. On top of the hill are two huts and a figure blowing on a conch shell.

155. GROUP OF TWO HOUSES WITH MEN ON POLES. Ixtlán del Rio region, Nayarit. Brownish clay with red, orange, black, and white paint. Height, 14"; diameter, 9". Collection Dr. and Mrs. George C. Kennedy, Los Angeles.

Spectators surround the men on poles. It is not improbable that the scene portrays a ceremony (*Juego del Volador*) still practiced by Totonacs and Otomi, in which four men in bird costumes are tied to the top of a high pole. By unwinding their ropes, they slowly descend, simulating the flight of birds. The underlying symbolism is related to the fertility cult and expresses the divine provenance of the crops (Kricke-berg, 1956, p. 232). A similar ritual survives among the Huichol. This piece is illustrated in *Präkolumbische Kunst*, item 944, pl. 84.

156. FUNERAL PROCESSION. / Ixtlán del Rio region, Nayarit. Brown clay with red, orange, white, and blue-gray paint. Height, 6 1/4". Collection Dr. and Mrs. George C. Kennedy, Los Angeles.

The scene is composed of a thatch-roofed house, seventeen people, several stacks of food, and the deceased—prepared for burial wrapped in blankets with feather decorations—carried by six persons. The group is modeled on a slab with six short legs.

157. FUNERAL PROCESSION. / Ixtlán del Rio region, Nayarit. Brown clay with red and white paint. Height, 5 1/2". Collection Dr. and Mrs. George C. Kennedy, Los Angeles.

The corpse is carried on the shoulders of attendants, and the procession is preceded by servants carrying plates with food offerings on their heads. Illustrated in *Präkolumbische Kunst*, item 955, pl. 85.

158. TWO-STORY HOUSE WITH OCCUPANTS. / Ixtlán del Rio region, Nayarit. Reddish-brown clay with white and brown paint. Height, 15 1/2". Collection Mr. and Mrs. Max J. Pincus, Pleasant Ridge, Mich.

The house has five rooms, a stairway, two birds, and twenty-two figures.

159. WOMAN HOLDING CHILD TO BREAST AND BOWL ON HEAD. / Southern Nayarit. Brownish-red clay with white paint. Height, 21". The May Department Stores Company, St. Louis, Mo.

160. OBESE WOMAN. / Nayarit. Cream and black on red clay. Height, 11³/₄". The Elsa Lanchester Laughton Collection, Hollywood, Calif.

161. FIGURE SEATED ON STOOL. / Nayarit. Brownish-red clay with black striations. Height, 13". Collection Stendahl.

Two supports of the stool merge with the figure's body, the other two are formed by the figure's legs. The hand-to-mouth attitude is characteristic of numerous "Naked Group" figures.

162. WOMAN AND TWO MEN. / Southern Nayarit. Red clay with black and white paint and bluish-gray patina. Height: 16", 21", 15¹/₂" respectively. Collection Mr. and Mrs. Edgar Dorsey Taylor, Los Angeles.

The seated man is playing a tortoise-shell drum with an antler striker. The men wear trunks and the woman a skirt. Ornamentation is indicated by paint and modeling.

163. WOMAN CARRYING BOWL ON SHOULDER. / Southern Nayarit. Dark-red clay with black and white paint. Height, 23¹/₂". Collection Mr. and Mrs. Ellsworth La Boyteaux, Orinda, Calif.

The figure wears a choker-type necklace, a characteristic of Late Preclassic Chupícuaro figurines, and multiple earrings. Her face and breasts are tattooed. The back is also tattooed, the design matching that seen on the bowl.

164. WOMAN WITH BOWL ON HEAD. / Vicinity Santiago Compostela, Nayarit. Burnished buff clay with red paint. Height, 9¹/₄". Collection Stendahl.

The bowl serves as a firing vent.

165. WARRIOR WITH CLUB AND SMALL JAR. / Southern Nayarit. Burnished painted clay. Height, 19³/₄". Private collection.

This figure belongs to the "Naked Group." Body paint substitutes for clothing.

166. FIGURE HOLDING RATTLE. / Nayarit, Jalisco border region. Cream-colored clay with red and black paint. Height, 17¹/₂". Collection Mr. and Mrs. Arthur C. Rosenberg, Chicago, Ill.

167. MAN WITH PUSTULES ON BODY. / Ixtlán del Rio region, Nayarit. Brown clay with black paint. Height, 6³/₄". Collection Dr. and Mrs. William F. Kaiser, Berkeley, Calif.

This may be the representation of a syphilitic.

168/169. KNEELING HUNCHED WOMAN HOLDING A BOWL (*two views*). / Ixtlán del Rio region, Nayarit. Tan clay with black and white paint. Height, 7¹/₄". Collection Stendahl.

The figure is dressed in skirt, headband, and ornaments.

170. MAN. / Southern Nayarit. Burnished red clay with traces of black and white paint. Height, 24". The Museum of Mouton-Rothschild, Pauillac, Gironde, France.

The figure is decorated with headdress, arm bands, scarifications on shoulders, earrings, and a shell necklace. Illustrated in *Präkolumbische Kunst*, item 968, pl. 87.

171. MAN SEATED ON A STOOL. / Southern Nayarit. Burnished orange-red clay. Height, 15³/₄". Collection Stendahl.

Low stools are associated exclusively with figures of the "Naked Group," which represents an ethnic group in West Mexico unknown in other parts of the country. Stools are believed to be a status symbol, as is the case in South America (Kirchhoff, p. 55). This figure was found in the same tomb with those shown in plate 172.

172. WARRIOR AND TWO WOMEN. / Southern Nayarit. Burnished clay with traces of black paint. Height: 17", 15", 19" respectively. Collection Stendahl.

The warrior wears a protective shirt and helmet of cotton and wickerwork and holds a club.

173. MAN HOLDING LARGE GOURD DRUM OR RASP. Ixtlán del Rio region, Nayarit. Burnished red and brown clay with black and white paint. Height, 5". Collection Proctor Stafford, Los Angeles.

174. MAN SEATED ON TWO-LEGGED STOOL. / Southern Nayarit. Light-brown clay with traces of black paint. Height, 15". Collection Mr. and Mrs. Saul Stanoff, Tarzana, Calif.

The object held to the mouth is either a smoking pipe or a flute.

175. MAN PLAYING ON GOURD RASP. / Southern Nayarit. Burnished brownish-black clay. Height, 16¹/₂". Collection Mr. and Mrs. Martin R. Needleman, Los Angeles.

176. MAN PLAYING AN EFFIGY-SHAPED RASP. / Ixtlán del Rio region, Nayarit. Dark-red clay with black and white paint. Height, 22". Collection Mr. and Mrs. Millard Sheets, Claremont, Calif.

The figure wears a pair of trunks, and a headdress held in place with an animal-skin fillet. Ornaments and body decoration are indicated by paint and modeling. Rasps are usually made of bone and rubbed with a piece of shell.

177. MAN. / Santiago Compostela region, Nayarit.

Burnished painted clay. Height, 18″. Collection John G. Bourne, Los Angeles.

178. WOMAN HOLDING SMALL DOG. / Ixtlán del Rio region, Nayarit. Painted clay. Height, 22″. Collection Dr. and Mrs. David I. Elterman, Los Angeles.

The woman wears a short skirt and her body is delicately painted.

179. MAN USING WALKING STICK. / Southern Nayarit. Painted clay. Height, 11½″. Collection Mr. and Mrs. Edwin L. Berkowitz, San Francisco.

180. EMACIATED MALE AND FEMALE FIGURES. / Ixtlán del Rio region, Nayarit. Painted clay. Height: 15¼″ and 13″. Private collection.

The male is drinking from a bowl using a tube (cf. *Arte precolombino del occidente de México*, pls. 3, 30, 31). The woman is stripping the kernels from an ear of corn. Both figures have numerous nose rings and earrings, elaborate hair arrangements, and facial tattooing.

181. JOINED COUPLE. / Ixtlán del Rio region, Nayarit. Orange clay with red, black, and white paint. Height, 18″. Collection Josef Müller, Solothurn, Switzerland.

Both male and female have elaborate facial tattooing and wear several nose rings and earrings protruding horizontally (those of the female are partly missing). The male holds a gourd rattle and the woman a bowl. Both are dressed in short mantles covering only one side of the body, and the woman wears a skirt.

182. MAN AND WIFE. / Southern Nayarit. Painted clay. Height: 18¾″ and 17½″. Collection Stendahl.

The man is a warrior holding a club and an ax. He wears a breechcloth, headgear, and ornaments, including a conch shell at his waist. The woman holds a bowl and wears a wraparound skirt and ornaments.

183. WOMAN WITH BOWL ON SHOULDER. / Ixtlán del Rio region, Nayarit. Painted clay. Height, 25″. Collection Stendahl.

The figure wears cotton garments and headband, numerous rings in earlobe and septum, rows of beads around her neck, and a crescent pendant.

184. STANDING WARRIOR. / Ixtlán del Rio, Nayarit. Painted clay. Height, 22″. Collection Dr. and Mrs. Irving F. Burton, Huntington Woods, Mich.

The figure is carrying a cudgel and wearing protective garments consisting of trunks, an animal skin around the body with the four feet and tail indicated on his back, and a leather helmet with a visor of feathers held in place by a leather fillet. He is richly ornamented and wears a conch shell at his waist.

185. KNEELING WOMAN WITH TWO CHILDREN AND BOWL OF FOOD, SEATED ON A TABLELIKE PROJECTION FROM THE BODY. / Ixtlán del Rio region, Nayarit. Brownish clay with red, orange, black, and white paint. Height, 13¼″. The Museum of Primitive Art, New York.

186. WARRIOR WITH PROTECTIVE ARMOR AND CLUB. / Ixtlán del Rio region, Nayarit. Brownish-red clay with black and white paint. Height, 24½″. Private collection.

Body protector and helme are made of cotton and wickerwork. The clubhead probabl contains inlaid bits of stone or obsidian.

187. EFFIGY VASE WITH HEAD OF RAIN-GOD. / Southern Nayarit. Buff clay with white and blue-green paint. Height, 4¾″. Collection Stendahl.

The widespread rain-god cult is manifest also in western Mexico in the small anthropomorphic vessels, often crudely made, but incorporating the essential iconographic features of the deity known elsewhere by his Nahuatl name as Tlaloc. The spout is modeled in three protruding sections which represent white heron feathers. The pleated paper ornament (*tlaquechpanyotl* or *amacuexpalli*) is normally worn at the back of the head, but here it covers the forehead; in other figures it may be attached to the center of the spout. The eyes are made of two hemispheres and encircled by blue paint. The nose is surmounted by the folded body of a serpent. Only the upper jaw and protruding teeth are shown.

188. DOG WITH ANTHROPOMORPHIC BODY. / Michoacán. Basalt. Height, 17″. American Museum of Natural History, New York.

The figure wears a bead necklace with a pectoral showing a human face.

189. BARKING DOG. / Ixtlán del Rio region, Nayarit. Tan clay with white paint. Height, 5½″. Collection Stendahl.

190. CHAC-MOOL FIGURE. / Michoacán. Postclassic period. Volcanic rock. Height, 28″. Collection Mr. and Mrs. Gordon Onslow-Ford, Inverness, Calif.

The so-called Chac-Mool figures depict a reclining person, often with his head turned to one side, who holds on his abdomen a round disk or a basin serving as a repository for offerings. It is often assumed that these figures, which were originated by the Toltecs, represent a deity. However, Jorge Acosta, foremost Mexican authority on the Toltec culture, considered these statues, together with the standard bearers and Atlantean figures, as ornamental products of a semireligious character.

191. JAGUAR SEAT. / Michoacán. Basalt. Height, 19″. Museum Rietberg, Zurich, Switzerland.

Parts of the legs and tail are missing. Several jaguar seats have been found in Toltec-period Chichén Itzá. A jaguar or coyote seat has been reported from Ihuatzio (Michoacán) in association with a Chac-Mool figure. The relationship between the two types of sculpture appears to be significant.

192/193. CLOISONNÉ DECORATED PEDESTAL BOWL (*two views*). / Michoacán. Postclassic period. Reddish-brown clay with polychrome. Height, 3³/₄". Collection Stendahl.

The decoration of the interior shows three long-nosed priests with feather headdresses. Two point a staff or stick at the ground, while the third holds the stick up. The position of the hands suggests a fire-drilling operation: the volutes emerging near the point of one of the sticks could be interpreted as smoke. The central field is quartered and could have directional significance, referring to the cardinal points. The exterior shows three similar long-nosed priests with bird headdresses and a stepped fret design on the base.

194. CLOISONNÉ DECORATED JAR. / Michoacán Postclassic period. Clay decorated in cloisonné technique with white, yellow, green, reddish-brown, and orange. Height, 8¹/₂"; diameter, 9". Collection Mr. and Mrs. Ellsworth La Boyteaux, Orinda, Calif.

The decorative motifs include geometric designs and seven stylized serpent heads. The rim, which is turned outward, depicts stepped fret designs.

195. CONCH SHELLS. / Nayarit. Postclassic period. Stuccoed and painted. Length, 10¹/₂". Collection Stendahl.

Conch shells were blown during an attack in order to frighten the enemy by their weird sound. They were also used in religious ceremonies throughout Mesoamerica.

196. TRIPOD BOWL. / Border of Michoacán and Guerrero. Toltec period. Buff clay with red, black, and cream paint. Height, 6"; diameter, 9³/₄". Collection Stendahl.

Geometric design with stepped fret (*xicalcoliuhqui*) rim decoration. The hollow rattle supports are in the shape of a human or animal leg.

197. MAN WITH ANIMAL MASK CARRYING A BOWL ON HIS BACK. / Jalisco. Basalt. Height, 21". Collection Mr. and Mrs. E. V. Staude, Los Angeles.

198. STANDING MALE. / Michoacán. Basalt. Height, 22". American Museum of Natural History, New York.

199. FIGURE. / Mezcala, Guerrero. Gray-green stone. Height, 14¹/₄". Collection Mr. and Mrs. Arthur N. Seiff, New York.

200. WOMAN. / Mezcala, Guerrero. Gray variegated stone. Height, 10¹/₂". Collection Stendahl.

201. SEATED FIGURE. / Mezcala, Guerrero. Mottled dark-green-and-white stone. Height, 4³/₄". Collection Mr. and Mrs. Dübi-Müller, Solothurn, Switzerland.

202. FIGURE. / Mezcala, Guerrero. Brownish-green stone with traces of red coloring. Height, 5¹/₄". Collection Mr. and Mrs. Arthur N. Seiff, New York.

203. PRISONER WITH ARMS TIED BEHIND BACK; GRASSHOPPER; ANIMAL. / Mezcala, Guerrero. White-and-green mottled stone. Height: 3¹/₄", 3¹/₄", 2³/₄". Animal: Collection Mr. and Mrs. Arthur N. Seiff, New York; Prisoner and Grasshopper: Collection Stendahl.

The motif of the seated prisoner with arms tied behind back is also found in Colima and Maya clay figures.

204. FROG. / Balsas River region, Guerrero. Cream-colored stone. Height, 5". Seattle Art Museum, Seattle, Wash.

The hemispherical perforations probably held inlaid objects.

205. MODEL OF A TEMPLE. / Mezcala, Guerrero. Andesitic serpentine. Height, 7¹/₈". The Museum of Primitive Art, New York.

The stairs are indicated at the bottom and a figure is lying on the top.

206. MODEL OF A TEMPLE. / Mezcala region, Guerrero. Gray-green stone. Height, 6". Collection Mr. and Mrs. Dübi-Müller, Solothurn, Switzerland.

The meaning of this artifact can be ascertained by comparison with similar objects. Only the façade of the temple is shown; some have a deity standing in the entrance and a staircase leading to the temple platform (cf. Franco, 1964, figs. 134–48). This piece is illustrated in *Präkolumbische Kunst*, item 863, pl. 71.

207. MASK SURMOUNTED BY TWO BIRDS' HEADS. / Mezcala, Guerrero. Dark-green stone. Height, 3³/₄". Collection Otto E. Meyer, San Francisco.

208. MASK. / Guerrero. Alabaster. Height, 5¹/₂". Collection Mack Gilman, Chicago, Ill.

209. SEATED MONKEY WITH TAIL UPRIGHT. / Mezcala, Guerrero. Grayish-white stone. Height, 5¹/₂". Collection Stendahl.

57. Man seated on four-legged stool.
Colima. Burnished red and ocher clay with traces of black paint. Height, 20".

58. Man and woman.
*Colima. Solid light-brown clay with traces of black
paint. Height: 14 ³/₄″ and 12 ¹/₂″.*

59. Acrobat.
Colima. Solid buff clay. Height, 3 ³/₄″.

60. Acrobat.
*Colima. Solid buff clay with black spattering.
Height, 3 ³/₄″.*

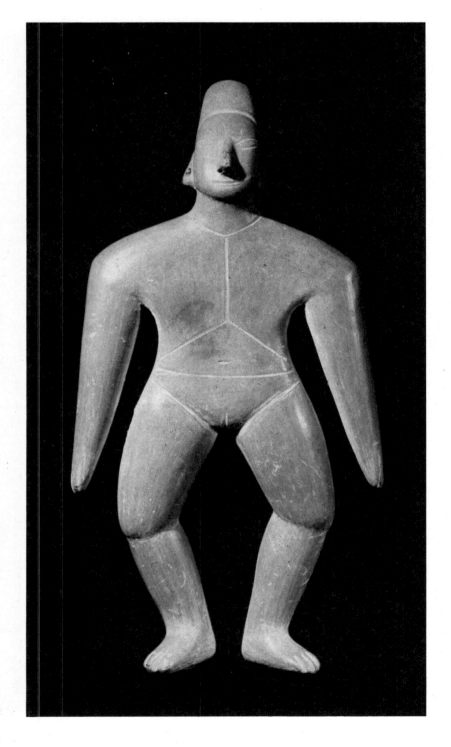

61. Woman.
Colima. Solid burnished cream clay. Height, 9 ⁷/₈″.

83

62. Dancer with bird mask and gourd rattles.
Colima. Solid ocher clay. Height, 6 1/2".

63. Dancing figure.
Colima. Solid buff clay. Height, 9 1/2".

64. Dancer with animal mask.
*Colima. Solid buff clay with black patination and
hollow head. Height, 6 1/4".*

65. Group of four small figurine-whistles.
*Colima. Reddish-brown clay with black patination.
Height, 7 to 8 3/8".*

66. Dance group, with two musicians with rattles and drum in center, circled by nine dancers with arms on each others' shoulders. *Colima. Solid buff clay with traces of black paint. Height, 7″; diameter, 9 1/2″.*

67. Mother with ten children. *Colima. Solid burnished cream clay. Height, 5 1/4″.*

68. Warrior with shield and weapon. *Colima. Buff clay with traces of black paint. Height, 5″.*

69. Man holding a boomerang-shaped object.
*Colima. Burnished red clay with traces of cream
and black paint. Height, 13 3/4".*

70. Musician and dancer.
*Colima. Brown-red burnished clay with residue of
black paint. Height, 18 1/4".*

71. Man holding a bowl in his hands.
*Colima. Burnished red and brown clay, with traces
of black paint. Incised. Height, 16 1/2".*

73. Acrobat in back-bend.
Colima. Burnished dark-red clay with traces of black negative painting. Height, 12 ¹/₂".

72. Man.
Colima. Burnished reddish-brown clay with traces of black paint. Height, 12".

74. Warriors with sling and stone missile.
Colima. Burnished red and tan clay with traces of black paint. Height, 11 ¹/₂".

75. Figure holding a bowl.
Colima. Burnished red and orange-red clay. Incised.
Height, 13 1/4".

76. Seated figure wearing mantle which covers front of body and is tied at back of neck. *Colima, Mexico. Brownish-red burnished clay. Height, 13 1/2".*

77. Man holding a large bowl.
Colima. Burnished red clay with incising. Height, 18 1/2".

78. Man with a load on his back supported with a tumpline. *Colima. Burnished black and brown clay. Height, 12 3/8".*

79. Man playing a drum.
Colima. Burnished brownish-red clay with residues of white chalky paint. Height, 16".

80. Water carrier.
Colima. Burnished red and brown clay with traces of black paint. Height, 14".

81. Man.
*Colima. Red and tan burnished clay with black
paint. Height, 11 3/4".*

82. Woman.
*Colima. Burnished red clay with traces of black
paint. Height, 13 1/4".*

83. Helmeted head.
Colima. Brownish-red clay with traces of black paint. Height, 10″.

84. Head.
Colima. Red clay with cream and black paint. Height, 9 1/2″.

85. Two men.
*Colima. Burnished red and tan clay. Height: left,
16 1/2"; right, 15 1/4".*

86/87. Hunchback (front and back view).
Colima. Burnished brownish-red clay with calcareous deposit. Height, 13 ³/₄".

88. Hunchback.
Colima. Burnished red clay. Height, 12 ³/₄″.

89. Hunchback.
Colima. Burnished red and tan clay with traces of black and incising. Height, 13 ³/₄″.

90. Hunchback.
Colima. Burnished brownish-red clay with traces of black paint. Incised. Height, 13 ¹/₄″.

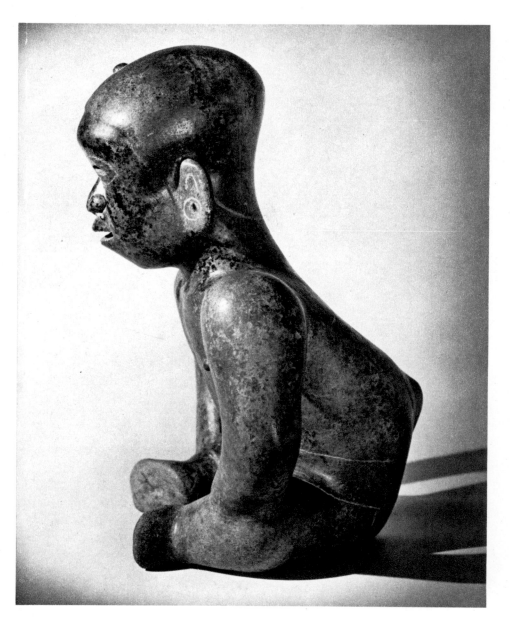

91. Iguana.
Colima. Black and cream on burnished red clay with calcareous deposit. Height, 6".

92. Dancing animals.
Colima. Burnished red clay with calcareous deposits. Height, 15".

93. Dog scratching itself.
Colima. Brownish-red clay with traces of black paint. Height, 11 3/4".

94. Dog effigy.
Colima. Burnished red clay. Height, 20".

95. Lobster.
Colima. Burnished red clay with calcareous deposit.
Height, 7 5/8".

96. Bird of prey holding snake in beak.
Colima. Burnished cream clay with black and red paint. Height, 9 ¹/₂".

97. Parrot.
Colima. Red and buff burnished clay. Height, 9 ¹/₂".

98. Double ducks.
Colima. Burnished red and tan clay with traces of black. Height, 7 ¹/₂".

99. Crab.
Colima. Burnished red clay. Height, 2 ¹/₄"; diameter, 4".

100. Coiled snake.
Colima. Burnished dark-red clay. Height, 5 1/2″; diameter, 10 1/2″.

101. Young bird.
Colima. Burnished brownish-red clay with traces of black. Height, 7″.

102. Bird in flight.
Colima. Brownish-red clay with traces of black. Height, 5 1/2″.

103. Globular jar with three kneeling-figure supports. *Colima. Burnished red clay with traces of black paint. Height, 9″; diameter, 10″.*

104. Jar.
Colima. Burnished brown clay with black deposits. Height, 9 ¹/₄″; diameter, 11 ¹/₄″.

105. U-shaped jar.
Colima. Brown-black mottled burnished clay. Height, 9 ⁵/₈″.

106. Stepped cylinder jar.
Colima. Burnished red clay with calcareous deposit.
Height, 9 $^1/_4$″; diameter, 9 $^1/_2$″.

107. Jug.
Colima. Burnished red and tan clay. Height, 10 $^3/_4$″.

108. Cylindrical vase with relief decorations.
Colima. Burnished brown clay. Height, 8 $^3/_4$″;
diameter, 7 $^1/_4$″.

109. Globular gadrooned jar with three parrot-shaped feet. *Colima. Burnished red clay with white paint. Height, 10″; diameter, 13 1/2″.*

110. Jar.
Colima. Burnished red clay. Height, 9 1/2″; diameter, 13″.

111. Spiked bowl with lid.
Colima. Brownish clay with traces of white paint. Height, 12″.

112. Jar.
Colima. Burnished brownish-red clay with calcareous deposit. Height, 8″; diameter, 11″.

113. Jar with eight human heads.
Colima. Burnished red and tan clay with traces of black paint. Height, 8″; diameter, 12″.

114. Jar with three iguana supports.
Colima. Burnished red and tan clay. Height, 14″; diameter, 10 ¹/₂″.

115. Mask.
Colima. Brown clay. Height, 9 ¹/₂″.

116/117. Incense burner with loop handle and
two joined figures riding a jaguar (two views).
*Colima. Red on buff clay with traces of black paint.
Height, 19 ¹/₄″.*

118/119. Incense burner with removable basin. *Colima. Reddish-brown clay with calcareous deposits. Height, 13".*

120. Model of a wooden drum (*teponaztli*).
Colima. Burnished red clay with calcareous deposit.
Height, 3″.

121. Tubular effigy incense burner with
appliquéd and incised decoration. *Colima.*
Early Postclassic period. Reddish-brown clay with
residues of white pigment. Height, 22 1/4″;
diameter, 13 1/2″.

122. Figure.
Colima. Carved bone. Height, 2″.

123. Woman.
Vicinity of Autlán, Jalisco. Solid buff clay with traces of white paint. Height, 9 1/2".

124. Man.
Vicinity of Autlán, Jalisco. Solid buff clay with traces of white paint. Height, 10".

125. Woman.
Vicinity of Autlán, Jalisco. Solid pinkish clay with traces of white paint. Height, 8 7/8".

126. Woman.
Michoacán. Buff clay with traces of white paint.
Height, 8 3/4″.

127. Seated hunchback.
Etzatlán region, Jalisco. Tan and dark-red clay.
Height, 10″.

128. Seated man holding bowl.
Etzatlán region, Jalisco. Cream and red clay.
Height, 8 ³/₄″.

129/130. Man; woman.
Vicinity of Ameca, Jalisco. Burnished tan clay
with red, black, brown, and red paint. Height of
man, 16 ³/₄″; of woman, 15 ¹/₂″.

131. Figure holding small club or stone knife.
Vicinity of Etzatlán, Jalisco. Burnished tan clay
with black paint. Height, 24 ¹/₂″.

132. Man carrying a ball he is ready to throw. *Vicinity of Ameca, Jalisco. Burnished cream clay with red paint. Height, 17".*

133. Warrior holding round missile. *Vicinity of Etzatlán, Jalisco. Burnished tan clay with black paint. Height, 10 3/4".*

134. Two women.
*Vicinity of Ameca, Jalisco. Burnished cream and
red clay with traces of black paint. Height: left,
10 1/4"; right, 8 5/8".*

135. Pair of joined female figures.
*Vicinity of Etzatlán, Jalisco. Buff clay with traces
of red, black, and cream paint. Height, 19".*

136. Woman with young girl on her lap.
Vicinity of Etzatlán, Jalisco. Burnished tan clay with red and black paint. Height, 8 1/8".

137. Obese woman.
Vicinity of Ameca, Jalisco. Burnished red and tan clay with traces of black paint. Height, 20 1/4".

138. Woman.
Vicinity of Etzatlán, Jalisco. Burnished brown and red clay with black and cream paint. Height, 19".

139. Woman holding small bowl.
*Etzatlán region, Jalisco. White on red clay with
traces of black. Height, 29".*

140. Warrior holding cudgel.
*Etzatlán region, Jalisco. Black and cream on red
clay. Height, 28 ¹/₂".*

141. Three warriors.
Vicinity of Ameca, Jalisco. Buff clay with red paint. Height of tallest, 18".

142. Animal effigy (probably of a dog).
Vicinity of Guadalajara, Jalisco. Burnished cream clay. Length, 10 1/4".

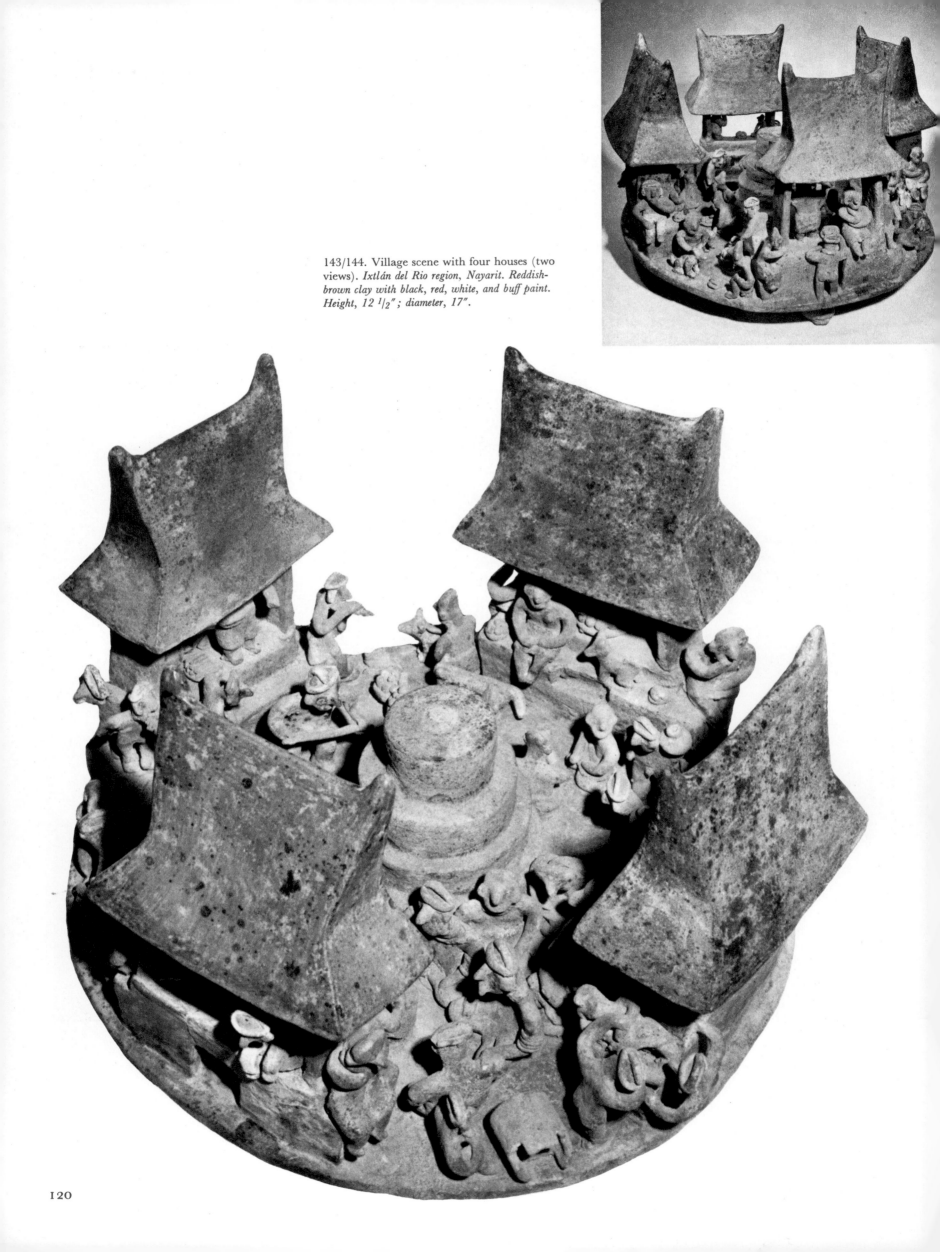

143/144. Village scene with four houses (two views). *Ixtlán del Rio region, Nayarit. Reddish-brown clay with black, red, white, and buff paint. Height, 12 1/2″; diameter, 17″.*

145. Four figures in a dance line.
Ixtlán del Rio region, Nayarit. Solid clay with traces of white, red, and black paint. Height, 3 3/4".

146. Village scene with three houses and a marriage ceremony. *Ixtlán del Rio region, Nayarit. Brown clay with black, white, and red paint. Height, 7"; diameter, 13".*

147. Dance group.
Ixtlán del Rio region, Nayarit. Solid clay with traces of black, white, and red paint. Height, 7".

148. Two-story house or shelter with eight occupants. *Nayarit. Solid clay with traces of black and cream paint. Height, 9 1/4".*

149. Two-story house with multiple-roof complex and nine occupants. *Ixtlán del Rio region, Nayarit. Clay with traces of red, yellow, white, and black paint. Height, 6 1/4".*

150. House complex with three roofs and
twelve occupants. *Ixtlán del Rio region, Nayarit.
Clay with traces of black and cream paint. Height,
7 1/4".*

151. Person reclining on pallet with attendant. *Ixtlán del Rio region, Nayarit. Brown clay with yellow, red, and black paint. Height, 3 1/2".*

152. House on platform with reclining person inside. *Ixtlán del Rio region, Nayarit. Reddish-brown clay with black, white, and orange paint. Height, 7".*

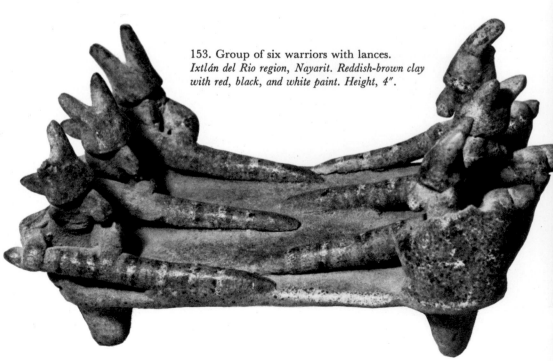

153. Group of six warriors with lances. *Ixtlán del Rio region, Nayarit. Reddish-brown clay with red, black, and white paint. Height, 4".*

154. Battle scene on hill.
*Ixtlán del Rio region, Nayarit. Brown clay with
red, white, yellow, and black paint. Height, 10".*

156. Funeral procession.
Ixtlán del Rio region, Nayarit. Brown clay with red, orange, white, and blue-gray paint. Height, 6 1/4".

155. Group of two houses with men on poles.
Ixtlán del Rio region, Nayarit. Brownish clay with red, orange, black, and white paint. Height, 14"; diameter, 9".

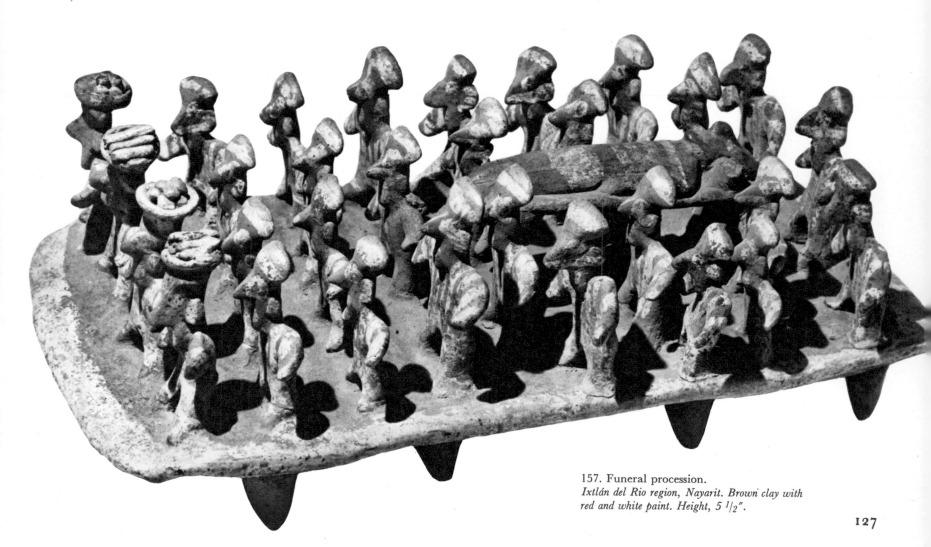

157. Funeral procession.
Ixtlán del Rio region, Nayarit. Brown clay with red and white paint. Height, 5 1/2".

158. Two-story house with occupants.
*Ixtlán del Rio region, Nayarit. Reddish-brown clay
with white and brown paint. Height, 15 1/2".*

161. Figure seated on stool.
*Nayarit. Brownish-red clay with black striations.
Height, 13".*

159. Woman holding child to breast and bowl
on head. *Southern Nayarit. Brownish-red clay
with white paint. Height, 21".*

160. Obese woman.
*Nayarit. Cream and black on red clay. Height,
11 3/4".*

129

162. Woman and two men.
Southern Nayarit. Red clay with black and white paint and bluish-gray patina. Height: 16", 21", 15 1/2" respectively.

163. Woman carrying bowl on shoulder.
Southern Nayarit. Dark-red clay with black and white paint. Height, 23 1/2".

164. Woman with bowl on head.
Vicinity Santiago Compostela, Nayarit. Burnished buff clay with red paint. Height, 9 1/4".

165. Warrior with club and small jar.
Southern Nayarit. Burnished painted clay. Height,
19 3/4".

166. Figure holding rattle.
Nayarit, Jalisco border region. Cream-colored clay
with red and black paint. Height, 17 1/2".

167. Man with pustules on body.
Ixtlán del Rio region, Nayarit. Brown clay with black paint. Height, 6 3/4".

168/169. Kneeling hunched woman holding a bowl (two views). *Ixtlán del Rio region, Nayarit. Tan clay with black and white paint. Height, 7 1/4".*

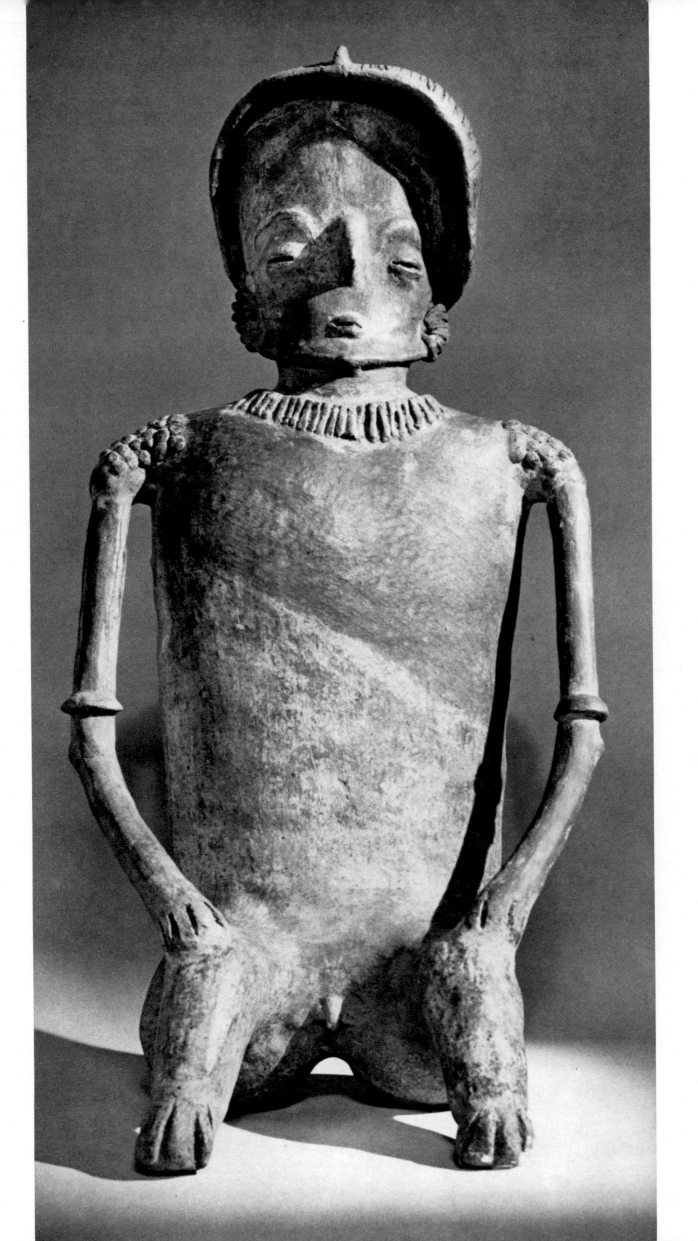

170. Man.
Southern Nayarit. Burnished red clay with traces of
black and white paint. Height, 24".

171. Man seated on a stool.
Southern Nayarit. Burnished orange-red clay.
Height, 15 ³/₄".

172. Warrior and two women.
Southern Nayarit. Burnished clay with traces of
black paint. Height: 17", 15", 19" respectively.

173. Man holding large gourd drum or rasp.
Ixtlán del Rio region, Nayarit. Burnished red and brown clay with black and white paint. Height, 5"

174. Man seated on two-legged stool.
Southern Nayarit. Light-brown clay with traces of black paint. Height, 15".

175. Man playing on gourd rasp.
Southern Nayarit. Burnished brownish-black clay. Height, 16 1/2".

176. Man playing an effigy-shaped rasp.
*Ixtlán del Río region, Nayarit. Dark-red clay with
black and white paint. Height, 22".*

177. Man.
*Santiago Compostela region, Nayarit. Burnished
painted clay. Height, 18″.*

178. Woman holding small dog.
Ixtlán del Rio region, Nayarit. Painted clay.
Height, 22".

179. Man using walking stick.
Southern Nayarit. Painted clay. Height, 11 1/2".

180. Emaciated male and female figures.
Ixtlán del Rio region, Nayarit. Painted clay.
Height: 15 1/4" and 13".

181. Joined couple.
Ixtlán del Rio region, Nayarit. Orange clay with
red, black, and white paint. Height, 18".

182. Man and wife.
Southern Nayarit. Painted clay. Height: 18 ³/₄"
and 17 ¹/₂".

183. Woman with bowl on shoulder.
Ixtlán del Rio region, Nayarit. Painted clay.
Height, 25".

184. Standing warrior.
Ixtlán del Rio, Nayarit. Painted clay. Height, 22".

185. Kneeling woman with two children and bowl of food, seated on a tablelike projection from the body. *Ixtlán del Rio region, Nayarit. Brownish clay with red, orange, black, and white paint. Height, 13 1/4".*

186. Warrior with protective armor and club. *Ixtlán del Rio region, Nayarit. Brownish-red clay with black and white paint. Height, 24 1/2".*

187. Effigy vase with head of rain-god.
Southern Nayarit. Buff clay with white and blue-green paint. Height, 4 3/4″.

188. Dog with anthropomorphic body.
Michoacán. Basalt. Height, 17″.

189. Barking dog.
Ixtlán del Rio region, Nayarit. Tan clay with white paint. Height, 5 1/2″.

190. Chac-Mool figure.
Michoacán. Postclassic period. Volcanic rock.
Height, 28".

191. Jaguar seat.
Michoacán. Basalt. Height, 19".

UPPER LEFT AND UPPER RIGHT
192/193. Cloisonné decorated pedestal bowl
(two views). *Michoacán. Postclassic period.
Reddish-brown clay with polychrome. Height, 3 ³/₄″.*

ABOVE
194. Cloisonné decorated jar.
*Michoacán Postclassic period. Clay decorated in
cloisonné technique with white, yellow, green,
reddish-brown, and orange. Height, 8 ¹/₂″;
diameter, 9″.*

ABOVE, CENTER
195. Conch shells.
*Nayarit. Postclassic period. Stuccoed and painted.
Length, 10 ¹/₂″.*

ABOVE
196. Tripod bowl.
*Border of Michoacán and Guerrero. Toltec period.
Buff clay with red, black, and cream paint. Height,
6″; diameter, 9 ³/₄″.*

197. Man with animal mask carrying a bowl
on his back. *Jalisco. Basalt. Height, 21″.*

198. Standing male.
Michoacán. Basalt. Height, 22″.

199. Figure.
*Mezcala, Guerrero. Gray-green stone. Height,
14 1/4".*

200. Woman.
*Mezcala, Guerrero. Gray variegated stone. Height,
10 1/2".*

201. Seated figure.
*Mezcala, Guerrero. Mottled dark-green-and-white
stone. Height, 4 ³/₄″.*

202. Figure.
*Mezcala, Guerrero. Brownish-green stone with
traces of red coloring. Height, 5 ¹/₄″.*

203. Prisoner with arms tied behind back;
grasshopper; animal. *Mezcala, Guerrero.
White-and-green mottled stone. Height: 3 ¹/₄″,
3 ¹/₄″, 2 ³/₄″.*

204. Frog.
Balsas River region, Guerrero. Cream-colored stone.
Height, 5".

205. Model of a temple.
Mezcala, Guerrero. Andesitic serpentine. Height, 7 1/8".

206. Model of a temple.
Mezcala region, Guerrero. Gray-green stone. Height, 6".

207. Mask surmounted by two birds' heads.
*Mezcala, Guerrero. Dark-green stone. Height,
3 3/4".*

208. Mask.
Guerrero. Alabaster. Height, 5 1/2".

209. Seated monkey with tail upright.
Mezcala, Guerrero. Grayish-white stone. Height, 5 1/2".

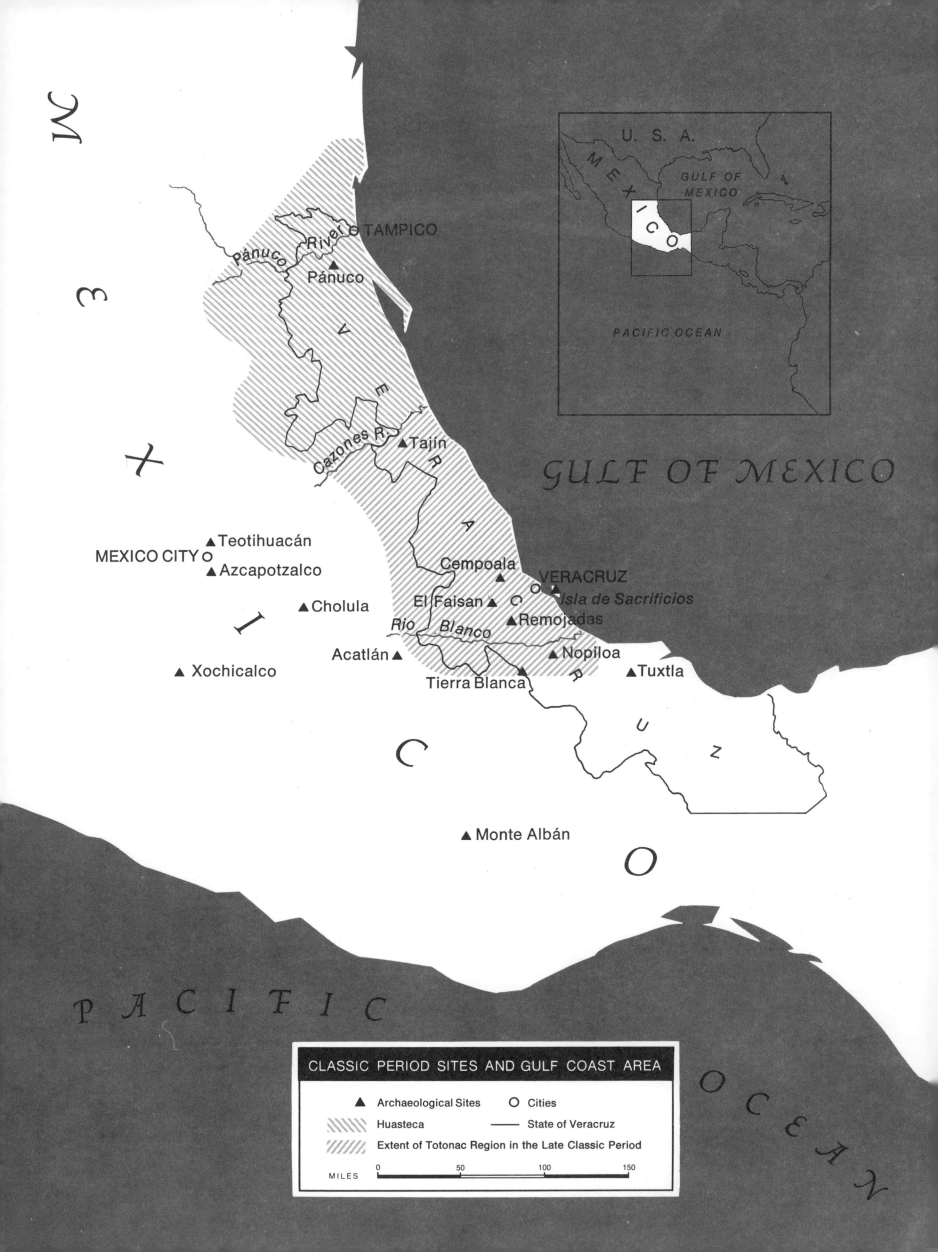

M
E
X
I
C
O

Pánuco River ○ TAMPICO
▲ Pánuco

V
E
R
A
Cazones R. ▲ Tajín
C
R
U
Z

▲ Teotihuacán
MEXICO CITY ○
▲ Azcapotzalco

Cempoala
▲
VERACRUZ
○ Isla de Sacrificios
El Faisan ▲
▲ Cholula
▲ Remojadas
Río Blanco
Acatlán ▲
▲ Nopiloa
▲ Tuxtla
Tierra Blanca ▲
▲ Xochicalco

▲ Monte Albán

GULF OF MEXICO

U.S.A.

MEXICO
GULF OF MEXICO

PACIFIC OCEAN

PACIFIC OCEAN

CLASSIC PERIOD SITES AND GULF COAST AREA

▲ Archaeological Sites   ○ Cities

Huasteca   State of Veracruz

Extent of Totonac Region in the Late Classic Period

MILES   0   50   100   150

I I I

THE CLASSIC PERIOD
IN MEXICO

The Classic Period in Mexico

Teotihuacán AND THE EARLY CLASSIC PERIOD

ABOUT THE THIRD CENTURY B.C. the great city of Teotihuacán in the northeastern part of the Valley of Mexico came into prominence. This settlement rapidly developed into a true urban center which in due course exerted profound influences over most of Mesoamerica, during a florescence known as the Classic period.

A recent mapping project, still in progress, has revealed that Teotihuacán, toward the end of its early period of occupation (Tzacualli phase), extended over more than three square miles and was the largest Formative period or Early Classic settlement of Mesoamerica. By the end of the first phase, or shortly afterwards, the Pyramid of the Sun had been built to its present height of 200 feet.

Early Teotihuacán shared the general characteristics of the Late Formative period, which is indicated by the form and decoration of the pottery and figurines. It was during the second phase (Miccaotli, about A.D. 150 to 250) that Teotihuacán assumed a leading role in Mesoamerican prehistory. Its truly urban character is revealed by a high degree of planning in the central area, in the middle of which stands the Ciudadela. This large plaza, with its pyramids and surrounding walls, is believed to have been the administrative center. Streets departing at right angles from the main causeway, the Street of the Dead, link the residential area with the ceremonial precinct. Toward the fringes of the city planning was less obvious. An interesting recent discovery is a large plaza, matching the one within the Ciudadela in size, and situated opposite it across the Street of the Dead. It is assumed that because of its extent and lack of high structures, this colossal plaza may have served as the city's market.

In addition to the numerous temples and palaces built for the religious hierarchy, there existed several large blocks with apartment buildings, one of which had no less than 176 connected rooms. These, and the innumerable objects—figurines, ornaments, sculptures, and tools—which have been unearthed, testify to an unprecedented aggregation of people in this area.

The architecture has an austere character, emphasized by simple straight lines and massive proportions. A structural element, first developed in Teotihuacán, is the sloping plane surmounted by a projecting cornice to form each of the vertical elements of the terraces. This element was widely diffused and elsewhere persisted into the fifteenth century, long after the fall of Teotihuacán.

The metropolis was an open city, without fortifications. The Classic period was a peaceful one, it would appear, except for minor raids and upheavals. This is also evident in the mural paintings, which depict deities or priests scattering seeds or bringing rain, but seldom present figures bearing arms. Tlaloc, the rain-god, was the predominant deity, which is understandable in view of the great dependence on water for agriculture. His cult and iconography derived from the Olmec rain-jaguar deity. During the Teotihuacán II period the rain-god cult merged with the cult of the Feathered Serpent. The latter was symbolized in the so-called Quetzalcoatl Pyramid, which subsequently was covered by a plain Early Classic structure. The Feathered Serpent cult was revived only after the fall of Teotihuacán, and given new direction as the Quetzalcoatl cult, whose main protagonist was the culture hero Ce Acatl Topiltzin Quetzalcoatl of Tula (Fiorescano, pp. 121–66).

Besides these main deities the Old God of Fire, a butterfly-god, and Xipe Totec, the fertility-god, were venerated. These gods symbolized the cosmic elements—water, wind, fire, and earth—and were eventually included in the Aztec pantheon. The profound religious orientation of Teotihuacán, seen in its art and architecture, implies an all-powerful priestly hierarchy which embodied strong secular powers. Under this rule, Teotihuacán attained a splendor never before reached, and which appeared in retrospect to the peoples of the later Postclassic period as the golden age of Mesoamerica.

The religiously oriented frescoes of Teotihuacán are invaluable records, for no pictorial manuscripts or codices survived from this period, although such undoubtedly must have existed.

Comparatively few examples of stone sculpture are preserved. An enormous stone image that stood in the temple on top of the Sun Pyramid was destroyed by the Spaniards in the early days of the Conquest. What remains of sculptural art excels in technique and monumentality. Architectural sculpture is refined and highly symbolic. Its aim was to impress the observer by means of multiple renderings of identical motifs. The serpent heads on the Quetzalcoatl Pyramid and the recently (1962) discovered bas-relief pillars of the Temple of the Butterflies (now more appropriately renamed Palace of Quetzalpapalotl) illustrate this point.

Traces of pigments indicate that originally these carvings were painted in various colors, which must have given them an entirely different and probably more fascinating aspect than is perceptible now.

Remarkable are the life-size stone masks, made of serpentine and other hard materials and highly polished. The inhabitants of Teotihuacán, although they were not the originators of this art, created these masks with great skill, the features resembling those of the "portrait type" figurines. The masks do not represent deities or living persons, and were exclusively used for funeral purposes.

Noteworthy is the absence of steles, widely used in the lowland Maya area and of such importance to the archaeologist for their inscriptions, which provide the calendric framework for the chronological ordering. The extensive research presently going on at Teotihuacán may perhaps unearth a stele or two, as happened recently at Xochicalco, where three steles were found in a cache, an unexpected reward after twenty years of exploration at that site. Ball courts are also, and strangely, missing at Teotihuacán; but perhaps some will be found one day, for most contemporaneous and later sites had at least one of these structures.

Teotihuacán sculpture has a unique flavor of its own. It was mainly confined to the type site, with the exception of the well-known stone incense burners bearing the image of Huehueteotl, the Old God of Fire, which occur also on the west coast, where they are doubtlessly a Teotihuacán inspiration.

The pottery of Teotihuacán, too, has its own peculiar features and developed into intricately decorated wares for ceremonial use. Of particular interest are the tall cylindrical vases with three feet, and flat-bottomed bowls with straight walls, which were decorated in very low relief, first by outlining the design with a sharp tool, then by scratching away the background. Another highly developed method of embellishing tripod vases was by coating them with a thin layer of stucco upon which the design was painted with various colors. The contours and details were often outlined in fine dark lines. Covarrubias called this method of decoration "paint cloisonné" and pointed out its very extensive geographical distribution and long use, ranging from the Formative period to the present day. In his opinion, the lacquer was a mixture of animal or vegetal resins and oils with clay and mineral pigments. After disintegration of the organic components during a long period of interment, only a thin layer supporting the paint is visible, giving the impression of painted stucco (Covarrubias, p. 95). Anna Shepard, on the other hand, found that stucco painting on pottery was applied over a coat of lime plaster after the vessel had been fired. She also noted that similar techniques, styles, and colors were used in ceramics and in mural painting, suggesting that in some cases vessel and mural painting was done by the same artist (Shepard, p. 178). These plano-relief-decorated and stuccoed-and-painted vessels and the murals are important sources for the study of Teotihuacán religious symbolism, which had attained a high level of sophistication.

The figurines are as abundant as in the preceding periods, if not more so, but instead of being entirely modeled by hand they were manufactured in molds. This procedure is a diagnostic of the Classic and of subsequent periods. The discovery of molds in the Teotihuacán archaeological zone, by those who supply the tourists with sometimes quite fanciful creations of supposedly authentic antiquities, has helped them to inject a genuine character into their products. One type of figurine is extraordinarily abundant, and, because of its broad forehead, great naturalism, and artistically rendered features, has been labeled the "portrait type." This denomination is not entirely accurate, for the stereotyped faces cannot be true portraits of individuals.

As a great religious and urban center, Teotihuacán was the focal point for extensive trade with other provinces and great centers that flourished simultaneously, such as Monte Albán (Oaxaca), Kaminaljuyú (Guatemala), and the Maya lowlands. Trade relations also extended to the Gulf coast region, particularly to central Veracruz and into western Mexico, including the Guerrero coast (Acapulco).

Trade objects consisted mainly of pottery vessels and stone artifacts which were exported in exchange for precious raw materials such as feathers of tropical birds, jade, and cotton. But religious and architectural concepts also were diffused, either directly or through Teotihuacán emissaries who had established colonies in foreign lands. This is verified by the existence of characteristic Teotihuacán features noticeable in architecture, sculpture, and artifacts in Colima (Armería), Jalisco (temple pyramid at El Ixtepete), Querétaro, and at Tajín and Cerro de las Mesas in Veracruz, as well as in many Valley of Mexico sites and at Kaminaljuyú and Tikal in Guatemala.

The civilizing influence of Teotihuacán during the Early Classic period was felt by some, and displaced other, seminomadic hunters of the northern frontier, thereby considerably expanding Mesoamerica in a northerly direction. It has been suggested that perhaps some of the civilized centers established there formed the target for the later invasions by these nomads, who, by the end of the seventh century, succeeded in sacking and burning Teotihuacán. Remains of carbonized beams, smoke stains on the white stucco-cement floors, and signs of willful destruction testify to the tragic end.

The destruction of the ceremonial buildings must have set in motion an exodus of the priests and of the highly skilled craftsmen who had been engaged by the priesthood in the construction and periodic renewal of the religious buildings. Thus deprived of its leadership, the metropolis ceased to function as a culture center. Its fringes continued to be inhabited by foreigners who produced a very different type of pottery, known as Mazapan ware, which is inferior in quality and artistry. Where did these specialized craftsmen go? Some probably joined an earlier established colony at Azcapotzalco, where they carried on the Classic traditions for two or three centuries. Another group migrated farther south and settled in the Puebla-Oaxaca region, joining the Mixtecs, while still others dispersed into Central America.

The fall of Teotihuacán had far-reaching political, religious, and economic consequences in the Mexican highlands during the Late Classic period. There remained several enclaves with Teotihuacán descendants whose skill contributed to the rise of regional cultures and art styles.

Xochicalco AND THE END OF THE CLASSIC PERIOD

Meanwhile other great centers, such as Xochicalco (near Cuernavaca in the state of Morelos) and Tajín (in north-central Veracruz), continued to flourish in the Classic pattern.

Xochicalco had strong ties with Teotihuacán and also absorbed elements from Oaxaca, the Maya area, and from Veracruz, blending them selectively into a pattern of its own. The adaptation of extraneous elements is evident in the relief carvings and in the kinds of offerings placed in caches beneath the sacred structures. The enormous feathered serpent carved on the exterior of the Main Pyramid is indicative of the revival of the Feathered Serpent cult, perhaps attempted by Teotihuacán priests who had taken refuge in Xochicalco. The amalgamation of Teotihuacán-, Zapotec-, and Nahua-style calendric glyphs which are carved on the newly discovered steles seems to indicate that Xochicalco was a center for the intellectual elite which harbored priests from other regions who had been displaced by the impending collapse of the Classic cultures, foreshadowed by the fall of Teotihuacán. The threat of approaching barbarians impelled the priests of Xochicalco to safeguard the records containing the essence of their priestly, divinatory, and calendric knowledge. Inscribed on steles (the first sculptures of this kind found in the central highlands), these monuments were secreted in a large cache beneath a temple platform. One of the steles had to be broken to be accommodated, but the fracture was executed in such a manner as to cause the least possible damage to the hieroglyphic text (Saenz, 1961).

Xochicalco is strategically located on a terraced hillside, surrounded by a rampart giving the impression of having been a fortress. Yet the site was abandoned without there being any signs of conquest or haste. Along the lower slopes, Late Classic Coyotlatelco and Toltec ceramic remains were found, pertaining to a later occupation by different peoples.

The Monte Albán Culture

The earliest cultures of the central valleys of Oaxaca, which began in about the ninth or tenth century before Christ, are characterized by Olmec culture motifs, seen not only in the low-relief "Danzante" carvings but also in ceramics. The Monte Albán I period was well advanced, typified by ceremonialism, hieroglyphic writing, a calendar, and flat-roofed stone tombs. The pottery, mostly gray in color, is well polished and decorated with incised lines. Toward the end of this period profound changes took place, due to incursions by peoples from Chiapas, and possibly from the Guatemala highland area, who apparently dominated the Valley of Oaxaca. Most of the ceremonial objects changed in style during the Monte Albán II period, while the domestic pottery persisted in patterns almost identical to those of the first period. The second-period style appears to be confined to Monte Albán proper and only a few other sites. Characteristic are the four-legged vessels, pot stands, and stuccoed-and-painted bowls.

Toward the beginning of the Christian era, Monte Albán II culture had fused with what remained of the earlier tradition, and new influences—this time from central Mexico, in particular the Puebla Valley and Teotihuacán—led to a new cultural alignment. Only at that time can the population of Monte Albán and of Oaxaca be identified with the Zapotecs.

Early Classic Monte Albán (Period III-A) is represented by a new architecture, characterized by sloping walls and superimposed vertical tablets, originally derived from Teotihuacán. Pottery decoration became highly stylized, consisting of engraved serpent motifs. The tomb complex became very elaborate. The dead were buried in stone-lined vaults with angular roofs. A number of tombs have antechambers and alfresco painted walls representing religious scenes.

The Monte Albán III-B period (Middle to Late Classic) was a time of great architectural development and expansion. Sculpture and pottery, however, declined in artistic quality. A very considerable concentration of population lived in the central valley, ruled by a priestly hierarchy from the hilltop of Monte Albán, where the people congregated only for religious ceremonies.

One of the characteristic manifestations of the Monte Albán culture is the funerary urn. It consists of a tall cylindrical vessel attached to a cross-legged figure with the hands resting on the knees. The torso is usually short and appears to be hidden by a huge breast-plaque. The face is sometimes covered by a mask and is usually surmounted by a large headdress. The pupils are indicated by holes and the mouth is open, showing the teeth. Ornaments were indicated by clay fillets or made separately in molds, as can be seen from the recurrence of motifs in the breast-plaques, ear ornaments, and headdresses. The large number of very similar urns and close adherence to an iconographical system reveal that they were mass-produced in an assembly line fashion.

The term "funerary urn," commonly applied to these effigies, is not entirely correct. They were discovered not only in tombs or in the antechambers of tombs, but also in caches beneath the floors of temple structures. Furthermore, in no instance did such vessels, when found in controlled excavations, contain bones or residues of cremations. The cylindrical vase was usually found to be empty, but on rare occasions contained small offerings of jade beads or shells. The function of the vase is therefore not clearly known. The figures attached to a large extent portray deities or priests in the attire of a specific god. Most frequently depicted is the rain-god, Cocijo, who always wears a mask and a medallion in the center of his headdress. Other personifications include deities of corn, a god with a bird headdress, who can be either male or female, and a butterfly deity. Some effigies lack the qualifying ornaments or symbols and have, instead, a tall conical headdress with two broad bands pending sideward over the shoulder. Such figures were the companions of the god effigies and are usually of smaller size.

The urns show a long and interesting evolution, having their roots in the Monte Albán I and II periods, antedating the Zapotec occupation of Monte Albán and the central valleys. During the entire Classic period (Monte Albán III-A and III-B), the urns had an important function in Zapotec ritual and were made in large numbers. They were discontinued with the decline of Monte Albán in A.D. 900 (Caso and Bernal).

The last Zapotec phase (Monte Albán IV) is not too well known, mainly because the political power of the Zapotecs declined and with it their artistic accomplishments. The pottery of this period is coarser and lacks innovations. By the middle of the thirteenth century the Mixtecs, with a distinctively different art tradition, began to infiltrate the area.

Central Veracruz

Another important culture center which continued to flourish after the collapse of Teotihuacán was at Tajín. It reached its climax in the Late Classic and extended its activity somewhat beyond the end of that period, perhaps because of its isolated location. The themes of the relief carvings which adorn its ball courts and other buildings involve religious concepts related to the solar cult, human sacrifice, and deities of the underworld. Tajín influence, extending mainly in a southeasterly direction, is evidenced, among other traits, by its characteristic decorative element, the interlaced scroll.

In the Tuxtlas region these influences crystallized into a unique art complex, typified by stone yokes, *hachas,* (flat stone heads), and *palmas* (palmate stones). These sculptures, which are related to the ball-game ceremonial, originated in the Early Classic period and were diffused in the Late Classic throughout the neighboring areas, the Valley of Mexico, and probably by a Pipil-Nicarao migratory wave as far as the Pacific slope of Guatemala and El Salvador. *Palmas* apparently originated later than yokes and *hachas* and are confined to Veracruz.

Some yokes are plain, others are carved, mainly on the exterior but sometimes inside as well. Carved specimens are generally restricted to Veracruz and most commonly represent a froglike creature, probably depicting a mythological earth monster.

Hachas are flattened heads reminiscent of the votive ax which gave them their name. Some have a tenon.

Palmas are tall, graceful forms, fan-shaped at the top, and have a concave base. They are decorated with various motifs, often zoomorphic, such as birds and alligators, or portray hands joined in a praying attitude.

The stylistic development of the figurines of Central Veracruz has been elucidated by intensive research in the past decade, mainly at Las Remojadas and Nopiloa (Medellín Zenil). The earliest types, reaching back to the twelfth century before Christ, were made in the same technique as coeval varieties of the central highlands, emphasizing solid bodies with oversized heads and rudimentary limbs. The features bear distinctive expressions which make them diagnostic for the area. They are often highlighted by the use of asphalt paint.

Figurines with smiling faces are a unique phenomenon of Mesoamerican art. Their prototype, in the form of small figurine-whistles of the Early Classic period, was first discovered at Las Remojadas, in the semiarid region near the modern town of Veracruz. During the Late Classic, these figurines become highly sophisticated and show geometric relief decoration on the forehead and on the skirts. Because of their expression, which ranges from calm introspective bliss to a mischievous grin, sometimes bordering on the idiotic, it has been suggested that they represent deities associated with dance, happiness, and music. Their posture, too, indicates motion. Other figurines portray the native Gulf coast deity, Xipe Totec, identified by the superimposed skin of the flayed victim which the priests used to wear in the ceremonies for this god. A hybrid Xipe-Tlazolteotl form occurs, in which the goddess wears a mask covering only the lower part of her face.

Exceptionally large-size figures also represent deities, among which Quetzalcoatl, in his aspect as wind-god, and the death-god are prominent.

Mayoid hollow figurine-whistles, which are moldmade in two parts and carefully joined, were fashioned of fine clay and bear a white stuccolike coat of paint. Human and animal motifs are common. This type, which is noted for its bulky appearance, blends with the Late Classic Maya figurine complex of the Campeche coast.

THE HUASTECS

At the time of the Spanish Conquest the Huasteca, a term which primarily designates a linguistic province, occupied chiefly the lowlands on the Gulf coast from the Tropic of Cancer to the Cazones River in northern Veracruz. In earlier times Huastec-speaking people extended farther west into the highlands of the Sierra Madre.

The oldest settlements in the Huasteca are contemporary with Early Formative villages of the Valley of Mexico, and their ceramic materials show affinities with the Maya area (Mamom phase of Uaxactún).

During the Classic period the Huastecs absorbed influences from Teotihuacán and the southern Gulf coast, but being a northern outpost of Mesoamerica, the area did not share all of the Classic culture traits.

Local developments in material culture persisted also during the Toltec period, when the Mixteca-Puebla style which spread over large parts of Mesoamerica left its mark also on the Huastec area. At that time the Huastecs developed an art style of their own, typified by stone sculpture and unique pottery forms. The early Postclassic low-relief stone carvings have a slablike appearance. Sculptures in the round developed later and followed the Toltec and Aztec pattern. Pottery in a style not found elsewhere in Mesoamerica was made with black-on-white decoration and in sophisticated forms, such as spouted effigy- and teapot-shaped vessels.

To the north and the northwest the Huastecs exerted a civilizing influence over the nomadic Chichimecs, and some of their culture traits found acceptance on the western coast of Mexico and in the southeastern United States.

The wind-god Quetzalcoatl, who is usually portrayed in Huastec attire, and the earth-goddess Tlazolteotl, both of whom became prominent in the Nahua pantheon of the central highlands, are very likely of Huastec origin. These people are also credited with the development of circular temples, which spread over much of Mesoamerica and which are generally associated with the wind-god.

The Classic Period in Mexico

Captions and Notes

PLATES 210–332

210. CYLINDRICAL BOWL WITH STUCCOED AND PAINTED DECORATION. / Teotihuacán, Valley of Mexico. Early Classic period. Brown clay with red, white, bluish-green, and black paint. Height, 5 1/2"; diameter, 5 3/4". Los Angeles County Museum of Natural History.

A priest with large eyes, personifying the rain-god, holds a staff from which he sprinkles three large drops onto a plant. His speech scroll is decorated with a flower to show that he is chanting or praying. This fertility rite is shown twice, with slight variation of detail.

211. TRIPOD BOWL WITH STUCCOED AND PAINTED DECORATION. / Teotihuacán, Valley of Mexico. Early Classic period. Brown ware painted green, white, and red, with thin black outlining. Height, 6 1/4"; diameter, 4 1/2". Private collection.

The shape of this vessel is unusual. The decoration depicts the stylized face of a butterfly deity. Eyes, proboscis, and an elaborate feather headdress can be discerned. This composition is very similar to that on a Teotihuacanoid tripod, also stuccoed and painted, from Kaminaljuyú, Guatemala (Kidder, Jennings, and Shook, fig. 207 h).

212. STUCCOED AND PAINTED CYLINDRICAL TRIPOD VASE. / Teotihuacán. Early Classic period. Brown clay with red, yellow, and green on dark-red background with black lines for details. Height, 5 1/2"; diameter, 5 3/4". Collection Mr. and Mrs. Ellsworth La Boyteaux, Orinda, Calif.

Two priests in rich regalia and with large speech scrolls are scattering seeds. The priests alternate with two large flowers in this scene, which is related to fertility rites.

213. CYLINDRICAL TRIPOD VASE. / Teotihuacán, Valley of Mexico. Early Classic period. Brown ware stuccoed and painted red, orange, green, white, and black. Height, 5 1/4"; diameter, 5 7/8". Collection Stendahl.

The highly stylized design twice shows the profile head of a priest with a sumptuous feather headdress and symbolic elements, including cotton tufts similar to appliqué representations on incense burners. It has hollow openwork slab supports. Two holes were drilled on either side of a crack below the rim so that a string could be inserted to tie up the break. This Pre-Columbian repair method was widely used. For a study of the distribution of the crack-lacing method, see Linné, 1934, pp. 210–11.

214. STANDING WOMAN. / Teotihuacán vicinity. Early Classic period. Volcanic stone. Height, 36". Philadelphia Museum of Art. The Louise and Walter Arensberg Collection.

There are traces of red and green paint over stucco. The position of the hands suggests that the figure held a wooden staff, bringing to mind the ceremonial bar in the hands of priests on Maya steles. Shirt and shoulder garment are fringed with feathers. A front view of this piece is illustrated in Kubler, 1954, fig. 2.

215. FIGURINE WITH CAPE. / Valley of Mexico. Late Formative period. Buff clay. Height, 6 1/2". Private collection.

The earliest Teotihuacán figurines were entirely modeled by hand (Tzacualli phase, Teotihuacán I). Further characteristics are the prognathism and the elaborate headdress formed by clay appliqués. The face has a masklike appearance because it is modeled of a slab of clay imposed over a core. The mouth is made by an incision, while eyes and nose are made of applied fillets.

216. HOLLOW FIGURINE WITH ANOTHER FIGURINE INSERTED IN ITS OPEN CHEST. / Valley of Mexico. Early Classic period. Buff paste with traces of yellow paint. Height, 10″. Collection Bill Pearson, San Francisco.

The head is moldmade and open in the back. Circular arm-stumps protrude on each side and are perforated in the center for the insertion of strings by which to attach the arms. The opening in the trunk was originally fitted with a slab cover (cf. Marquina, pl. 35). The flat moldmade figure representing an adult female with an elaborate headdress was attached to the back of the opening before firing. The interior figurine is painted white (feathers and beads on headdress), blue (background of head and torso), and red and yellow (flowers). The legs of the main figure are missing; they were probably attached with strings. This piece is illustrated in *Indigenous Art of the Americas*, fig. 123.

217. STANDING FIGURINE WITH RINGS AROUND THE EYES. / Santiago Ahuizotla, Valley of Mexico. Early Classic period. Buff clay with white paint. Height, 5″. Collection Stendahl.

The rings around the eyes suggest that this figure is related to the rain-god, the supreme deity of Teotihuacán. The body is covered by an oval plaque depicting an owl and surrounded by feathers. At the top is the head of the bird; in the center a shield with a hand and two crossed spears. Between the tops of the spears, which are decorated with cotton balls, and the stone tips, are the owl's wings. The triangular object below the shield is the characteristic tail design of owl representations. The hand-owl-spear composition had symbolic significance and occurs also on plano-relief pottery and on murals. For a comparative analysis of this symbol, see von Winning, 1948, pp. 129–32.

218. PAIR OF DANCERS. / Valley of Mexico. Early Classic period. Buff clay. Height, 4″. Collection Stendahl.

The basic type of figurine of the preceding phases (see plate 215) continued to be made during the Classic period, but the heads were now made exclusively from molds. The greater realism of their features earned them the somewhat misleading term "portrait type" (*tipo retrato*), although they were not true portraits, but stereotyped and mass-produced images. The bodies are slim and schematic and it has been suggested that they were clad in paper or pieces of cotton. These pieces are illustrated in *Präkolumbische Kunst*, item 725, pl. 58.

219. EFFIGY JAR REPRESENTING HUEHUETEOTL, THE OLD GOD. / Veracruz. Early Classic period. Thin orange ware. Height, 12″. Museum of the American Indian, Heye Foundation, New York.

A similar vessel is illustrated in Dockstader, pl. 25.

220. PLANO-RELIEF-DECORATED CYLINDRICAL VASE (*two views*). / Valley of Mexico. Early Classic period. Orange-brown clay. Height without supports, 5 1/2″; diameter, 9 1/2″. Collection William P. Palmer.

The decoration shows a priest with animal headdress and a large speech scroll to which are attached flowers and the imbricated year symbol. With one hand he scatters water, in the other he holds a pouch. He is accompanied by an eagle with spread wings, whose headdress forms a panel containing half-stars (water symbols). Priest and eagle occur twice on this vessel in similar design. The lower border shows alternating water drops and shields. The hollow slab feet and 20 per cent of the vessel are reconstructed.

221. SEATED OLD MAN WITH BASIN ON HIS HEAD. / Texcoco region, Valley of Mexico. Volcanic tuff. Height, 17″. Collection Mrs. Edith Hafter, Zurich, Switzerland.

The old man is seated cross-legged, bent forward, hands resting on his knees. The legs form a ring support. His body is very short and slim and is hidden behind the large face and two large ear disks. The cheeks are sunken and his mouth partially toothless. The basin on his head, intended for burning incense, is decorated with diamond-shaped elements alternating with four rectangular elements, which symbolize fire. Figures of clay carrying a bowl on their head for the burning of incense are known from the Late Formative period and represent the Old God, one of the earliest deities, also venerated during the Classic period and known among the Aztecs as Huehueteotl. In the Teotihuacán culture these *incensarios* were made in considerable quantities, exclusively of stone and with little variation in basic features.

222. INCENSE BURNER IN TWO PARTS. / Santiago Ahuizotla, Valley of Mexico. Middle to Late Classic period. Brown clay, ornaments painted red, yellow, and green. Height, 29″. Collection Stendahl.

The burner has been reconstructed. The hourglass-shaped vessel at the bottom is covered by an inverted bowl with flaring walls. Its flat base is perforated and supports a clay tube in the rear which serves as a chimney. A number of separately molded clay plaques depicting motley butterflies, water symbols, and feather ornaments are attached to a framework of clay slabs and surround the mask of the deity in the center. Originally the prefired appliqués were adhered by means of small blobs of clay, after which the entire burner was fired a second time. This mode of attachment did not prevent the appliqués from becoming detached during their long interment. Therefore, the reconstruction of these very complex incense burners is almost always somewhat arbitrary. The butterfly designs relate this *incensario* to the butterfly-god, one of the important deities of Teotihuacán and Monte Albán that continued to be worshiped up to the time of the Conquest. The butterfly is associated with flames and fire; hence it is not surprising that it was often used for the decoration of incense burners.

223/224. Mask (*two views*). / Puebla. Early Classic period. Black steatite. Height, 8 1/2 ". Collection Mr. and Mrs. Robert A. Rowan, Pasadena, Calif.

Masks were worn as pectorals, as shown on small Teotihuacán clay figurines, and were connected with funeral rites.

225. Male Figure. / Puebla. Early Classic period. Dark-green steatite. Height, 9 ". Collection Mr. and Mrs. Bernard J. Reis, New York.

226. Mask. / Central Mexico. Early to Middle Classic period. Blue-green steatite. Height, 5 3/4 ". Collection Stendahl.

227. Funerary Urn. / Oaxaca. Monte Albán III-A. Brown clay. Height, 25 1/2 ". Southwest Museum, Los Angeles.

This unusually large urn shows a young man seated cross-legged with the incised flap of his loincloth between his knees. He holds a bowl containing a foamy liquid (probably pulque) indicated by two lateral volutes. His headdress is partly missing, but from comparison with similar specimens it can be assumed that it consisted of a simple conical cap, from which pend two broad bands which as shown here reach both shoulders. The back of the figure is in the shape of a tall cylindrical vessel. Noteworthy is the rendering of the face, which is not covered by the ubiquitous mask. The ornament above the forehead is a stylized representation of a jaguar's nose and jaw, an element widely known from Zapotec epigraphy as Glyph "C" and common on funerary urns. The lack of the facial mask, the flaps of the cap, and the relative simplicity in the ornamentation are diagnostics of a group of urns known as "companions" because they lack details which associate them iconographically with deities. The urn pictured here is one of an established subgroup whose stylistic evolution is discussed by Caso and Bernal, pp. 119–36.

228. Fragment of a Funerary Urn Depicting the Bat-God. / Oaxaca. Classic period. Brown clay. Height, 6 3/4 ". Thomas Gilcrease Institute of American History and Art, Tulsa, Okla.

A prominent deity of the Zapotec pantheon was the bat-god, whose features are often mistaken for those of a jaguar. The bat-god had wide distribution in Mesoamerica and appears in pictorial manuscripts and on pottery in the Maya and the Mixtec-Puebla areas. From complete specimens on vessels and urns it is evident that the god was shown in human form attired in the disguise of a bat. Diagnostic is the alignment of the teeth of the upper jaw, while those of the lower jaw are covered by the protruding tongue. A further diagnostic is the rendering of the nose.

229. Figurine Vase. / Oaxaca. Monte Albán I. Gray clay. Height, 8 ". American Museum of Natural History, New York.

The face of the deity peers from the opened beak of a bird. The incised design on the beak is frequently depicted in profile. Caso and Bernal (1952) have noted the existence of a young god with a bird helmet associated with braziers as early as Monte Albán I.

230. Effigy Jar. / Oaxaca. Monte Albán I. Burnished gray clay. Height, 5 1/8 "; diameter, 3 3/4 ". Collection Mr. and Mrs. Hasso von Winning, Los Angeles.

Incisions below the eyes probably indicate tears (weeping-eye motif). The headband is similar to that on a brazier from Monte Negro (Monte Albán II) illustrated in Caso and Bernal, fig. 483 a.

231. Funerary Urn Representing the Butterfly-God. / Oaxaca. Monte Albán III-A. Clay with brownish-red paint. Height, 9 ". Dayton Art Institute, Dayton, Ohio.

The face of the god projects beneath the upturned proboscis of a butterfly and is flanked by its eyes. The headdress undoubtedly reflects Teotihuacán affinities. A similar urn is described in detail by Caso, 1949, pp. 78–95; see also Caso and Bernal, fig. 507.

232. Urn of a Masked Goddess. / Oaxaca. Monte Albán II. Gray clay. Height, 11 1/2 ". Collection Dr. and Mrs. William F. Kaiser, Berkeley, Calif.

Urns of this type are rare. They are characterized by a serpentine oral mask, long narrow eyes, and breasts indicated by incised nipples and curved lines. Caso and Bernal (p. 163; fig. 286) named this type "Goddess 8. Z" because a glyph resembling the Zapotec day sign "Z" combined with the numeral 8 is engraved on the skirt of one of the pieces. Boos (p. 133) maintains this archaeological name in his classification and traces the stylistic evolution through Monte Albán periods III-A and III-B. This urn possibly represents the feminine counterpart of the "God with the Buccal Mask of the Serpent."

233. Duck Pot. / Oaxaca. Monte Albán, Early Classic period. Clay, polished black and incised. Height, 5 5/8 "; length, 13 1/2 ". Collection Dr. and Mrs. William F. Kaiser, Berkeley, Calif.

A similar effigy from the Mixteca is tentatively ascribed to the Monte Albán II or III-A period (Paddock, 1966, p. 178, fig. 194).

234. Funerary Urn. / Oaxaca. Monte Albán III-A. Brown clay. Height, 25 3/4 ". Collection Dr. and Mrs. George C. Kennedy, Los Angeles.

The stylized jaguar's jaw (Glyph "C") appears on the headdress of an aged man with wrinkled face and sunken cheeks. This urn, like that shown in plate 227, belongs to the "Companion group with the Glyph 'C' on their heads."

235. STANDING JAGUAR. / San Rafael Tenenyecac, Tlaxcala. Classic period. Basalt. Height, 36″. Yale University Art Gallery. Gift of the Olsen Foundation.

The jaguar figure wears a sumptuous feather headdress, and his loincloth is tied in a knot with symmetrically projecting ends. Eight rectangular carvings on his body contain a crosslike element which is frequently found on Zapotec steles, signifying turquoise or precious stone. "Three Turquoise" was the name of a jaguar deity commonly depicted at Monte Albán. The provenance of this relief slab is clearly established and supports previously established cultural relations between the Valley of Puebla and Monte Albán.

236. FUNERARY URN. / Oaxaca. Monte Albán III-A. Gray clay. Height, 25″. Nelson Gallery–Atkins Museum, Nelson Fund, Kansas City, Mo.

The very ornate headdress of the seated deity is characterized by a bird mask in the center, flanked by two human heads peering from the wide-open beaks of birds, and by wings and feathers. The mouth is hidden behind a nose ornament. The figure holds a staff and an incense pouch and wears a large buckle fringed with longitudinal sections of olivella shells. The rectangular plaque between the legs is the embroidered flap of the loincloth (cf. Caso and Bernal, fig. 346). The numerous ornaments were molded separately and attached before firing.

237. FUNERARY URN REPRESENTING COCIJO, THE RAIN-GOD. / Oaxaca. Monte Albán III. Gray clay. Height, 13″. Collection Dr. and Mrs. Franklin D. Murphy, Los Angeles.

The deity represented is one of the oldest in the pre-Zapotec pantheon, and its evolution can be traced from Monte Albán I times.

238. FUNERARY URN. / Oaxaca. Classic period, Monte Albán III-A. Brown clay. Height, 26″. Collection Dr. and Mrs. William F. Kaiser, Berkeley, Calif.

The large urn shows a seated god with the buccal mask of the serpent. He holds a jar from which emerges a cloud or water symbol.

239. STANDING MAN. / Central Veracruz. Early Classic period. Buff clay. Height, 34″. Collection Stendahl.

The front flap on his loincloth is broken off, as is some former projection in the middle of the chest. A series of holes in the top of the head probably served to hold hair, feathers, or such adornment. Enlarged pre-auricular appendages are indicated. The knife-edged deformation of the shank bones is referred to as "saber shin" (*see also* plate 72).

240. HUMAN EFFIGY VASE WITH SPOUT. / Remojadas region, Veracruz. Preclassic period. Tan clay with red and black paint. Height, 10 1/2″. Collection Mr. and Mrs. Kirk Douglas, Beverly Hills, Calif.

Similarities with the large hollow figurines from Tlatilco

and Texmelucan are noticeable. An identical specimen is illustrated in Medellín Zenil, pl. 8.

241. SEATED OLD GOD OF FIRE. / Remojadas region, Veracruz. Early Classic period. Buff clay with black resin paint. Height, 14″. Collection Stendahl.

The bearded figure carries a receptacle on his head, as do the stone fire-gods of Teotihuacán.

242. FIGURE SEATED CROSS-LEGGED, WITH CONVENTIONALIZED HEADDRESS. / Remojadas region, Veracruz. Early Classic period. Brown clay with black resin paint. Height, 13 1/2″. Collection Mr. and Mrs. Vincent Price, Los Angeles.

The posture is typical of the Early Upper Remojadas figurines that represent the long-nosed god whose legs form a ring base with hands resting on the knees. The headdress is a conventionalization of the bird headdress of the figurine type mentioned. Usually, two slablike wings protrude diagonally, with the bird's head in the center looking down. The coffee-bean eyes are another characteristic of the style. The stylistic evolution of these figurines was established by Medellín Zenil, who believes them to be representations of the solar deities. The torso and arms are decorated with bands and bosses.

243. SEATED WOMAN WITH BULBOUS LEGS. / Talome region, Veracruz. Early Classic period. Tan clay with black resin paint. Height, 18″. Collection Morton D. May, St. Louis, Mo.

The perforations on the head are possibly for the insertion of hair or feathers.

244. STANDING WOMAN. / Remojadas region, Veracruz. Early Classic period. Buff clay with traces of black and red paint. Height, 25 1/4″. Collection Mr. and Mrs. Ellsworth La Boyteaux, Orinda, Calif.

The woman wears a wraparound skirt, feathered headdress, and ear, neck, and arm ornaments.

245. THREE FIGURES. / Remojadas region, Veracruz. Early Classic period. Buff clay with black resin paint. Height of tallest, 26″. Left and center, Collection Stendahl; right, Collection Mr. and Mrs. Milton S. Fox, New York.

The figures wear short-sleeved shirts decorated with appliqués; the headdresses are held on by chin straps. Heels are extended to enable the figures to stand. In the backs of the heads are square openings.

246. SEATED FIGURE WITH JAGUAR HEADDRESS. / Remojadas region, Veracruz. Early Classic period. Buff clay with red and black resin paint. Height,

18". Collection Mr. and Mrs. Ellsworth La Boyteaux, Orinda, Calif.

The lower part of the face is covered by a mask, commonly found on small figurines from Remojadas representing Xipe-Tlazolteotl. The mask (*metzxayacatl*) is considered to be part of the skin from the thigh of a slain victim.

247. STANDING MAN WITH SHELLS ON HIS BELT. / Tlacotalpan region, Veracruz. Early Classic period. White on reddish-brown clay. Height, 27 1/4". Collection Stendahl.

The pectoral band is a trait usually associated with the laughing-face figurines. Belts, from which hang shells cut open at the outer end, occur also in Zapotec wares of the early III-B period (cf. Caso and Bernal, figs. 346, 396).

248. HEAD OF JAGUAR. / Acatlán de Pérez Figueroa, Oaxaca. Early Classic period. Buff clay. Height, 11 1/2". Collection Dr. and Mrs. William F. Kaiser, Berkeley, Calif.

The head is a fragment of a large figure that was probably in a seated position.

249. DOG. / Remojadas region, Veracruz. Early Classic period. Buff clay with black resin paint. Height, 10 1/2". Collection Mr. and Mrs. Robert A. Rowan, Pasadena, Calif.

250. PAIR OF SEATED DOGS. / Tlacotalpan region, Veracruz. Early Classic period. Buff clay. Height: 16 1/2" and 26" respectively. Collection Dr. and Mrs. George C. Kennedy, Los Angeles.

Both dogs wear neckpieces and appear to be howling.

251. HEAD OF BEARDED AGED MAN. / Acatlán de Pérez Figueroa, Oaxaca. Early Classic period. Buff clay. Height, 15". Denver Art Museum, Denver, Colo.

On this figure's headdress is an inverted mask. The headdress and facial features, particularly the eyes and nose, are comparable with a funerary urn representing the bearded god "Two Jaguar" (Caso and Bernal, fig. 365).

252. SEATED FEMALE. / Tierra Blanca region, Veracruz. Early Classic period. Grayish clay. Height, 31". Collection Stendahl.

253. CHIEFTAIN CARRIED ON A LITTER BY FOUR ATTENDANTS. / Remojadas region, Veracruz. Early Classic period. Buff clay with traces of black resin paint. Height, 18 3/4". Los Angeles County Museum of Natural History.

The throne consists of a platform with a scaffold of the type known as Remojadas Xipe-Tlazolteotl figures (cf. Medellín

Zenil, pl. 39). Noteworthy is the posture of the litter bearers, who support it with one hand.

254. SEATED MALE. / Acatlán de Pérez Figueroa, Oaxaca. Early Classic period. Grayish clay. Height, 28". Collection Mr. and Mrs. E. V. Staude, Los Angeles.

The position of the right hand denotes a gesture of reverence. The features of this figure indicate a blend of Zapotec and Veracruz styles.

255/256. STANDING MAN (*front and back view*)./ Tlacotalpan region, Veracruz. Early Classic period. White on reddish-brown clay. Height, 47". Collection William P. Palmer.

The figure wears a nose rod and a nose plaque. The apertures in the back were made to prevent him from cracking during firing.

257/258. STANDING PRIEST CLAD IN THE SKIN OF A FLAYED VICTIM (*front and back view*)./ Vicinity of Alvarado, Veracruz. Early Classic period. Reddish clay. Height, 34 1/2". Private collection.

The scales represent the skin of a sacrificial victim whose chest had been opened in honor of the god Xipe Totec. *See also* plates 360 and 361.

259. SEATED BALLPLAYER. / Remojadas region, Veracruz. Early Classic period. Buff clay. Height, 27". Collection Mr. and Mrs. Jules Berman, Beverly Hills, Calif.

The figure wears a plain yoke around his waist, to which a jaguar effigy head is affixed by means of a cord under the lower lip. There is a protective apron worn under the yoke, and the headdress consists of a chin-tied and a forehead-tied band. The yoke is modeled from the inside of the hollow figure, while the jaguar head is applied. The right arm is restored.

260. LARGE SKELETAL FIGURE WITH DEATH'S-HEAD. / Central Veracruz. Early Classic period. Buff clay. Height, 28". Collection Stendahl.

Hands and feet have a clawlike appearance; the limbs show superimposed bones. Large hollow hand-modeled figurines called "Monumental Ware" have been reported from Early Classic deposits at Cerro de las Mesas, where they are a local development. A monumental figure measuring about forty inches, in the shape of an *incensario* representing Quetzalcoatl, was discovered in a cache in Zempoala, Veracruz, and dated beginning of the sixteenth century (García Payon, pp. 57–65). Apparently this was a treasured heirloom, hurriedly secreted upon the arrival of the Spaniards.

261. "LAUGHING FACE" TYPE FIGURINE HOLDING A RATTLE. / Los Cerros region, Veracruz. Late

Classic period. Buff clay. Height, 19″. Collection Mr. and Mrs. Ellsworth La Boyteaux, Orinda, Calif.

The face, body, and arms were molded separately. The head and arms are tenoned and were fitted into the body while the clay was still wet. The front teeth are mutilated by filing.

262. MAN WITH CONICAL HEADDRESS AND SHIELD. / Tierra Blanca region, Veracruz. Late Classic period. Buff clay with traces of red paint. Height, 8″. Collection Stendahl.

This moldmade warrior and the one in plate 263 wear a long shirt instead of the customary breechcloth. The design on the shield consists of two juxtaposed animal heads.

263. MAN WITH A LARGE JAGUAR HEADDRESS. / Tierra Blanca region, Veracruz. Late Classic period. Buff clay with traces of red paint. Height, 6³/₄″. Collection Stendahl.

The figure is moldmade. The man peers through the open jaws of the jaguar. He wears a broad necklace composed of tubular objects and a rectangular pectoral commonly associated with jaguar representations. A round shield with pendant, made of the same material as the necklace, is attached to his arm.

264. STANDING MAN WITH BIRD MASK AND WINGS. / Tierra Blanca region, Veracruz. Classic period. Tan clay with traces of red paint. Height, 6¹/₄″. Collection Stendahl.

The moldmade figure is holding a bannerlike device in his right hand.

265. KNEELING MOTHER AND CHILD. / Nopiloa, Veracruz. Late Classic period. Black on cream clay. Height, 9″. Collection Stendahl.

This is a moldmade hollow figurine of the "laughing face" type.

266. WOMAN CARRYING CHILD. / Nopiloa, Veracruz. Late Classic period. Black on buff clay. Height, 6¹/₂″. Collection Stendahl.

The woman's face on this moldmade rattle shows remarkable realism. Her pupils are set so that she appears to be looking toward the child—a very unusual feature in Mesoamerican art, which emphasizes either full frontal or profile expression. The child is supported by a shawl slung around the woman's shoulders and tied with a large knot in front.

267. PAIR OF "LAUGHING FACE" TYPE MALE FIGURINES. / Central Veracruz. Late Classic period. Buff clay with traces of polychrome. Height: 17″ and 17¹/₄″ respectively. Collection Dr. and Mrs. William F. Kaiser, Berkeley, Calif.

Both figures hold rattles in their hands, a characteristic of the Los Cerros II phase (Paz and Medellín Zenil, p. 40).

268. STANDING FIGURE. / El Faisan, Veracruz. Classic period. Buff clay with red and black paint. Height, 12″. Collection Mr. and Mrs. Ned Tanen, Los Angeles.

The figure wears a cape, skirt, and feathered headdress. The head is moldmade but the body is hand-modeled, with two peg supports on the back.

269. ANTHROPOMORPHIC WHISTLING JAR. / Veracruz. Early Postclassic (?) period. Orange clay with black and brown paint. Height, 10¹/₂″. Collection Stendahl.

The lips of the person are puckered as if he were whistling. The whistle is hidden below the crest, in the back of the head. The spout was probably somewhat taller. Whistling jars have a wide distribution, from Central Mexico to Salvador, and range from Late Preclassic to Early Postclassic times.

270/271. EARTHENWARE CUP WITH CARVED RELIEF DECORATIONS (*two views*). / Central Veracruz. Early Classic period. Dark-brown clay with calcareous deposits. Height, 6¹/₂″. City Art Museum of Saint Louis, St. Louis, Mo.

The decoration consists of two standing figures in loincloths and headdresses and two acrobats performing on a low platform with supports. An "acrobat" in a similar position on a Maya stele made of lime plaster, from the Municipio Cardenas, is now in the Tabasco Museum at Villahermosa.

272. "LAUGHING FACE" TYPE FIGURINE WITH JOINTED LIMBS. / Nopiloa, Veracruz. Late Classic period. Reddish-yellow clay with creamy-yellow slip and residues of a pasty white paint. Height, 12³/₄″. Collection David Nagata, New York.

The torso is covered with an elaborately carved Maya style design that represents a cross-legged seated figure with a voluminous headdress. For a detailed description, see von Winning, "Two Figurines with Movable Limbs from Veracruz, Mexico."

273. FOUR-BARREL FLUTE DECORATED WITH HUMAN EFFIGY HEAD. / Central Veracruz. Late Classic period. Red on buff clay. Length, 21¹/₂″. Museum of the American Indian, Heye Foundation, New York.

274. CARVED BACK OF A MIRROR. / Veracruz. Early Classic period. Slate. Diameter, 6¹/₄″. American Museum of Natural History, New York.

A priest, with his head tilted back, is shown with a speech scroll emanating from his mouth. He holds a serpent staff in his hand. A jaguar's head with forelegs is shown in a manner that would seem to indicate that the person is clad in the skin of this animal. The numerous small drill holes probably served for the attachment of the stucco-based pigments.

275. BOWL WITH MOLDMADE RELIEF DECORATION. / Tierra Blanca region, Veracruz. Late Classic period. Brownish-red clay. Height, 4 1/4″; diameter, 6 1/2″. Collection Stendahl.

The decoration, made with two molds, depicts nine persons arranged in four groups. Their anatomical proportions are distorted and they are somewhat clumsily portrayed. Each face is different, but their foreheads all recede sharply. Each person is differentiated in dress, ornaments, and attitude; no weapons are depicted. Apparently some historical event is commemorated in this scene, which shows the submission of two chieftains.

276. CARVED BACK OF A MIRROR. / Tlaxcala. Early Classic period. Slate, with traces of cinnabar. Height, 5″. American Museum of Natural History, New York.

A priest is shown in rich attire, holding an incense pouch in his hand. The reverse side is smooth except for scratches in various directions, which were probably made for better adherence of the pyrite mirror. For a discussion of mirror backs, see Covarrubias, pp. 185–86 and fig. 82.

277. FIGURE OF A MONKEY TIED TO A PLATFORM ORIGINALLY ON WHEELS. / Tierra Blanca region, Veracruz. Late Classic period (Upper Remojadas II). Light-brown fine clay with almost completely weathered gray slip. Height, 5 1/2″. Los Angeles County Museum of Natural History.

Attached to the bottom of the platform are two clay axle housings. The wheels are restored and were probably undecorated. For a detailed description, see von Winning, 1960, pp. 65–67.

278. FLUTE. / Joachin, Veracruz. Late Classic period. White on red clay. Length, 12 3/4″. Collection Stendahl.

The tune of the flute can be varied by means of a clay pellet that rolls back and forth inside the tube. The head probably represents a plumed serpent. The disk is decorated with winglike elements.

279/280. HEMISPHERICAL BOWL DECORATED WITH LOBSTERS AND AQUATIC BIRDS (two views). / Central Veracruz. Late Postclassic period (Cerro Montoso style). Reddish-brown on cream clay with orange-red rim. Diameter, 7 1/4″. American Museum of Natural History, New York.

281. POLYCHROME TRIPOD DISH WITH HUMAN FIGURE. / South-central Veracruz. Late Classic period. Black, red, orange, and white on cream clay. Diameter, 10 1/2″. American Museum of Natural History, New York.

The male figure wears an unusual headdress which extends in front and in back. The white volutes represent the knots that tie the different strands together. Similar knots are shown on the front and back of his loincloth. The thumbs of both hands clearly indicate Teotihuacán influence, whereas the entire composition represents a local tradition within the greater Veracruz art style. The border decoration depicts long-beaked birds.

282. BOWL. / San Andrés de Tuxtla, Veracruz. Late Classic period. Orange and black on buff clay. Height, 3 1/2″; diameter, 9″. American Museum of Natural History, New York.

The decoration consists of two winged insectlike creatures.

283/284/285. BOWL INCISED WITH TWO MONKEYS AND TWO JAGUARS (three views). / Central Veracruz. Late Classic period. Burnished orange and tan clay. Height, 3″; diameter, 7 3/4″. Collection Stendahl.

286. CRESTED HEAD-TYPE Hacha REPRESENTING A BIRD (VULTURE?). / Central Veracruz. Classic period. Basalt. Height, 14″. Collection Mr. and Mrs. Dübi-Müller, Solothurn, Switzerland.

287. CRESTED HEAD-TYPE Hacha. / Central Veracruz. Classic period. Basalt. Height, 15″. Collection Dr. and Mrs. William F. Kaiser, Berkeley, Calif.

The ornaments of the headdress, depicting the upper jaw, eye, and nose decoration of an animal (serpent?), have a strong resemblance to Teotihuacán pictorial style.

288. Hacha REPRESENTING A BIRD'S HEAD. / Central Veracruz. Classic period. Volcanic rock. Height, 14 1/2″. Seattle Art Museum, Seattle, Wash.

289. PLAIN Hacha. / Veracruz. Classic period. Volcanic rock. Height, 19″. Collection Mr. and Mrs. Fred Olsen, Guilford, Conn.

290. Hacha WITH IGUANA ON HEAD. / Central Veracruz. Classic period. Basalt. Height, 8″. Collection Stendahl.

The tail of the iguana is shown on the reverse side of the hacha.

291. HEAD. / Central Veracruz. Postclassic (?) period. Basalt. Height, 10″. Collection Stendahl.

The tenon in back is covered with white mortar, indicating that the head was at one time an architectural ornament.

292. HEAD WITH ENGRAVED DESIGN ON CHEEKS AND LOOP HANDLE IN BACK. / Veracruz, Mexico. Classic period. Onyx marble (alabaster). Height, 7 1/4″. The Museum of Primitive Art, New York.

A loop handle in the back conveys that this piece was probably used in ceremonial ball games.

293. *Hacha* IN THE SHAPE OF A STYLIZED BIRD's HEAD. / Central Veracruz. Classic period. Basalt. Height, 9 1/2″. Collection Mr. and Mrs. Dübi-Müller, Solothurn, Switzerland.

294. *Hacha* WITH MONKEY-SHAPED HEAD. / Central Veracruz. Classic period. Basalt. Height, 9″. Collection Charles Ratton, Paris.

295. *Hacha* FORM REPRESENTING HEAD OF AN ANIMAL. / Central Veracruz. Classic period. Brown sandstone. Height, 7″. The Dumbarton Oaks Collections, Washington, D.C.

296. *Hacha* SHOWING A BENT LEG (POSSIBLY OF AN ACROBAT). / Central Veracruz. Classic period. Onyx marble (alabaster) with traces of red paint. Height, 15 1/2″. Collection Bruno Adriani, Carmel, Calif.

297. UNFINISHED HUMAN FIGURE. / Central Veracruz. Classic (?) period. Limestone. Height, 16 1/2″. Collection Stendahl.

298. *Hacha* IN THE SHAPE OF AN ANIMAL's HEAD (DEER ?). / Central Veracruz. Classic period. Basalt. Height, 11 1/2″. Collection Mrs. Albert Newman, Chicago, Ill.

299/300. *Hacha* WITH TWO DIFFERENT PROFILES (*two views*). / Central Veracruz. Classic period. Andesite. Height, 12″. The Dumbarton Oaks Collections, Washington, D.C.

One side of the face shows a bulbous (closed?) eye surmounted by a shell. The eye on the other side is normal, the tongue extends across the cheek. The dualism in this sculpture is a religious concept expressed also on certain clay figurines.

301/302. PLAIN PALMATE STONE (*two views*). / Central Veracruz. Classic period. Diorite. Height, 16 1/2″. Collection Morton D. May, St. Louis, Mo.

303. PALMATE STONE WITH BAT DESIGNS. / Veracruz. Classic period. Basalt. Height, 15 7/8″. Collection Hugh Allison Smith, Metairie, La.

The design is separated into two parts by a volute to which is attached a wing-shaped element consisting of knotted bands. Two bats are shown in the upper section. One of these animals is devouring a string of jade beads (symbolizing something precious). Below, a third bat is facing a crawling human figure apparently emerging from a shell. The bat is a not unusual decorative motif on *palmas* (cf. Covarrubias, pl. 42).

304. PALMATE STONE WITH LARGE NOSE ORNAMENT AND SPEECH SCROLL. Veracruz. Classic period. Volcanic stone. Height, 25 3/4″. Private collection.

This is an intermediate form between a *palma* and a *hacha*.

305. PALMATE STONE WITH HUMAN FACE BENEATH A SERPENT HEADDRESS. / Veracruz. Classic period. Volcanic stone. Height, 24 3/8″. Private collection.

An intermediate form between a *palma* and a *hacha*.

306. PALMATE STONE WITH INTERLACED SCROLLS. / Central Veracruz. Classic period. Basalt. Height, 16 1/2″. Private collection.

Similar decoration occurs on *palmas* no. 25 and 27 illustrated by Proskouriakoff, 1954, fig. 8.

307. *Palma* SHOWING A MAN WEARING A YOKE ABOUT THE WAIST. / Nautla region, Veracruz. Classic period. Volcanic rock. Height, 21″. Thomas Gilcrease Institute of American History and Art, Tulsa, Okla.

Ekholm (1949, p. 8 and fig. 1 a) comments on the "small triangular knob extending out from the front of the yoke. This appears to represent a thin stone head fastened to the yoke . . . in this case the projecting knob . . . might have been intended for an animal head."

308. PALMATE STONE WITH SCULPTURED MALE HOLDING A SERPENT STAFF. / Veracruz. Classic period. Basalt. Height, 17″. Collection Mr. and Mrs. Francis V. Crane, Marathon, Fla.

Above the sculptured figure is a human face with protruding bifurcated tongue carved in low relief.

309/310. *Palma* (*two views*). / Xico-Coatepec region, Veracruz. Classic period. Volcanic stone. Height, 32 1/2″. American Museum of Natural History, New York.

The design on the front shows, in addition to the typical scrollwork, two entwined serpent bodies with bird-shaped heads. In the center is a shell pendant similar to the Quetzalcoatl emblem. The design on the back shows two figures with speech scrolls. Proskouriakoff (1954) notes their unorthodox arrangement and believes it indicates a possible decadent trend and hence a late development of this sculpture.

311. YOKE FRAGMENT. / Central Veracruz. Classic period. Granite. Height, 5″. Dayton Art Institute, Dayton, Ohio.

About one-half of the yoke is missing. The head on the right peers from the jaws of a death's-head, shown by the fleshless lower jaw. The heads of all three figures have closed eyes and mouths, probably indicating death.

312. END OF A YOKE FRAGMENT. / Veracruz. Classic period. Granitic rock. Height, 5 1/2″. Collection Mr. and Mrs. James W. Alsdorf, Winnetka, Ill.

The head peers from beneath the upper jaw of a serpent.

313/314. YOKE WITH INTERIOR CARVING (*with schematic drawing*). / Central Veracruz. Classic period. Granitic rock. Height, 4 1/2″; length, 15″; width, 12″. Collection Stendahl.

The decoration represents a terrestrial monster with curved arms and claws. A shell is shown above the nose. The eyes are directly above the jaws and at a lower level than the nose. The exterior is grooved.

315/316. YOKE (*two views*). / Central Veracruz. Classic period. Brownish-green diorite. Height, 5″; length, 15 1/2″; width, 14 1/2″. The Museum of Primitive Art, New York.

The representation is that of a crouching froglike terrestrial monster. Faces are carved on the sides and the ends.

317. MONKEY EFFIGY VASE. / Central Veracruz. Postclassic period. Onyx marble (alabaster). Height, 6 7/8″; diameter, 6″. Thomas Gilcrease Institute of American History and Art, Tulsa, Okla.

This vase resembles the famous obsidian vessel from Texcoco in the Museum of Anthropology, Mexico City. Caso described it as a monkey trying to raise itself while carrying a vessel— " . . . for that reason he has one leg bent, while the other is firmly planted to start the upward movement. The tail of the monkey is used as a rope with which to carry the vessel, and the vessel itself is the body of the animal" (1938, pp. 41–42).

318/319. YOKE WITH TWO ENTWINED LONG-NECKED BIRDS (*two views*). / Veracruz. Classic period. Green diorite with traces of red paint. Height, 4 1/2″; length, 16″; width, 14 3/4″. American Museum of Natural History, New York.

The wings of the birds (vultures?) in the center are shown beneath their heads. Similar birds are carved on the exterior ends.

320/321. YOKE WITH THREE EXTERIOR FACES (*two views*)./ Central Veracruz. Classic period. Diorite. Height, 5″; length, 17″; width, 15″. Collection Bruno Adriani, Carmel, Calif.

322. STANDING MAN. / Veracruz. Postclassic period (Huastec). Volcanic stone. Height, 53″. Collection Josef Müller, Solothurn, Switzerland.

323. STELE REPRESENTING A RAIN-GOD. / Northern Veracruz. c. A.D. 1000. Stone. Height, 48″. Yale University Art Gallery. Gift of Mr. and Mrs. Fred Olsen.

The figure holds a staff and an incense pouch. Proskouriakoff, who published the sculpture, notes the Late Classic Maya posture (1954, p. 86 and fig. 9 f).

324. SCULPTURED MARKER SHOWING A FEATHERED SERPENT ON EACH SIDE. / Central Veracruz. Classic period. Andesite. Height, 36″. Collection Stendahl.

It seems that the serpent is transfixed by an arrow, the point of which protrudes below the left eye. Similar representations occur in the pictorial manuscripts, in the Codex Borgia, for example, and Seler (1963, I, pp. 72–74) has interpreted them as symbols for blood.

325/326. TWO STANDING BALLPLAYERS WEARING YOKES AND KNEEPADS, AND HOLDING STRIKING DEVICES. / Pánuco area, Veracruz. Classic period. Solid buff clay with traces of black resin paint. Height: 11 1/4″ and 16 3/8″ respectively. Collection Stendahl.

327. SPOUTED EFFIGY JAR. / Northern Veracruz. Late Postclassic period. Red and black on buff clay. Height, 8 1/2″. Galerie Israel, Tel-Aviv.

328. DEITY WITH CONICAL HAT. / Northern Veracruz. Postclassic period. Sandstone. Height, 69″. Collection Mr. and Mrs. Vincent Price, Los Angeles.

329. FIGURE LEANING ON A STAFF. / Northern Veracruz. Postclassic period. Sandstone. Height, 22 1/2″. Collection Morton D. May, St. Louis, Mo.

This male figure is resting his elbow on a prismatic staff which is wrapped diagonally with leather (?) straps. One side of the figure shows the wrinkled face and thorax of an aged person, while the face and chest on the other side are those of a youth.

330. FIGURE LEANING ON A STAFF. / Northern Veracruz. Postclassic period (Huastec). Sandstone. Height, 34 3/8″. The Museum of Primitive Art, New York.

331. QUETZALCOATL WITH THE MASK OF THE WIND-GOD. / Northern Veracruz. Postclassic period (Huastec). Sandstone. Height, 43″. The Elsa Lanchester Laughton Collection, Hollywood, Calif.

332. MAIZE-GODDESS. / Northern Veracruz. Postclassic period (Huastec). Sandstone. Height, 45″. Collection Mr. and Mrs. Gordon Onslow-Ford, Inverness, Calif.

Characteristic is the large rectangular headdress (*amacalli*), with tassels (shown here in rectangular shape) pending over the sides of the head. Chicomecoatl and other fertility and earth deities wear this headdress together with the large ro-settes shown both in front and in back. The *amacalli* is a crown made of paper and is commonly depicted in the codices as a diagnostic of the deities mentioned.

210. Cylindrical bowl with stuccoed and painted decoration. *Teotihuacán, Valley of Mexico. Early Classic period. Brown clay with red, white, bluish-green, and black paint. Height, 5 1/2″; diameter, 5 3/4″.*

211. Tripod bowl with stuccoed and painted decoration. *Teotihuacán, Valley of Mexico. Early Classic period. Brown ware painted green, white, and red, with thin black outlining. Height, 6 1/4″; diameter, 4 1/2″.*

212. Stuccoed and painted cylindrical tripod vase. *Teotihuacán. Early Classic period. Brown clay with red, yellow, and green on dark-red background with black lines for details. Height, 5 1/2″; diameter, 5 3/4″.*

213. Cylindrical tripod vase. *Teotihuacán, Valley of Mexico. Early Classic period. Brown ware stuccoed and painted red, orange, green, white, and black. Height, 5 1/4″; diameter, 5 7/8″.*

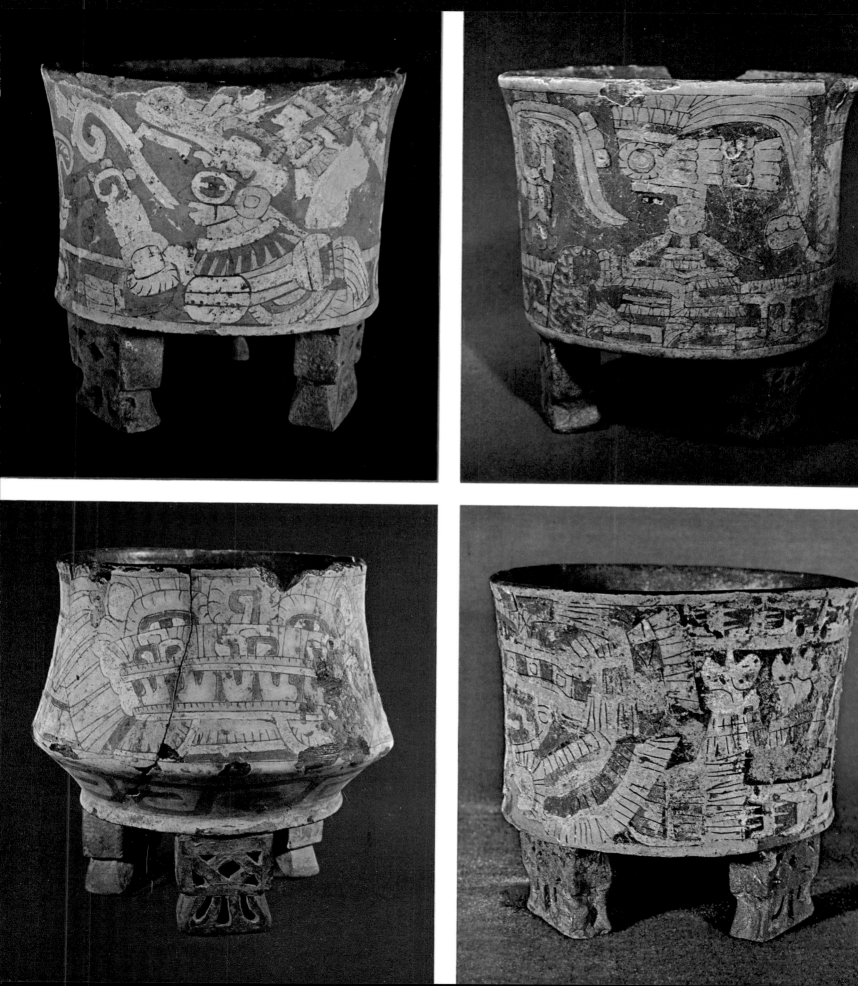

214. Standing woman.
Teotihuacán vicinity. Early Classic period. Volcanic stone. Height, 36".

BELOW, LEFT TO RIGHT

215. Figurine with cape.
Valley of Mexico. Late Formative period. Buff clay. Height, 6 1/2".

216. Hollow figurine with another figurine inserted in its open chest. *Valley of Mexico. Early Classic period. Buff paste with traces of yellow paint. Height, 10".*

217. Standing figurine with rings around the eyes. *Santiago Ahuizotla, Valley of Mexico. Early Classic period. Buff clay with white paint. Height, 5".*

218. Pair of dancers.
Valley of Mexico. Early Classic period. Buff clay. Height, 4".

219. Effigy jar representing Huehueteotl, the old god. *Veracruz. Early Classic period. Thin orange ware. Height, 12″.*

220. Plano-relief-decorated cylindrical vase
(two views). *Valley of Mexico. Early Classic
period. Orange-brown clay. Height without supports,
5 1/2"; diameter, 9 1/2".*

221. Seated old man with basin on his head.
Texcoco region, Valley of Mexico. Volcanic tuff.
Height, 17".

222. Incense burner in two parts.
Santiago Ahuizotla, Valley of Mexico. Middle to Late Classic period. Brown clay, ornaments painted red, yellow, and green. Height, 29".

223/224. Mask (two views).
Puebla. Early Classic period. Black steatite. Height, 8 1/2".

225. Male figure.
Puebla. Early Classic period. Dark-green steatite. Height, 9".

226. Mask.
Central Mexico. Early to Middle Classic period. Blue-green steatite. Height, 5 3/4".

227. Funerary urn.
*Oaxaca. Monte Albán III-A. Brown clay. Height,
25 1/2".*

228. Fragment of a funerary urn depicting the
bat-god. *Oaxaca. Classic period. Brown clay.
Height, 6 3/4".*

229. Figurine vase.
Oaxaca. Monte Albán I. Gray clay. Height, 8".

230. Effigy jar.
*Oaxaca. Monte Albán I. Burnished gray clay.
Height, 5 1/8"; diameter, 3 3/4".*

231. Funerary urn representing the butterfly-god. *Oaxaca. Monte Albán III-A. Clay with brownish-red paint. Height, 9″.*

232. Urn of a masked goddess.
Oaxaca. Monte Albán II. Gray clay. Height, 11 1/2″.

233. Duck pot.
Oaxaca. Monte Albán, Early Classic period. Clay, polished black and incised. Height, 5 5/8″; length, 13 1/2″.

234. Funerary urn.
Oaxaca. Monte Albán III-A. Brown clay. Height, 25 3/4″.

235. Standing jaguar.
San Rafael Tenenyecac, Tlaxcala. Classic period.
Basalt. Height, 36″.

236. Funerary urn.
Oaxaca. Monte Albán III-A. Gray clay. Height,
25″.

237. Funerary Urn Representing Cocijo. the
Rain-God. *Oaxaca. Monte Albán III. Gray clay.*
Height, 13″.

238. Funerary urn.
Oaxaca. Monte Albán III-A. Brown clay. Height,
26".

239. Standing man.
Central Veracruz. Early Classic period. Buff clay.
Height, 34".

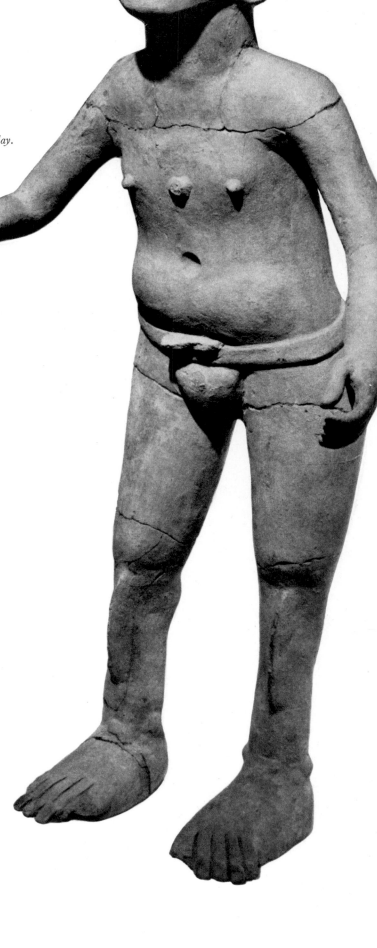

240. Human effigy vase with spout.
Remojadas region, Veracruz. Preclassic period. Tan
clay with red and black paint. Height, 10 1/2".

241. Seated old god of fire.
Remojadas region, Veracruz. Early Classic period.
Buff clay with black resin paint. Height, 14".

242. Figure seated cross-legged, with
conventionalized headdress. *Remojadas region,*
Veracruz. Early Classic period. Brown clay with
black resin paint. Height, 13 1/2".

243. Seated woman with bulbous legs.
Talome region, Veracruz. Early Classic period. Tan
clay with black resin paint. Height, 18".

244. Standing woman.
Remojadas region, Veracruz. Early Classic period.
Buff clay with traces of black and red paint. Height,
25 1/4".

245. Three figures.
Remojadas region, Veracruz. Early Classic period.
Buff clay with black resin paint. Height of tallest, 26".

246. Seated figure with jaguar headdress.
Remojadas region, Veracruz. Early Classic period.
Buff clay with red and black resin paint. Height,
18″.

247. Standing man with shells on his belt.
Tlacotalpan region, Veracruz. Early Classic period.
White on reddish-brown clay. Height, 27 1/4″.

248. Head of jaguar.
*Acatlán de Pérez Figueroa, Oaxaca. Early Classic
period. Buff clay. Height, 11 1/2"*

249. Dog.
*Remojadas region, Veracruz. Early Classic period.
Buff clay with black resin paint. Height, 10 1/2".*

250. Pair of seated dogs.
*Tlacotalpan region, Veracruz. Early Classic period.
Buff clay. Height: 16 1/2" and 26" respectively.*

251. Head of bearded aged man.
Acatlán de Pérez Figueroa, Oaxaca. Early Classic period. Buff clay. Height, 15″.

252. Seated female.
Tierra Blanca region, Veracruz. Early Classic period. Grayish clay. Height, 31″.

253. Chieftain carried on a litter by four attendants. *Remojadas region, Veracruz. Early Classic period. Buff clay with traces of black resin paint. Height, 18 3/4".*

254. Seated male.
Acatlán de Pérez Figueroa, Oaxaca. Early Classic period. Grayish clay. Height, 28".

255/256. Standing man (front and back view). *Tlacotalpan region, Veracruz. Early Classic period. White on reddish-brown clay. Height, 47".*

257/258. Standing priest clad in the skin of a flayed victim (front and back view). *Vicinity of Alvarado, Veracruz. Early Classic period. Reddish clay. Height, 34 1/2".*

259. Seated ballplayer. *Remojadas region, Veracruz. Early Classic period. Buff clay. Height, 27".*

260. Large skeletal figure with death's-head. *Central Veracruz. Early Classic period. Buff clay. Height, 28".*

261. "Laughing face" type figurine holding a rattle. *Los Cerros region, Veracruz. Late Classic period. Buff clay. Height, 19".*

BELOW, LEFT TO RIGHT

262. Man with conical headdress and shield. *Tierra Blanca region, Veracruz. Late Classic period. Buff clay with traces of red paint. Height, 8".*

263. Man with a large jaguar headdress. *Tierra Blanca region, Veracruz. Late Classic period. Buff clay with traces of red paint. Height, 6 3/4".*

264. Standing man with bird mask and wings. *Tierra Blanca region, Veracruz. Classic period. Tan clay with traces of red paint. Height, 6 1/4".*

265. Kneeling mother and child. *Nopiloa, Veracruz. Late Classic period. Black on cream clay. Height, 9".*

266. Woman carrying child. *Nopiloa, Veracruz. Late Classic period. Black on buff clay. Height, 6 1/2".*

COLORPLATE, OPPOSITE

267. Pair of "laughing face" type male figurines. *Central Veracruz. Late Classic period. Buff clay with traces of polychrome. Height: 17" and 17 1/4" respectively.*

268. Standing figure.
*El Faisan, Veracruz. Classic period. Buff clay with
red and black paint. Height, 12".*

269. Anthropomorphic whistling jar.
*Veracruz. Early Postclassic(?) period. Orange clay
with black and brown paint. Height, 10 1/2".*

270/271. Earthenware cup with carved relief decorations (two views). *Central Veracruz. Early Classic period. Dark-brown clay with calcareous deposits. Height, 6 1/2″.*

272. "Laughing face" type figurine with jointed limbs. *Nopiloa, Veracruz. Late Classic period. Reddish-yellow clay with creamy-yellow slip and residues of a pasty white paint. Height, 12 3/4″.*

274. Carved back of a mirror.
Veracruz. Early Classic period. Slate. Diameter, 6 $^1/_4$".

275. Bowl with moldmade relief decoration.
*Tierra Blanca region, Veracruz. Late Classic
period. Brownish-red clay. Height, 4 $^1/_4$";
diameter, 6 $^1/_2$".*

273. Four-barrel flute decorated with human
effigy head. *Central Veracruz. Late Classic period.
Red on buff clay. Length, 21 $^1/_2$".*

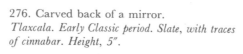

276. Carved back of a mirror.
Tlaxcala. Early Classic period. Slate, with traces of cinnabar. Height, 5".

277. Figure of a monkey tied to a platform originally on wheels. *Tierra Blanca region, Veracruz. Late Classic period (Upper Remojadas II). Light-brown fine clay with almost completely weathered gray slip. Height, 5 1/2".*

278. Flute.
Joachin, Veracruz. Late Classic period. White on red clay. Length, 12 3/4".

279/280. Hemispherical bowl decorated with
lobsters and aquatic birds (two views).
*Central Veracruz. Late Postclassic period (Cerro
Montoso style). Reddish-brown on cream clay with
orange-red rim. Diameter, 7 1/4".*

281. Polychrome tripod dish with human
figure. *South-central Veracruz. Late Classic period.
Black, red, orange, and white on cream clay.
Diameter, 10 1/2".*

282. Bowl.
San Andrés de Tuxtla, Veracruz. Late Classic period. Orange and black on buff clay. Height, 3 1/2"; diameter, 9".

283/284/285. Bowl incised with two monkeys and two jaguars (three views). *Central Veracruz. Late Classic period. Burnished orange and tan clay. Height, 3"; diameter, 7 3/4".*

286. Crested head-type *hacha* representing a
bird (vulture?). *Central Veracruz. Classic period.
Basalt. Height, 14".*

287. Crested head-type *hacha.
Central Veracruz. Classic period. Basalt. Height,
15".*

210

288. *Hacha* representing a bird's head.
*Central Veracruz. Classic period. Volcanic rock.
Height, 14 1/2".*

289. Plain *hacha.*
Veracruz. Classic period. Volcanic rock. Height, 19".

290. *Hacha with iguana on head.
Central Veracruz. Classic period. Basalt. Height,
8".*

291. Head.
*Central Veracruz. Postclassic(?) period. Basalt.
Height, 10".*

292. Head with engraved design on cheeks
and loop handle in back. *Veracruz, Mexico.
Classic period. Onyx marble (alabaster). Height,
7 1/4".*

293. *Hacha* in the shape of a stylized bird's
head. *Central Veracruz. Classic period. Basalt.
Height, 9 1/2".*

294. *Hacha* with monkey-shaped head.
Central Veracruz. Classic period. Basalt. Height, 9".

295. *Hacha* form representing head of an
animal. *Central Veracruz. Classic period. Brown
sandstone. Height, 7".*

296. *Hacha* showing a bent leg (possibly of an acrobat). *Central Veracruz. Classic period. Onyx marble (alabaster) with traces of red paint. Height, 15 1/2".*

297. Unfinished human figure. *Central Veracruz. Classic(?) period. Limestone. Height, 16 1/2".*

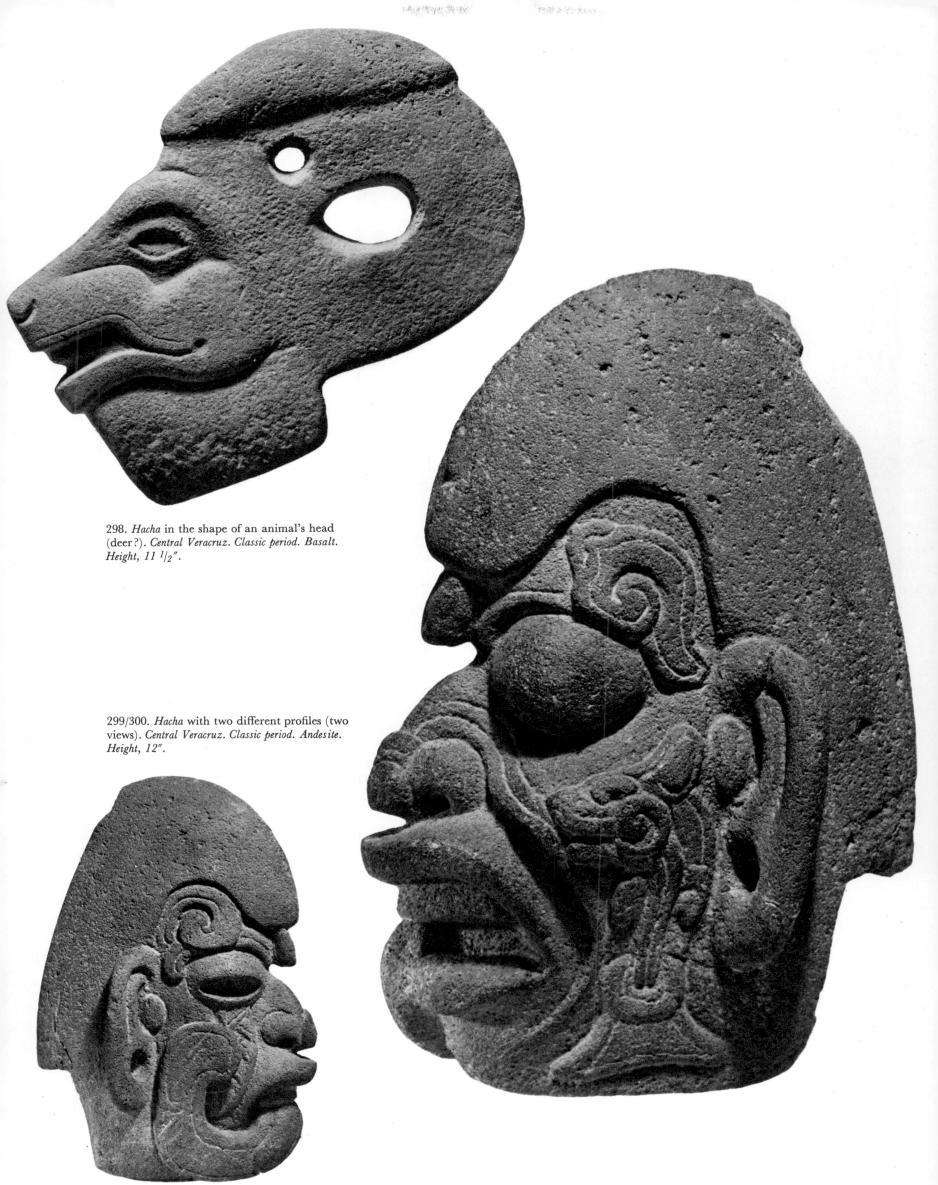

298. *Hacha* in the shape of an animal's head
(deer?). *Central Veracruz. Classic period. Basalt.
Height, 11 1/2″.*

299/300. *Hacha* with two different profiles (two
views). *Central Veracruz. Classic period. Andesite.
Height, 12″.*

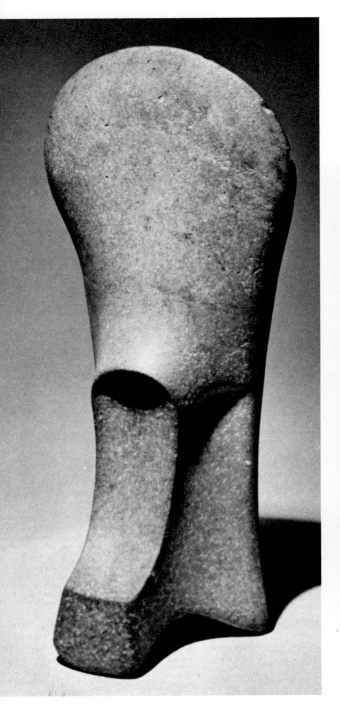

301/302. Plain palmate stone (two views). *Central Veracruz. Classic period. Diorite. Height, 16 1/2".*

303. Palmate stone with bat designs. *Veracruz. Classic period. Basalt. Height, 15 7/8".*

216

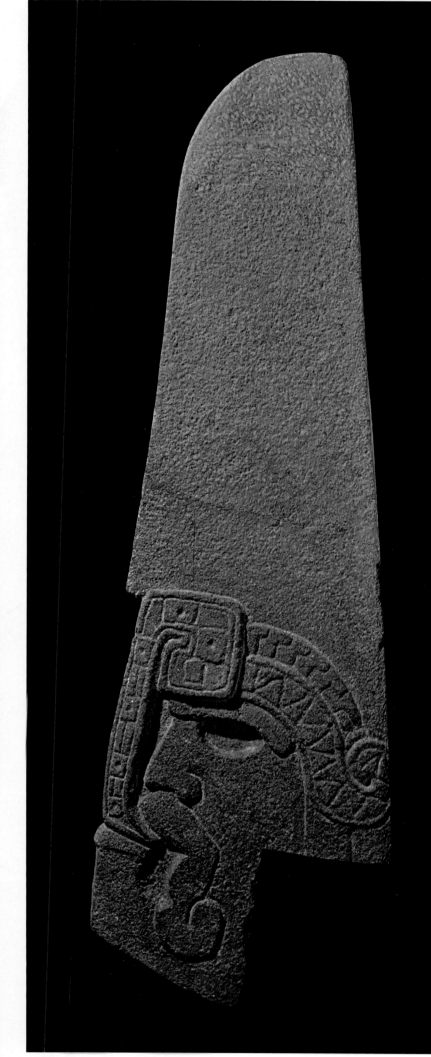

304. Palmate stone with large nose ornament
and speech scroll. *Veracruz. Classic period.*
Volcanic stone. Height, 25 3/4".

305. Palmate stone with human face beneath
a serpent headdress. *Veracruz. Classic period.*
Volcanic stone. Height, 24 3/8".

306. Palmate stone with interlaced scrolls. *Central Veracruz. Classic period. Basalt. Height, 16 ¹/₂″.*

308. Palmate stone with sculptured male holding a serpent staff. *Veracruz. Classic period. Basalt. Height, 17″.*

307. *Palma* showing a man wearing a yoke about the waist. *Nautla region, Veracruz. Classic period. Volcanic rock. Height, 21″.*

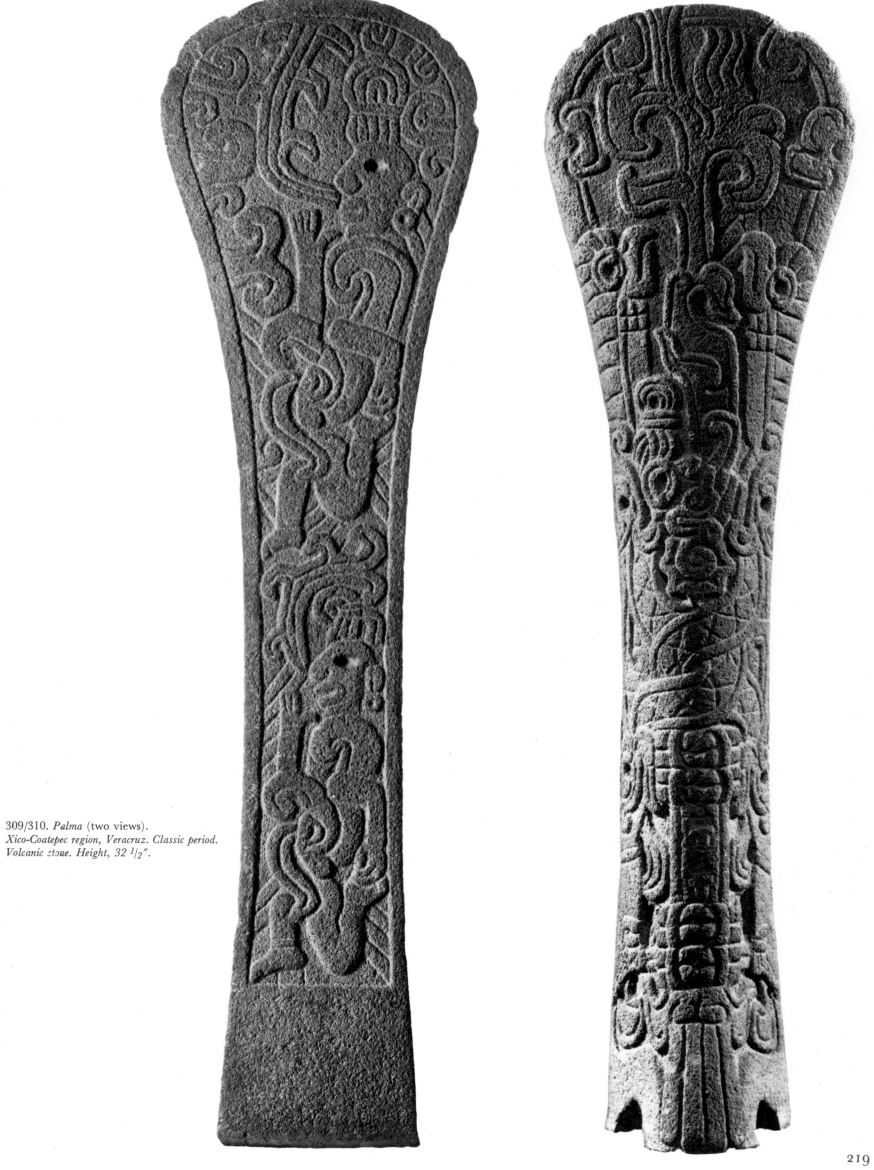

309/310. *Palma* (two views).
Xico-Coatepec region, Veracruz. Classic period.
Volcanic stone. Height, 32 ¹/₂".

311. Yoke fragment.
Central Veracruz. Classic period. Granite. Height, 5".

312. End of a yoke fragment.
Veracruz. Classic period. Granitic rock. Height, 5 1/2".

313/314. Yoke with interior carving (with
schematic drawing). *Central Veracruz. Classic
period. Granitic rock. Height, 4 1/2"; length, 15";
width, 12".*

315/316. Yoke (two views).
*Central Veracruz. Classic period. Brownish-green
diorite. Height, 5″; length, 15 ¹/₂″; width,
14 ¹/₂″.*

320/321. Yoke with three exterior faces (two views). *Central Veracruz. Classic period. Diorite. Height, 5″; length, 17″; width, 15″.*

317. Monkey effigy vase.
Central Veracruz. Postclassic period. Onyx marble (alabaster). Height, 6 7/8″; diameter, 6″.

318/319. Yoke with two entwined long-necked birds (two views). *Veracruz. Classic period. Green diorite with traces of red paint. Height, 4 1/2″; length, 16″; width, 14 3/4″.*

322. Standing man.
Veracruz. Postclassic period (Huastec). Volcanic stone. Height, 53″.

323. Stele representing a rain-god.
Northern Veracruz. c. A.D. 1000. Stone. Height, 48″.

324. Sculptured marker showing a feathered serpent on each side. *Central Veracruz. Classic period. Andesite. Height, 36″.*

325/326. Two standing ballplayers wearing yokes and kneepads, and holding striking devices. *Pánuco area, Veracruz. Classic period. Solid buff clay with traces of black resin paint. Height: 11 1/4″ and 16 3/8″ respectively.*

327. Spouted effigy jar.
Northern Veracruz. Late Postclassic period. Red and black on buff clay. Height, 8 1/2″.

328. Deity with conical hat.
Northern Veracruz. Postclassic period. Sandstone.
Height, 69".

329. Figure leaning on a staff.
Northern Veracruz. Postclassic period. Sandstone.
Height, 22 1/2".

331. Quetzalcoatl with the mask of the wind-god. *Northern Veracruz. Postclassic period (Huastec). Sandstone. Height, 43".*

332. Maize-goddess.
Northern Veracruz. Postclassic period (Huastec). Sandstone. Height, 45".

330. Figure leaning on a staff.
Northern Veracruz. Postclassic period (Huastec). Sandstone. Height, 34 3/8".

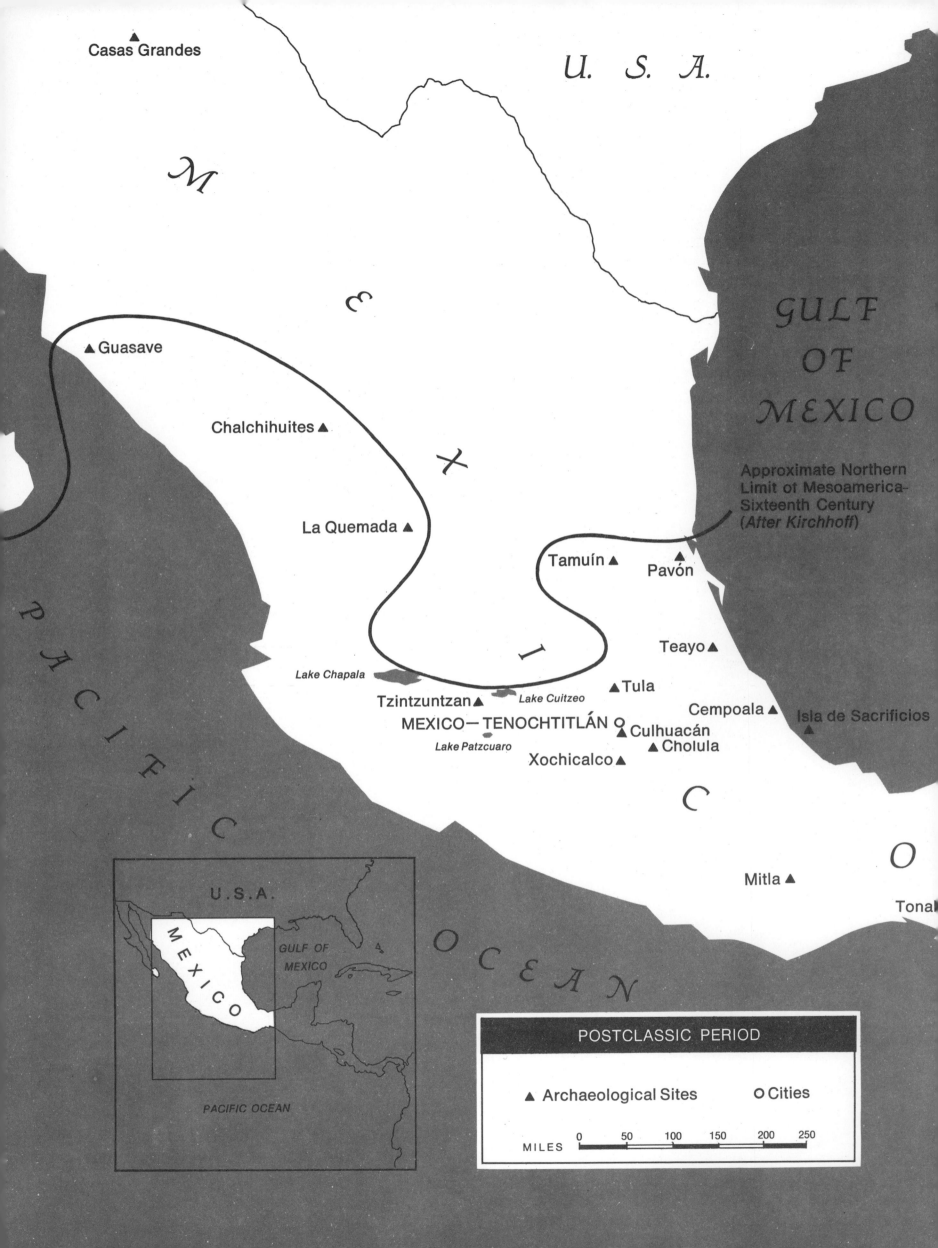

Casas Grandes ▲

U. S. A.

M

GULF

OF

MEXICO

▲ Guasave

e

Chalchihuites ▲

X

Approximate Northern
Limit of Mesoamerica-
Sixteenth Century
(*After Kirchhoff*)

La Quemada ▲

Tamuín ▲   Pavón ▲

I

Teayo ▲

Lake Chapala

▲ Tula

Tzintzuntzan ▲   *Lake Cuitzeo*

Cempoala ▲   Isla de Sacrificios ▲

MEXICO— TENOCHTITLÁN ○   ▲ Culhuacán

Lake Patzcuaro   ▲ Cholula

Xochicalco ▲

C

P A C I F I C

O

Mitla ▲

Tona

U.S.A.

MEXICO

GULF OF
MEXICO

O C E A N

PACIFIC OCEAN

POSTCLASSIC PERIOD

▲ Archaeological Sites   ○ Cities

MILES   0   50   100   150   200   250

IV

THE POSTCLASSIC PERIOD
IN MEXICO

The Postclassic Period in Mexico

The Mixtecs

WHEREAS THE ZAPOTECS were apparently unified under a central power located at Monte Albán, the Mixtecs, whose early antecedents are somewhat obscure, were established in many fertile valleys in western Oaxaca during the Late Classic period, in dozens of small city-states. The history and genealogy of their ruling families is known from a number of pictorial manuscripts which have fortunately survived the ravages of time. The dynasties of the rulers of Tilantongo in the Upper Mixteca have been traced back to A.D. 692 by Alfonso Caso. During that time the Mixteca was largely under the influence of Monte Albán and Teotihuacán. By the end of the tenth century Mixtec culture seems to have been well established in the southern part, but the characteristic features —its distinctive art style and excellent craftsmanship—became dominant only after A.D. 1350, and continued to the Conquest.

The development of this new great art style was not only due to the Mixtecs, but was also fostered by the important ceremonial center of Cholula and the southern Puebla region. The hallmark of this vigorous development is the excellent polychrome pottery which spread over extensive parts of Mesoamerica. The themes painted on the lacquered vessels consist of mythological personages, serpent and eagle motifs, some of which are paralleled in the pictorial manuscripts, among which the Codex Borgia group ranks as the outstanding accomplishment. Superb artistry and craftsmanship are also evident in ceremonial objects carved in bone or precious stone, mosaic inlays, and feather ornaments. It has become customary to label such masterpieces as "Mixtec," although many of them may be attributed to one or another of several local substyles within the Puebla-Mixteca macrostyle. Metalworking in gold and silver, however, was confined to the Mixteca proper. Since Cholula was also the seat of a powerful merchant guild, it has been considered to have held a major role in the spreading of this style over much of Mesoamerica, from Sinaloa in the north to Nicaragua.

Tula and the Toltecs

Turning once again to the Valley of Mexico at the close of the Classic period, it is evident that the infiltration of nomadic hordes brought about the disintegration of the political and cultural fabric. The invaders, who were of Nahuatl linguistic and ethnic affiliation, soon adopted the more civilized ways of life of the peoples whom they conquered. They became sedentary, and eventually a more secularly oriented era began, known as the Postclassic.

Toward the middle of the tenth century the Tolteca-Chichimecs, one of the dominant tribal aggregations, established themselves in Culhuacán (now a suburb of Mexico City), and settled later in Tula (Hidalgo). There they were joined by descendants of the old Teotihuacán refugees, the Nonoalca, who were skilled artisans and sculptors. Thus Tula developed into a powerful culture center, where the warrior spirit of the nomads, blended with the newly oriented Quetzalcoatl cult, exerted its civilizing influence over the neighboring Nahua tribes and far beyond.

The early history of Tula and the Toltecs is not too well known. Quetzalcoatl was the supreme deity. One of his high priests, who had assumed the name of Quetzalcoatl, was particularly instrumental in retaining the orthodoxy of this cult and eventually became immortalized as the culture hero Quetzalcoatl. He was opposed by a rising faction that intended to introduce new rites and re-establish the practice of human sacrifice, and he finally had to flee Tula. Quetzalcoatl's downfall is dramatically related in various Spanish chronicles (Tozzer, pp. 29–30).

Essentially this personality was the victim of the struggle between the adherents of the gods of the older religion, represented by Quetzalcoatl (the Feathered Serpent) and Tlaloc on one side, and those of the new cult centering on Tezcatlipoca and Huitzilopochtli, who later became the war-god of Tenochtitlán, on the other. The losers migrated to the lake shores of the Valley of Mexico, settled in Cholula and in Chichén Itzá (Yucatan). Quetzalcoatl went east to Tlillan Tlapallan, "the land of red color", where he lived on as a legendary figure who would supposedly return someday in the future and bring better times. The last king of Tula fled the capital in A.D. 1168, when new waves of nomadic Chichimecs from the north penetrated the central highlands and sacked and burned Tula.

The militaristic spirit of the Toltecs is best reflected in their monumental stone sculpture. Lapidary art took its inspiration from the earlier styles of Teotihuacán, Tajín, and Xochicalco, but also betrays Mixteca-Puebla influence. There are few images of deities, and Tezcatlipoca, whose cult vanquished Quetzalcoatl, is not represented at all. Toltec sculpture is mainly confined to Tula and is characterized by entirely new forms. Atlantean figures, standard bearers, and Chac-Mool figures begin to occur for the first time in this period. Warrior figures rather than priests decorate the huge round or square columns and bench friezes. The figures impress by their monumentality, rigidity, and the sustained repetition of identical motifs. Brilliant colors to highlight the details are well preserved on the reliefs of the benches surrounding the interiors of large buildings.

The savage destruction of Tula possibly accounts for the loss of a great many sculptures; some are known to have been taken to Tenochtitlán, where they were placed in a special temple housing foreign deities. Outside of Tula, Toltec sculpture is far more abundant at Chichén Itzá.

The Aztecs

The influx of the barbarian Chichimecs from the north and the west that caused the fall of the Toltec empire was accompanied by an emigration of Toltec artisans into eastern Mexico during the twelfth and thirteenth centuries. The movement of the latter accounts for the wide dispersal of the Chac-Mool figures, which range all over Mesoamerica from Tzintzuntzan in Michoacán to Yucatan and El Salvador. The newcomers to the Central Plateau were eager to emulate Toltec traditions and claim Toltec ancestry, which was equivalent to being civilized. The repute of Toltec pre-eminence was long remembered during these times of political turmoil as a golden age. Its heritage, blended with the militant vitality of the invaders, bred a magnificent and awe-inspiring sculptural style during the Late Postclassic period in central Mexico. The master craftsmen of the Puebla-Mixteca region, who had attained great proficiency in pictorial renderings on pottery and codices, contributed much toward this development. Full-time specialized artisans, organized in guilds, were attracted by the wealth of Tenochtitlán, the Aztec capital, which had emerged as the dominant power from the long struggle among the feuding remnants of the old Toltec domain.

Despite the large-scale destruction by Spanish missionaries, whose religious zeal in eradicating the "works of Satan" was unbridled, a great number of large and small stone sculptures survives. The enormous quantity of examples of lapidary art which must have existed prior to the arrival of the Spaniards is also hinted by the detailed descriptions compiled by Sahagún and other chroniclers, who marveled at the magnificence of indigenous works of art made of stone, pottery, precious metals, and other materials.

A number of Toltec-period innovations, such as the Chac-Mool and Atlantean figures, standard bearers, and friezes with warrior processions, were integrated in the Aztec pattern but with minor modifications.

Compared with Toltec sculpture, that of the Mexico-Aztecs shows more naturalism and greater perfection, particularly during the last century before the Spanish Conquest. The stone images personify to a large extent deities, with emphasis on the portrayal of fertility-gods, and show a deep preoccupation with mortality, evident in the skeletal emblems. The sculptors adhered closely to the iconographic system founded on earlier traditions and codified by the all-powerful priesthood.

The religious function of stone sculpture is highlighted by frequent use of calendric symbols, and, on the larger images, by carvings of a standardized version of the earth monster on the underside, which is normally not visible. A similar practice is noticeable in Classic Zapotec monuments at Monte Albán, where recent relocation and consolidation of monumental sculptures revealed previously unknown glyphic inscriptions on the underside (Acosta, p. 28).

The "official" Aztec sculpture, as Nicholson called it (p. 20), dealt not only with religious subjects, but also included animal figures carved in the round, as for example feathered serpents, coyotes, grasshoppers, and many others. All these animals were portrayed with great realism.

The variety of themes, the use of hard, fine-grained basalts, and conscientious elaboration of detail combined with great mastery in design and technique give Aztec stone sculpture a privileged place among the many impressive monuments of Mesoamerican art.

The ceremonial pottery of the Postclassic period in central Mexico reached a high degree of sophistication under the skillful hands of artisans in the Mixteca-Puebla region, including Cholula.

In the Late Postclassic period, Texcoco, Chalco, and Mexico-Tenochtitlán made polychrome pottery locally in large quantities.

The domestic black-line-decorated orange ware, with abstract curvilinear and later with naturalistic designs, was first developed in Culhuacán. In time these thick wares, bearing designs drawn in broad lines, changed to very thin, well-made dishes, embellished with very fine lines executed with great precision. These wares, known as Aztec pottery, spread over great parts of Mesoamerica in the wake of the Mexica conquests.

The clay figurines of the Postclassic period were made in molds, as during the Classic. They are mostly flat and less refined than the Teotihuacán specimens. The portrayal of features and accouterments depends more on painting applied to a chalky base than on modeling. There appears to have been less emphasis on manufacture of clay figurines during the Toltec period than during the last two centuries prior to the Conquest. The favorite subject among Aztec figurines is the figure of a woman holding a child. Deities, warriors, animals, even models of temples, were made in quantity. Other clay artifacts include flutes, Panpipes, whistles, stamps, and vast numbers of moldmade spindle whorls of various shape and decoration.

The Postclassic Period in Mexico

Captions and Notes

PLATES 333–397

333. MOSAIC MASK. / Yucatan. Postclassic period. Turquoise, jade, tortoise- and conch-shell intarsia, applied with vegetable resin to a carved wooden form. Height, 5 3/4". The Dumbarton Oaks Collections, Washington, D. C.

The teeth are jaguar and filed human; bound hair once formed a headdress and beard. A red, lacquerlike material colors the ears, nostrils, and mouth. The series of drilled holes on the outer edges suggests that the mask was tied on the personage before burial. A leather or fabric tab hung from the mask's jaw to cover the lower portion of the wearer's face. The tradition of such "half masks" began with the Archaic cultures in the Valley of Mexico. This mask shows striking similarities to the murals of Santa Rita Corozal and Tulum, which are related in design to the pre-Conquest Mixtec codices from the Mexican highlands.

334. HUMAN SKULL WITH MOSAIC INLAY. / Southwest Chiapas. Late Postclassic period. Turquoise, shell, and gold-copper alloy. Height, 8 1/2". Collection Wright S. Ludington, Santa Barbara, Calif.

The facial decoration, particularly the disk on either side of the head, is characteristic of the death-gods as shown in the codices. Human skulls with mosaic inlays rank among the masterpieces of Puebla-Mixtec art. The clay in which the skull was encased held the decorations in place to make possible the restoration.

335. FUNERAL MASK. / Southwest Chiapas. Late Classic period. Jadeite, mosaic, and shell. Height, 9". Collection Mr. and Mrs. Francis V. Crane, Marathon, Fla.

The separately carved components were found in a tomb located in a ceremonial structure. Originally mounted on a wood or plaster support, the mask probably had covered the face of a deceased dignitary. The present reconstruction was made on a base of clay at the time of discovery. The background for the eyes is made of shell. Similar jade death masks are known from Palenque and can be assumed to represent portraits of the persons with whom they were buried.

336. CARVED PLAQUE. / Central Mexico. Postclassic period. Brownish jade with traces of cinnabar. Height, 5". Collection Stendahl.

A standing personage flanked by two attendants shown in profile.

337. VASE WITH STRAIGHT FLARING SIDES AND TRIPOD STEPPED SLAB SUPPORTS. / San Jerónimo de Juárez, Guerrero. Postclassic period. Alabaster with traces of cinnabar. Height, 7 3/8"; diameter, 7 1/4". Private collection.

Inside the vase were found two shells and the carved jade plaque seen in plate 338. The tripod supports are similar to those found on Mixtec pottery of the late period.

338. CARVED PLAQUE. / San Jerónimo de Juárez, Guerrero. Postclassic period. Light-green jade with traces of cinnabar. Height, 3 1/4". Private collection.

A human head whose asymmetrical headdress shows a serpent with a human head held in its jaws.

339. MASK. / Central Mexico. Late Postclassic period. Clay with polychrome decoration. Height, 5 3/4". Philadelphia Museum of Art. The Louise and Walter Arensberg Collection.

This piece is illustrated in Kubler, 1954, fig. 25.

340. MASK WITH FRAGMENTS AND TRACES OF MOSAIC. / Provenance unknown. Late Postclassic period. Wood and turquoise. Height, 8". Portland Art Museum, Portland, Ore. William Sargent Ladd Collection.

The face had been completely covered with small pieces of turquoise and, perhaps, shell. The tight-fitting head cover, which represents the hair, is diagnostic of Late Aztec stone sculpture.

341. PITCHER WITH POLYCHROME DECORATION. / Cholula, Puebla. Late Postclassic period. Clay. Height, 10″. Thomas Gilcrease Institute of American History and Art, Tulsa, Okla.

A priest attired in jaguar skin is seated on a small bench and holds a ladle with burning incense. Behind the priest is a feathered serpent whose head emerges from the jaguar's jaws.

342. GLOBULAR JAR WITH SPOUT. / Cholula, Puebla. Late Postclassic period. Polychrome clay. Height, 11 1/4″. Thomas Gilcrease Institute of American History and Art, Tulsa, Okla.

Stylized design of a serpent's head, composed of upper jaw with three fangs, eye, and elaborate headdress. Instead of the lower jaw, two elements with bifurcated ends are shown, one of which probably represents the tongue. Several circular hatched elements surround the design and represent downy balls of feathers, the traditional symbol of sacrifice. The spout was originally connected with the rim, probably by a slab of clay.

343/344. CYLINDRICAL VASE WITH ENGRAVED FIGURES (*with schematic detail*). / Found in Guerrero. Late Classic period. Alabaster. Height, 7 5/8″; diameter, 7 7/8″. Collection Josef Müller, Solothurn, Switzerland.

The lip and openwork rim decoration have been partly reconstructed (*see* schematic detail). The vessel was repaired in ancient times by the crack-lacing method, as is shown by the pairs of holes drilled on either side of the vertical fissures. The decoration is incised in shallow lines and shows two individuals attired in capes. One has a feathered serpent headdress, the other has his hair tied up with a beaded band. Both individuals have long nose ornaments. Two serpents coil around the rim of the vessel, their heads and feathered tails entwined on either side of the figures. A third serpent emerges from the foot of the person to the right, who wears a jaguar claw as breast ornament. An extraordinary feature of this vessel is a perfectly straight perforation through the entire wall beginning at the top of the rim, with an opening on the inside at the bottom. This duct was apparently planned beforehand, because the wall of the vessel is slightly thicker along the vertical plane that houses the perforation. The function of this duct is not clear, but it brings to mind the duct which connects the crypt with the upper sanctuary of the Temple of the Inscriptions at Palenque and which is believed to have served as a symbolic link between the buried priest-ruler and the religious rites performed in the temple above.

345. PLATE WITH POLYCHROME DECORATION. / Cholula, Puebla. Late Postclassic period. Clay. Diameter, 9″. Thomas Gilcrease Institute of American History and Art, Tulsa, Okla.

The center motif depicts an eagle studded with blood-stained flint knives, the emblems of sacrifice and war. Stepped frets encircle the design. The rim decoration shows four birds' heads with minor variations in detail, but all have a curled crest which is typical of the conventionalized rendering of pheasants or quail.

346. PEDESTAL BOWL WITH TWO JAGUAR HEADS. / Cholula style. Late Postclassic period. Polychrome clay. Height, 4 1/4″; diameter, 8 1/2″. Collection Stendahl.

347. PEAR-SHAPED PEDESTAL VASE. / Cholula, Puebla. Late Postclassic period. Brown clay with polychrome decoration and glossy surface. Height, 11″. Los Angeles County Museum of Natural History.

Eagle heads, feathers, and stepped frets decorate the upper part. Hearts, death's-heads, shields, and hands cover the body.

348. PEDESTAL JAR WITH FLARING NECK. / Cholula, Puebla. Late Postclassic period. Brown clay with polychrome decoration and glossy surface. Height, 8 3/4″. Collection Stendahl.

The neck is decorated with motifs similar to those seen in plate 347. An eagle's head with wide-open beak and a circular arrangement of feathers is shown twice on the globular body. The pedestal is decorated with cloud symbols framing a row of *chalchihuitl* (jade).

349. MACUILXOCHITL ("FIVE FLOWER"), THE GOD OF DANCE, SONG, AND GAMES. / Region of Teotitlán del Camino, Oaxaca. Postclassic period. Polychrome clay. Height, 25″. Collection Mrs. Edith Hafter, Zurich, Switzerland.

Macuilxochitl is closely related to Xochipilli, the god of happiness and, in a larger sense, of agriculture and the sun. He is distinguished by facial decoration, surrounding the mouth, which shows a human hand with fingers—hence the determinative "five"; here the decoration is stylized. The close-fitting headdress, another characteristic, consists of a stylized bird's head crowned by five bunches of feathers. Such figures apparently were used as incense burners, the copal smoke emanating from the openings in the body and the mouth.

350. NECKLACE. / Southwest Chiapas. Late Postclassic period. Cast gold. Length, 10 1/4″. The Dumbarton Oaks Collections, Washington, D.C.

Twenty small turtle shells, each with three straps and three bells.

351. NECKLACE. / Southwest Chiapas. Late Postclassic period. Cast gold. Length, 15 1/2″. The Dumbarton Oaks Collections, Washington, D.C.

Sixteen ovoid elements, each with three bells, are stylized representations of turtle shells.

352. EAR ORNAMENT. / Southwest Chiapas. Late Post-classic period. Cast gold and turquoise. Height, 2 1/2". The Dumbarton Oaks Collections, Washington, D.C.

The eyes are inlaid with turquoise. From the earlobes pend almond-shaped ornaments which are the traditional emblem of the gods of dance and of the pulque gods. In the codices this ornament is painted white to indicate that it was carved of shell. From the beard pends a plaque with three bells.

353. NECKLACE OF EIGHTEEN SKULLS. / Southwest Chiapas. Late Postclassic period. Cast gold and turquoise. Length, 14". The Dumbarton Oaks Collections, Washington, D.C.

The skulls have articulated jaws and alternate ones have inlaid turquoise eyes.

354. NECKLACE OF FROGS. / Southwest Chiapas. Late Postclassic period. Cast gold and turquoise. Length, 17". Collection Jan Mitchell, New York.

The charcoal and clay core of the casting process is still retained in the body of each frog.

355. NECKLACE OF FIFTEEN BELLS. / Southwest Chiapas. Late Postclassic period. Cast gold and shell beads. Length, 17". Collection Mr. and Mrs. Francis V. Crane, Marathon, Fla.

356. RING WITH JAGUAR HEAD. / Southwest Chiapas. Late Postclassic period. Cast gold. Diameter, 1". Collection Mr. and Mrs. Paul Geier, Rome, Italy.

This piece is illustrated in *Präkolumbische Kunst*, item 812, p. 99.

357. NECKLACE. / Southwest Chiapas. Late Postclassic period. Thirty-seven rock crystal beads and ten amethyst beads; crystal dog's-head pendant. Length, 15". Collection Stendahl.

358. FRAGMENT OF SQUARE WALL PANEL. / Tula, Hidalgo. Postclassic period. Lime plaster. Height, 22". Los Angeles County Museum of Natural History.

Tlaloc, the rain-god, is seen standing with his head in profile. In his hand he holds one of his emblems, the serpent, signifying lightning. The spaces next to the serpent are filled with scrollwork commonly seen in Toltec style sculptures.

359. HEAD FRAGMENT. / Central Mexico. Postclassic period. Volcanic rock. Height, 15". The Museum of Primitive Art, New York.

The headdress consists of a variation of the *miotli* motif, the year sign composed of trapeze and ray, which is seen on Toltec period Tlaloc sculptures (cf. Seler, 1908, figs. 31, 32).

360/361. STATUE REPRESENTING SACRIFICE TO XIPE TOTEC, "OUR LORD THE FLAYED ONE." / Tula, Hidalgo. c. A.D. 1000–1168. Painted, soft fine lime mortar. Height, 16". Collection Mr. and Mrs. Robert A. Rowan, Pasadena, Calif.

Xipe Totec is one of the older gods of the Mexican pantheon, but a very important one, who was venerated from the beginning of the Classic period (first century B.C.) to the time of the Spanish Conquest. He is the god of spring, of seed time, and also the patron god of jewelers. Sacrifices in his honor were to assure that the earth would cover itself once more with a new layer of vegetation. The figure represents a priest clad in the flayed skin of a sacrificial victim. A mask of skin covers the face and part of the back of the head, exposing only the eyes and mouth of the bearer. The teeth consist of a piece of carved shell inserted in the mouth. Holes penetrating the victim's skin at the back of the head and on his chest and back indicate that a cord or strap was inserted to pull the skin tightly over his body.

362. RECEPTACLE WITH FOUR RELIEF-DECORATED PANELS. / Tula, Hidalgo. c. A.D. 1000–1168. Coarse lime mortar. Reconstructed. Height, 20". Collection Mr. and Mrs. Robert A. Rowan, Pasadena, Calif.

This boxlike receptacle was found together with the Xipe figure also pictured in plates 360 and 361. All four sides are decorated, and each one is framed by a molding. Calendrical symbols and figures of priests, warriors, and gods are among the motifs. The function of the box can only be conjectured, but by analogy with similar stone boxes left by the Aztecs, who succeeded the Toltecs of Tula and continued the lapidary tradition of their predecessors, it is not improbable that it served to preserve the ashes of a deceased warrior of high rank, who had died in battle or in sacrifice and was given the highest honors.

363. FEATHERED SERPENT RELIEF. / Xochicalco, Morelos. Postclassic period. Volcanic stone. Height, 36". Heeramaneck Galleries, New York.

Representations of feathered serpents, although frequently identified with Quetzalcoatl, their namesake, do not always symbolize the creator-god, whom they preceded in time. In this carving a striking similarity is seen with a rock carving on the Cerro de la Malinche near Tula, Hidalgo, where Quetzalcoatl is presented in front of a feathered serpent in identical position. The lower right-hand quarter of the panel is restored.

364/365. POTTERY MOLD AND DRAWING OF A CAST MADE THEREOF. / Tultitlán, State of Mexico. Maya-Toltec style, twelfth or thirteenth century A.D. Fine-grained brown clay. Height, 7 1/4". Collection Stendahl.

The curvature of the mold shows that it was intended to decorate a large cylindrical vase about 6 1/4" in diameter. On such a vase the design could have been fitted four times if the entire surface was to be covered. The intricate decoration shows two sumptuously attired persons. The higher-ranking one, holding a staff and a fan, stands on a dais and directs his speech to a masked companion whose upturned face and outstretched hands indicate submissiveness. No weapons are shown; thus the persons are either priests or chieftains, but not warriors. Most of the stylistic details have much in common with the lapidary art of the Mexican or Toltec phase at Chichén Itzá. For a detailed description of the designs, see von Winning, 1962.

366/367. STANDARD BEARER (*two views*). / Tula, Hidalgo. Postclassic period. Volcanic tuff. Height, 36″. Collection Stendahl.

The hands of the figure are joined, forming a hole through which a pole with some emblem was inserted. These sculptures, of Toltec origin, were placed firmly (as the broad base conveys) on either side of temple balustrades. A circular ornament forming the brooch of the belt, also frequent in Toltec sculpture, is of Teotihuacán origin, where it is depicted on plano-relief-decorated pottery. Standard bearers occur throughout the Toltec culture and were also used by the Aztecs.

368/369. COILED SERPENT (*two views*). / Tula, Hidalgo. Postclassic period. Dark-green igneous rock. Height, 23″. Philadelphia Museum of Art. The Louise and Walter Arensberg Collection.

This piece is illustrated in Kubler, 1954, pl. 35.

370/371. BIFACE SCULPTURE WTIH MAN, JAGUAR, SERPENT, AND BIRD MOTIF ON ONE SIDE, AND BURDEN CARRIER ON THE OTHER (*two views*). / Mexico D.F. Postclassic period. Andesite. Height, 30″. Los Angeles County Museum of Natural History.

The combination of human, bird, and jaguar features is known under various names (e.g., monster mask or man-bird-serpent) and is of Toltec origin. Frequent renderings of this sort are known from Tula and the Mexican period at Chichén Itzá. It is doubtful whether this sculpture is a late Aztec creation; it could very well have been among the "art treasures" which the Aztecs salvaged after the fall of Tula and brought to Tenochtitlán, a procedure known from documentary sources. On the back is a kneeling figure with animal mask carrying a burden with tumpline across the forehead held in place by the hand. This method of carrying still survives in present-day Mexico and Guatemala. The burden consists of a model of a temple, shown in profile, with double-tiered base, walls, and flat roof (cf. similar representations in Codex Nuttall 2, 17, 25, 31, 50, 78, and Codex Laud 44). Eleven disks surrounding the temple have calendrical significance in the Aztec-Mixtec system, i.e., not in the earlier Classic period bar-and-dot system.

372/373. HOURGLASS-SHAPED INCENSE BURNER WITH MOLDED APPLIQUÉS (*two views*). / Valley of Mexico. Late Postclassic period. Buff clay, restored. Height,

22″; diameter, 18¹/₂″. Thomas Gilcrease Institute of American History and Art, Tulsa, Okla.

The decoration consists of three parts: 1. The bands with circular elements on rim, waist, and base, which are a characteristic decoration on incense burners. 2. Molded designs embodying fire and water symbols, which cover three-quarters of the vessel; stylized appliqués projecting from the rim. 3. The front, which shows a rosette (probably indicating a knot) fringed with representations of small shells alternating with jade circles. The central designs of the rosette contain V-shaped elements symbolizing the sun. Below are streams of water. The Y-shaped elements on the upper plaques represent smoke (fire). The decoration also occurs in pictorial manuscripts and is an expression of the dichotomy of fire and water, which had great importance in ancient Mexican thought, symbolizing *yaoyotl* (war). This Late Postclassic incense burner shows an adherence to techniques of ornamentation used in Classic Teotihuacán (see plate 222). The only other hourglass-shaped and appliqué-decorated incense burner, to our knowledge, is on display at the National Museum in Mexico City. It was reportedly found at Palmillas, Veracruz, and shows late Mexican influence.

374. WARRIOR WITH JAGUAR HEADDRESS. / Valley of Mexico. Mazapan culture, Postclassic period. Ocher clay with remnants of white and reddish paint. Restored. Height, 31″. Collection Stendahl.

The figure is in two parts, with the head tenoned into the torso. Parts of the headdress are restored. This piece is illustrated in *Präkolumbische Kunst*, item 740, pl. 60. A life-sized clay figure similar to this one was first reported in a Mazapan culture context (from the Xolalpan house ruin at Teotihuacán) by Linné, 1934, pp. 83–84, fig. 113; it is on display in the museum at Teotihuacán. The figures have identical nose ornaments, arm ribbons, and closed eyes.

375. EAGLE DEVOURING A HUMAN HEART. / Central Mexican highlands. Early Postclassic period. Painted terra-cotta relief, 27¹/₂ ×29¹/₂″. The Metropolitan Museum of Art, New York. Gift of Frederick E. Church, 1893.

These relief carvings, showing an eagle holding a human heart, with three appendages representing blood, are a characteristic motif on the temple platforms at Tula and Toltec-period Chichén Itzá. There the eagles, symbolizing the sun, alternate with prowling jaguars, symbols of earthly power. Both creatures were the totems of two warrior orders which assumed great importance in Aztec times. Eagle knights and jaguar knights captured the victims to be sacrificed to the sun, which could be nourished only by the most precious liquid man had to offer—his blood. The depiction of the eagle with a human heart is therefore of religious significance. (A similar relief slab is reproduced in Keleman, plate 63 b.)

376. SEATED PERSON. / Castillo de Teayo, Veracruz. Late Postclassic period. Laminated sandstone.

Height, 31 5/8″. The Metropolitan Museum of Art, New York.

The position of the right hand seems to indicate that the figure was used as a standard bearer and was placed at the top of the stairs of a temple platform.

377. HEAD OF THE RAIN-GOD TLALOC. / Valley of Mexico. Late Aztec period. Lava and residues of lime plaster with red and blue paint. Height, 24″. Collection Stendahl.

The sculpture is cylindrical, reminiscent of the shape of clay Tlaloc effigy vessels. The rain-god is characterized by the *atzatzontli*, a crown of heron feathers tied by two twisted cords; the peculiar nose composed of twisted serpent bodies which also form the upper lip; four large upper teeth; and the broad flat ornament (usually made of folded paper) attached to the back of the neck (*tlaquechpanyotl*). In this sculpture, and also in the specimen in the Arensberg collection (Kubler, 1954, fig. 32), the neck ornament is attached to the sides because of the cylindrical shape, and the pleated folds are indicated by parallel lines. Here they are seen behind the scrolls representing clouds. The back of the piece is plain, except for the crown and a strand of braided hair.

378. SEATED FIGURE WITH THE MASK OF THE WIND-GOD. / Valley of Mexico. Late Postclassic period. Basalt. Height, 15 1/2″. Collection Josef Müller, Solothurn, Switzerland.

Among several characteristics of Quetzalcoatl in his aspect as the wind-god Ehecatl are the peaked cap, the protruding buccal mask, and the curved ear ornaments.

379. TLALOC, THE RAIN-GOD. / Valley of Mexico. Postclassic period. Basalt. Height, 20″. Collection Stendahl.

The characteristic mask of the rain-god consists of two entwined serpents forming the nose and encircling the eyes. Tied to his head is a crown of heron feathers, their whiteness implying the clouds in the sky. The plaque in the back of his head is a formalized rendering of the pleated paper ornament (*tlaquechpanyotl* or *amacuexpalli*) known to be a symbol of fertility-gods. The cavity in his chest is suggestive of the placement of offerings (cf. plate 386).

380. FERTILITY GODDESS, PROBABLY CHICOMECOATL. / Valley of Mexico. Late Postclassic period. Basalt. Height, 30″. Collection Josefowitz, Switzerland.

The emblems of this statue identify it as a maize deity venerated under the name Chicomecoatl ("Seven Serpent"). On her head is a paper house (*amacalli*), a rectangular device that when worn ritualistically by the priest consisted of a framework covered with bark paper and adorned with rosettes from which pend long strips of paper. Between the rosettes are four vertical elements which correspond to the *miotli* seen in the codices, forming a trapeze and ray, which are a solar and year symbol. This symbol relates the deity to the harvesting cycle. She wears the *quechquemitl* with tasseled edges and the *cueitl* (skirt). The right hand is shaped to sustain a staff (*chicahuaztli*), a common emblem of fertility deities; the left hand holds two ears of maize.

381. HEAD. / Central Mexico. Late Postclassic period. Porous volcanic rock. Height, 11 1/2″. Private collection.

382. PERSON CARRYING A STONE IMAGE. / Vicinity Mexico City. Late Postclassic period. Volcanic rock. Height, 17″. Collection Stendahl.

A person (*Macehual*) clad in a loincloth carries a stone sculpture by means of a thick, twisted tumpline (cf. plate 371). The burden represents a maize deity (*Chicomecoatl*) typified by a large rectangular headdress combined with two rosettes and two corncobs held at the side of the head.

383. CIRCULAR BASIN DECORATED WITH DEATH'S-HEADS. / Valley of Mexico. Late Postclassic period. Basalt. Height, 9 1/2″; diameter, 24″. Collection Stendahl.

The skulls, which are tied together to form a string, and the braided bands on the upper and lower edge are symbols of sacrifice which identify the bowl as a *cuahxicalli*, destined for receiving human hearts and blood offered to the sun. The carving on the inside represents the *zacatapayolli*, a bundle of hay into which the bloodstained bone awls were stuck during the penitent self-sacrificial blood-drawing ceremony. The basin is half restored. A similar basin is illustrated in Kubler, 1954, pl. 43. For a drawing of a *zacatapayolli*, see Caso, 1927, figs. 69, 70 a, b.

384. MAN. / Central Mexico. Late Postclassic period. Basalt. Height, 32 1/2″. Collection Stendahl.

The position of the fingers indicates that this figure served as a standard bearer.

385. KNEELING OLD WOMAN. / Mexico City. Late Postclassic period. Basalt. Height, 13 3/4″. Collection Pierre Langlois, Paris.

386. KNEELING WATER-GODDESS. / Valley of Mexico. Postclassic period. Basalt. Height, 13 1/2″. Collection Stendahl.

Chalchiuhtlicue is the goddess of terrestrial waters (as distinguished from rain and vegetation) and companion of Tlaloc. Characteristic is the multiple headband decorated with jade beads indicating streams of water. The headband is tied at the back of the head, the strands falling to the waist. Her hair is tied on the sides. She wears jade ear disks which are tasseled to emphasize their preciousness. The eyes were probably inlaid with shell. The cavity in the chest is unusually large and deep and was probably intended for the placement of offerings. The goddess wears the typical skirt, *cueitl*, consisting of a rectangular piece of cotton material tied around the waist.

387. RECLINING JAGUAR. / Valley of Mexico (?). Late Postclassic period. Basalt. Height, $4^7/_8$". Brooklyn Museum, New York.

388. AGED MAN SEATED ON BENCH. / Valley of Mexico. Late Postclassic period. Basalt. Height, $24^1/_2$". Thomas Gilcrease Institute of American History and Art, Tulsa, Okla.

The circular design between the legs indicates the knot of the loincloth (*maxtlatl*), the customary male attire.

389. EARTH MONSTER. / Valley of Mexico. Late Postclassic period. Basalt. Depth, 9"; diameter, 43". Collection Stendahl.

This sculpture has been about two-fifths restored. It depicts Tlaltecuhtli, the earth-god who devours the bundles containing the bodies of the dead. Here he is seen in his guise as a monstrous toadlike animal. His human arms and legs are decorated with skulls and owls, symbols of death, and his hands and feet have claws instead of toes and fingers. The large skull in the center depicts the buckle of a leather belt which holds the skirt of the god. Such a buckle (*tezcacuitlapilli*) is characteristic of many Toltec and Aztec deities, and is always worn on the back. The human head at the bottom is undoubtedly the face of the sun-god. This is not as paradoxical as it may seem, but expresses the concept of *tlachitonatiuh*, the "devoured sun" that hides inside the earth to illuminate the subterranean world. The back of the sculpture is flat and undecorated.

390. COILED SERPENT. / Texcoco, Valley of Mexico. Late Postclassic period. Basalt. Height, 11". Chicago Natural History Museum, Chicago, Ill.

391. COILED SERPENT. / Valley of Mexico. Late Postclassic period. Basalt. Height, $9^1/_2$". Collection Dr. and Mrs. William F. Kaiser, Berkeley, Calif.

392. TENONED SERPENT HEAD. / Mexico City. Late Postclassic period. Basalt. Height, $25^1/_2$". Collection Stendahl.

The tenon implies that the serpent head once adorned the lower end of a balustrade, an architectural trait derived from the Toltecs.

393. HOURGLASS-SHAPED VASE WITH APPLIQUÉS. / Valley of Mexico. Late Postclassic period. Polychrome clay. Height, 26". Thomas Gilcrease Institute of American History and Art, Tulsa, Okla.

A human face projects from the widely opened beak of a bird. The pectoral shows a serpent.

394/395. ENGRAVED DEER-BONE FRAGMENT (*with schematic drawing*). / Cholula, Puebla. Late Postclassic period. Length, $3^1/_2$". Collection Stendahl.

The incised design, which is filled with black paint, shows the wind-god, Ehecatl; a figure which probably represents Huehuecoyotl, the Old Coyote; and a face with a speech scroll. The fourth motif is too incomplete to be determined, but possibly represents the day sign 4 *ollin*. One end of the bone was cut diagonally and carefully smoothed. For a detailed description, see von Winning, "An Incised Bone Artifact from Cholula, Mexico."

396/397. INCISED BONE RATTLE OR MUSICAL RASP (*with schematic drawing*). / Culhuacán, Valley of Mexico. Late Postclassic period. Human femur. Length, 12". Royal Ontario Museum, University of Toronto, Canada.

Bone rattles or musical rasps, known as *omichicahuaztli*, provided musical accompaniment in Aztec funeral ceremonies for dead warriors. The delicately incised designs consist of symbols of war, sacrifice, blood, and death arranged in a single composition having seven major parts: solar disk and starry sky; shield beneath the sky; eagle-warrior figure; figure clad in slain victim's skin; earth monster; blood streams; and darts. All the elements shown can be explained by comparison with figures in the Aztec codices and stone monuments and are a typical expression of the religious symbolism relating to the death of warriors in late Aztec times, just preceding the Conquest. For a detailed description, see von Winning, 1959 ("A Decorated Bone Rattle from Culhuacán, Mexico").

333. Mosaic mask.
Yucatan. Postclassic period. Turquoise, jade, tortoise, and conch shell intarsia, applied with vegetable resin to a carved wooden form. Height, 5 3/4".

334. Human skull with mosaic inlay.
Southwest Chiapas. Late Postclassic period.
Turquoise, shell, and gold-copper alloy. Height, 8 ¹/₂".

335. Funeral mask.
Southwest Chiapas. Late Classic period. Jadeite,
mosaic, and shell. Height, 9".

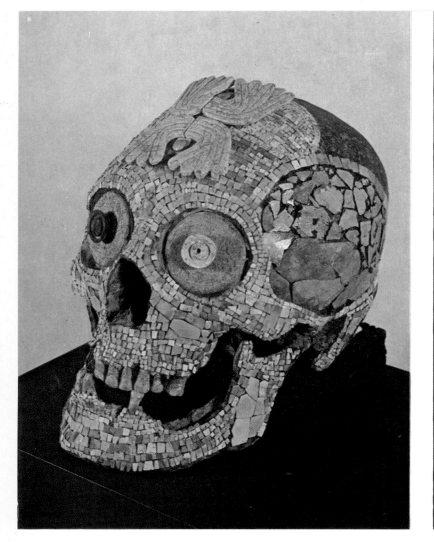

339. Mask.
Central Mexico. Late Fostclassic period. Clay with polychrome decoration. Height, 5 3/4".

340. Mask with fragments and traces of mosaic. *Provenance unknown. Late Postclassic period. Wood and turquoise. Height, 8".*

336. Carved plaque.
Central Mexico. Postclassic period. Brownish jade with traces of cinnabar. Height, 5".

337. Vase with straight flaring sides and tripod stepped slab supports. *San Jerónimo de Juárez, Guerrero. Postclassic period. Alabaster with traces of cinnabar. Height, 7 3/8"; diameter, 7 1/4".*

338. Carved plaque.
San Jerónimo de Juárez, Guerrero. Postclassic period. Light-green jade with traces of cinnabar. Height, 3 1/4".

341. Pitcher with polychrome decoration.
Cholula, Puebla. Late Postclassic period. Clay.
Height, 10".

342. Globular jar with spout.
Cholula, Puebla. Late Postclassic period. Polychrome
clay. Height, 11 1/4".

343/344. Cylindrical vase with engraved
figures (with schematic detail). *Found in*
Guerrero. Late Classic period. Alabaster. Height,
7 5/8"; diameter, 7 7/8".

345. Plate with polychrome decoration.
Cholula, Puebla. Late Postclassic period. Clay.
Diameter, 9".

346. Pedestal bowl with two jaguar heads.
Cholula style. Late Postclassic period. Polychrome
clay. Height, 4 1/4"; diameter, 8 1/2".

347. Pear-shaped pedestal vase.
Cholula, Puebla. Late Postclassic period. Brown
clay with polychrome decoration and glossy surface.
Height, 11".

348. Pedestal jar with flaring neck.
Cholula, Puebla. Late Postclassic period. Brown
clay with polychrome decoration and glossy surface.
Height, 8 3/4".

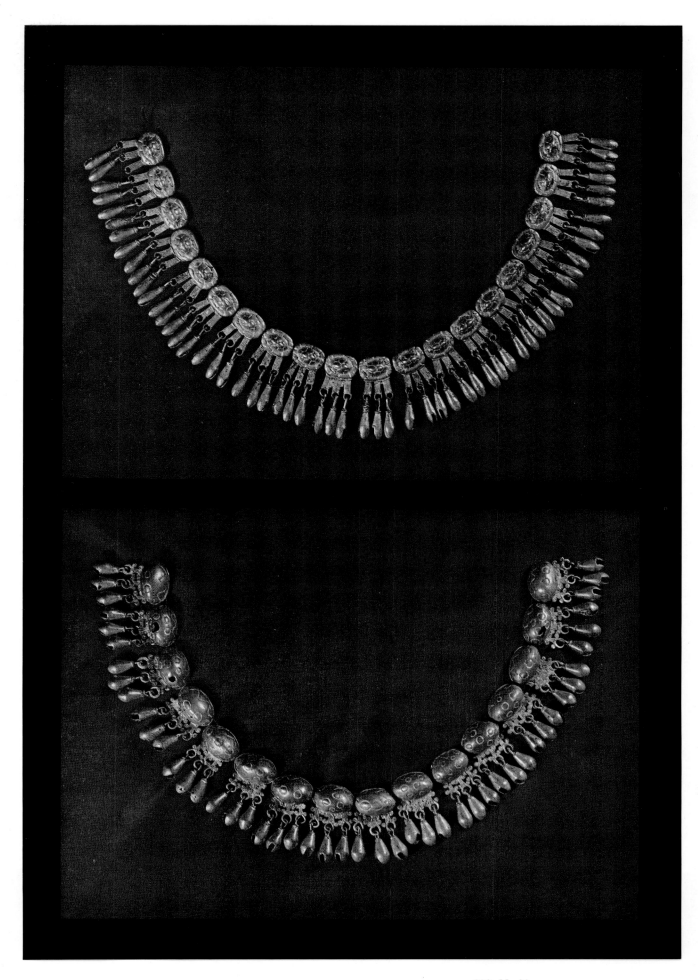

350. Necklace.
Southwest Chiapas. Late Postclassic period.
Cast gold. Length, 10 1/4".

351. Necklace.
Southwest Chiapas. Late Postclassic period.
Cast gold. Length, 15 1/2".

349. Macuilxochitl ("five flower"), the god of
dance, song, and games. *Region of Teotitlán del
Camino, Oaxaca. Postclassic period. Polychrome
clay. Height, 25".*

251

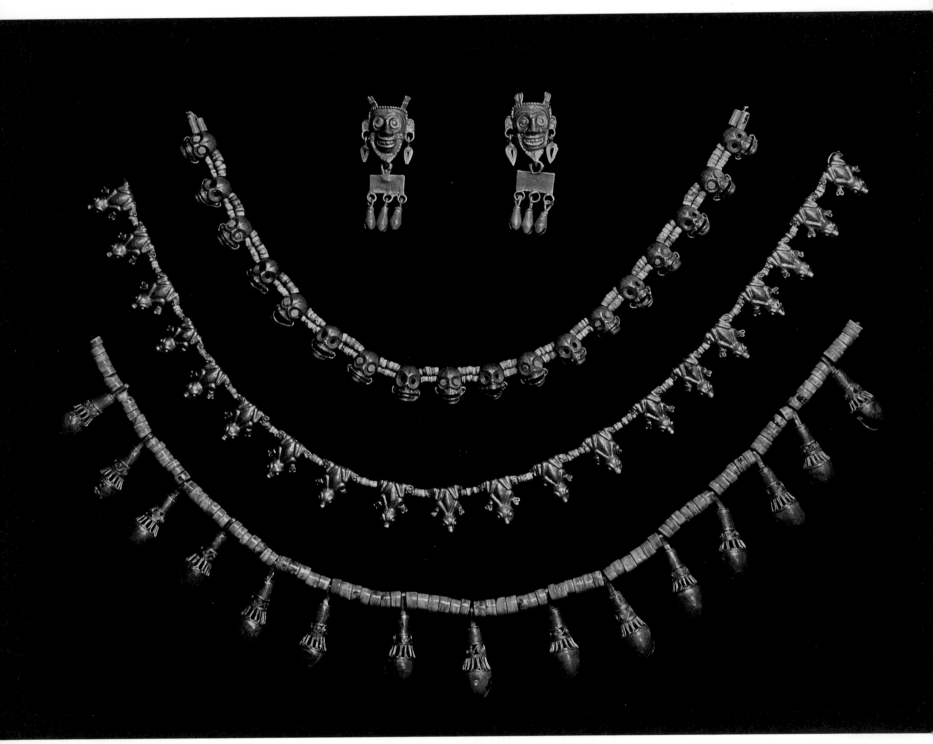

352. Ear ornament.
Southwest Chiapas. Late Postclassic period. Cast gold and turquoise. Height, 2 ¹/₂″.

353. Necklace of eighteen skulls.
Southwest Chiapas. Late Postclassic period. Cast gold and turquoise. Length, 14″.

354. Necklace of frogs.
Southwest Chiapas. Late Postclassic period. Cast gold and turquoise. Length, 17″.

355. Necklace of fifteen bells.
Southwest Chiapas. Late Postclassic period. Cast gold and shell beads. Length, 17″.

356. Ring with jaguar head.
Southwest Chiapas. Late Postclassic period. Cast gold. Diameter, 1".

357. Necklace.
Southwest Chiapas. Late Postclassic period. Thirty-seven rock crystal beads and ten amethyst beads; crystal dog's-head pendant. Length, 15".

358. Fragment of square wall panel.
Tula, Hidalgo. Postclassic period. Lime plaster.
Height, 22".

359. Head fragment.
Central Mexico. Postclassic period. Volcanic rock.
Height, 15".

360/361. Statue representing sacrifice to
Xipe Totec, "our lord the flayed one" (side
and back views). *Tula, Hidalgo. c. A.D. 1000–
1168. Painted, soft fine lime mortar. Height, 16″.*

OPPOSITE PAGE

362. Receptacle with four relief-decorated
panels, surmounted with the figure illustrated
opposite. *Tula, Hidalgo. c. A.D. 1000–1168.
Coarse lime mortar. Reconstructed. Height, 20″.*

363. Feathered serpent relief.
*Xochicalco, Morelos. Postclassic period. Volcanic
stone. Height, 36".*

364/365. Pottery mold and drawing of a cast made thereof. *Tultitlán, State of Mexico. Maya-Toltec style, twelfth or thirteenth century A.D. Fine-grained brown clay. Height, 7 1/4".*

366/367. Standard bearer (two views).
Tula, Hidalgo. Postclassic period. Volcanic tuff.
Height, 36".

368/369. Coiled serpent (two views).
Tula, Hidalgo. Postclassic period. Dark-green
igneous rock. Height, 23".

370/371. Biface sculpture with man, jaguar,
serpent, and bird motif on one side, and
burden carrier on the other (two views).
Mexico D.F. Postclassic period. Andesite. Height,
30".

372/373. Hourglass-shaped incense burner with molded appliqués (two views). *Valley of Mexico. Late Postclassic period. Buff clay, restored. Height, 22″; diameter, 18 1/2″.*

374. Warrior with jaguar headdress. *Valley of Mexico. Mazapan culture, Postclassic period. Ocher clay with remnants of white and reddish paint. Restored. Height, 31″.*

375. Eagle devouring a human heart.
Central Mexican highlands. Early Postclassic period.
Painted terra-cotta relief, 27 1/2 × 29 1/2".

376. Seated person.
Castillo de Teayo, Veracruz. Late Postclassic
period. Laminated sandstone. Height, 31 ⁵/₈".

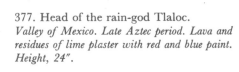

377. Head of the rain-god Tlaloc.
*Valley of Mexico. Late Aztec period. Lava and
residues of lime plaster with red and blue paint.
Height, 24".*

378. Seated figure with the mask of the wind-
god. *Valley of Mexico. Late Postclassic period.
Basalt. Height, 15 1/2".*

379. Tlaloc, the rain-god.
Valley of Mexico. Postclassic period. Basalt. Height, 20".

380. Fertility goddess, probably Chicomecoatl.
Valley of Mexico. Late Postclassic period. Basalt. Height, 30".

381. Head.
Central Mexico. Late Postclassic period. Porous volcanic rock. Height, 11 1/2".

382. Person carrying a stone image.
Vicinity Mexico City. Late Postclassic period. Volcanic rock. Height, 17".

383. Circular basin decorated with death's-heads. *Valley of Mexico. Late Postclassic period. Basalt. Height, 9 1/2"; diameter, 24".*

384. Man.
*Central Mexico. Late Postclassic period. Basalt.
Height, 32 1/2".*

385. Kneeling old woman.
Mexico City. Late Postclassic period. Basalt.
Height, 13 3/4".

386. Kneeling water-goddess.
Valley of Mexico. Postclassic period. Basalt.
Height, 13 1/2".

387. Reclining jaguar.
Valley of Mexico(?). Late Postclassic period.
Basalt. Height, 4 7/8".

388. Aged man seated on bench.
*Valley of Mexico. Late Postclassic period. Basalt.
Height, 24 1/2".*

389. Earth monster.
Valley of Mexico. Late Postclassic period. Basalt.
Depth, 9″; diameter, 43″.

390. Coiled serpent.
Texcoco, Valley of Mexico. Late Postclassic period.
Basalt. Height, 11″.

391. Coiled serpent.
Valley of Mexico. Late Postclassic period. Basalt.
Height, 9 1/2″.

392. Tenoned serpent head.
Mexico City. Late Postclassic period. Basalt.
Height, 25 1/2″.

273

393. Hourglass-shaped vase with appliqués.
*Valley of Mexico. Late Postclassic period.
Polychrome clay. Height, 26″*

394/395. Engraved deer-bone fragment (with
schematic drawing). *Cholula, Puebla. Late
Postclassic period. Length, 3 1/2″.*

274

396/397. Incised bone rattle or musical rasp
(with schematic drawing). *Culhuacán, Valley of
Mexico. Late Postclassic period. Human femur.
Length, 12″.*

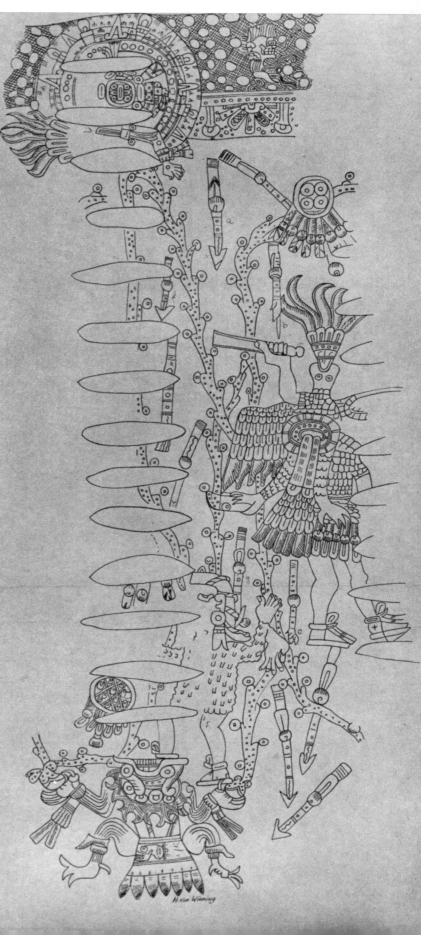

V

ART OF THE MAYA AREA

Art of the Maya Area

Formative and Classic Maya

THE MAYA AREA extends over the southeastern half of Mesoamerica and comprises the states of Tabasco and, partly, Chiapas; the Yucatan Peninsula; Guatemala; British Honduras and the western part of Honduras; and El Salvador. A major portion of this vast territory consists of lowlands where the centers of greatest development are located.

During the Early Formative period, both lowlands and highlands were probably inhabited by peoples who depended on a hunting and gathering economy (M. D. Coe, 1963, p. 33). In the Middle Formative period the spread of Olmec civilization left its mark on much of southeastern Mesoamerica and stimulated the development of a new art style that flourished during the Late Formative and which is eminently represented at Izapa. The sophisticated low-relief sculptures of this very important and large center, located in southern Chiapas, portray a rain-god derived from the Olmec jaguar deity, which suggests that Izapan civilization originated in the Olmec heartland (ibid., pp. 34–35). Its monumental architecture features large temple mounds, steles, altars, and hieroglyphic writing, not only at Izapa proper but also at sites along the Pacific slope of Guatemala and the highlands.

There is much in Early Classic Maya art that is derived from Izapa civilization. Toward the end of the Late Formative period, certain ceramic features were introduced into the Maya area, probably from the south, including the swollen tetrapod (a bowl with four thick legs), spouted vessels, and negative painting. These extraneous influences blended with regional culture patterns and unfolded, during the Classic period, into a great civilization with a higher degree of cultural homogeneity than that of the Mexican mainland.

For descriptive purposes the Maya area is divided into a northern, central, and southern region. The central region, which is the heartland of typical Classic Maya development, extends from the most southeastern Maya site, Copán, to the most western, Palenque, and consists of low, densely forested land. The homogeneity of the lowland Maya is demonstrated by stylistic uniformity. For more than five hundred years the Maya carved steles with calendric inscriptions and used stone-and-mortar architecture with the corbeled vault. Other distinctive traits are the carefully recorded astronomic observations and the extreme complexity and ordered beauty of Maya symbolic art.

Maya culture was on a higher intellectual and aesthetic plane than the art of Central Mexico, although the northern neighbors of the Maya may have been superior in many materialistic aspects, such as the size of structures, complexity in political organization, and extent of irrigation agriculture. But Maya art is unique in its excellence of craftsmanship. This suggests emphasis on quality rather than on quantity, on refinement rather than on monumentality.

The great Mayanist J. E. S. Thompson (1956, p. 88) thinks that the Maya of the Classic period formed a loose federation of autonomous "city-states," ruled by a small caste of priests and nobles who were united by ties of kinship and whose religious motivation was paramount. Thus the Maya followed the Central Mexico pattern where the civil ruler held certain priestly functions, while the high priest, almost equal in rank, devoted himself exclusively to religious matters, which among the Maya in particular involved much astronomical knowledge.

However, there is little evidence of true cities in the Maya area. The Maya "cities" of the Classic period were ceremonial centers consisting of extensive platforms or pyramidal structures supporting temples and "palaces" facing a central courtyard. Since the slash-and-burn method of agriculture was the only practical one in the lowlands, these centers could not have supported large concentrated populations. Neither were there great concentrations of house mounds anywhere. The Maya lived in scattered hamlets over the entire habitable area and congregated at regular intervals at the temple sites, which were inhabited by the priest-rulers and their retainers.

Maya art, like the art of western Mesoamerica, was primarily a religious art and can be fully understood only within the religious context. Ornamentation of pottery, sculpture, and artifacts is conventionalized and symbolic and is applied with a strong feeling for balance and symmetry. Intricate and closely spaced composition often makes it difficult to appreciate the realistic content of Maya art. Careful scrutiny and an effort at analysis are necessary to appreciate the subtleties of lines and planes which on cursory observation seem cluttered and meaningless.

Classic Maya pottery is distinguished by the inventiveness and mastery that characterize other Maya craft products, and closely adheres to Mesoamerican ceramic traditions. The potter's wheel was unknown, but a device known as the *kabal*, a small wooden cylinder on which the pottery is coiled and turned by the potter's feet, was in use and is still employed in modern Yucatan.

Various techniques of surface decoration were used. Mold-pressed ornaments, usually in panels or in two-piece molds, appliqués of hand-modeled ornaments, various methods of carving and excising, fine-line incising, as well as multicolor painting, are among the many elaborate techniques which reached a high degree of perfection. These methods are not restricted to the Maya area, however, although the finished products have a characteristic Maya appearance. Molding, for instance, seems to have been introduced in the Late Classic period, having had an earlier beginning in the Mexican highlands.

Polychrome decoration reached its apogee in the Late Classic period. Black outlining of red and yellow areas was frequently used and seems to have replaced an earlier practice of outlining by incised lines. The most elaborate naturalistic style centered in the northern foothills of the Guatemala highlands (at Chamá), where it was applied to cylindrical vases and flat dishes. A dynamic style of figure painting was developed by the Jaina school in northern Campeche.

Toward the end of the Classic period, and during the beginning of the Postclassic, two diagnostic wares appeared which are securely anchored in the time sequence and therefore serve to cross-date ceramic sequences in other areas outside the Maya region: Plumbate and Fine Orange pottery.

Plumbate, the only Mesoamerican ware with a glazelike surface, first appeared during the Late Classic period in southern Guatemala and parts of Chiapas. It now seems certain that it was produced in only one place—on the border of Guatemala and Chiapas. Some later forms, of the Early Postclassic period, portray exclusively Mexican deities, thereby indicating that they were made by Nahua- and not by Maya-affiliated peoples. It has also been suggested (communication by G. F. Ekholm) that Maya-speaking people could have made the pottery for a "Nahua market." These god and animal effigies were traded over the whole of Mesoamerica, as far north as Tepic in northwestern Mexico and as far south as Nicaragua. The greater number of these vessels are concentrated in the Guatemala highlands and western El Salvador; that is, in the proximity of their center of manufacture. By A.D. 1200 the trade ceased abruptly and Plumbate was no longer manufactured (Thompson, 1956, p. 184).

Fine Orange ware (not to be confused with coarse-tempered Thin Orange) is unique among Mesoamerican pottery because of its fine-textured orange paste, which contains no temper. The ware has a spotty distribution and ranges in time from the Maya Late Classic to the Conquest. The early forms originated in the Usumacinta drainage (Jonuta), or in southwestern Campeche, and are decorated with scroll-like patterns arranged in panel bands with broad black stripes as background. During the transitional period following the Classic this ware occurred in the Petén lowlands of Guatemala, decorated with carved glyphs accompanying panels with human figures. In the Early Postclassic its location shifted to the coast of Campeche and the Isla de Sacrificios, a burial center off the port of Veracruz. Cylindrical vases with pedestals and pyriform vases with bulbous feet are among the most common shapes. These persisted, with some variation in ornamentation, along the coast of Tabasco and southwestern Campeche until the Conquest.

FIGURINES

Manufacture of clay figurines rose to greatest perfection on the northwest coast of Campeche during the Late Classic. Graves on the small island of Jaina and the nearby island site of Uaymil have been found to contain hundreds of figurines of unsurpassed quality. The virtuosity in creating portraitlike features, combined with scrupulous concern for detail, enhance the realism of these figures. They were painted in bright colors, including the famous Maya blue. These clay sculptures reveal a great deal about the life of the Maya of the Classic period, their dress and ornaments, their ceremonial paraphernalia and weapons, but perhaps best of all their physiognomies. The persons are shown in different attitudes and occupations, as dancers, musicians, ballplayers, warriors, dwarfs, slaves, tortured individuals, and priest-rulers.

Many of the figurines were hand-modeled and solid, which is quite exceptional for this era of Mesoamerica, in which molding techniques prevailed. Tall and slender, with projecting headdresses made from appliqués, these solid figurines have a serene yet dynamic quality. Regal in their appearance are the standing or cross-legged types wearing a large shell suspended from the neck. Scarification around the chin, and artificial prolongation of the nose bridge to project it above the forehead—probably achieved by artificial padding with tree gum—were Maya ideals of beauty and distinction (Groth-Kimball, p. xiv). Ear ornaments consisting of jade disks, in some cases supplemented by a transverse rod, were faithfully reproduced in the clay figurines. Textiles must have been very intricate and colorful, to judge from the ornate garments.

The traditional male costume was a loincloth of varying width, which in its broadest form resembles a kilt. Tasseled belts, sometimes hung with shells, were also worn. It seems strange, however, that footgear is entirely neglected in clay figurines, while the monumental sculptures depict elaborate sandals with heel guards. These sandals have been recognized as a valuable criterion for stylistic development in stone carvings (Proskouriakoff, 1950, pp. 81–87).

Facial expressions show a high degree of individuality, so much so that they could be regarded as portraits. Advanced age is shown by sunken cheeks, toothless mouths, and deep wrinkles. Contrast in age is expressed in pairs showing an aged male fondling a young girl. Scenes of this kind are also painted in the Codex Dresden (pl. xxi, c), a ritualistic-astronomical almanac, and therefore have ceremonial connotations. Few figurines can be pronounced to represent deities. The majority portray members of the elite, both male and female, and the religious aspects appear to be subordinated.

In addition to the hand-modeled solid figurines, Jaina is renowned for its moldmade figures, which are often provided with a mouthpiece to serve as a whistle. However, it is doubtful that they were intended primarily as musical instruments. The figurine-whistle tradition was strongly developed along the Gulf coast of Veracruz, generally featuring women with raised hands, painted a creamy white. This type is related to the laughing-face complex of the Nopiloa region and probably diffused into Campeche during the Early Classic period. The Jaina artists refined the stereotyped expressionless features. They also employed the method, believed to have been introduced from Veracruz, of attaching arms and legs with strings, which gives the figures a dynamic effect.

Other foreign traits, including several from Teotihuacán, were assimilated by Jaina, such as asymmetrical headdresses, facial pads, faces showing life and death in juxtaposition, jaguar helmets, obese persons, and the pedestal or three-quarter form of figurines.

The apogee of what might well be called the Jaina school was reached during the latter part of the Late Classic period, according to its pottery style and two monuments with calendric inscriptions (Proskouriakoff, 1950, p. 190). The beginnings probably fall in the Early Classic, and, with the abandonment of the Classic centers in the Maya area, Jaina also ceased its activities. It is likely that the Jaina craftsmen were driven out by a progressive lowering of the coastal shelf which inundated their abodes, and that they moved east into the Puuc region, where they contributed their skill toward the continuance of these centers into the beginning of the Toltec period.

STONE CARVINGS

The monumental stone sculpture of the lowland area is closely related to the architecture, and together they represent the most spectacular achievements of Maya art. Altars and steles with human figures and calendric inscriptions were carved at regular intervals throughout the area for more than five centuries. The similarly attired and positioned human figures and the general uniformity of the glyphic inscriptions strikingly reveal the homogeneity and great conservatism of Maya culture during the Classic period.

Jade had a great value in Mesoamerica and was obtained from stream beds in the mountains of Guatemala and Chiapas. It was worked into human figures, pendants, necklaces, and other ornaments. Alabaster was rarely used and only a few bowls, intricately carved and painted, are known (Von Winning, 1963, p. 113). Shell and bone were formed into ornaments whose Maya origin can be recognized by the style of decoration.

Postclassic Maya

THE DRASTIC CHANGES that took place in Mesoamerica between A.D. 900 and 1000 also include the abandonment of the ceremonial centers in the Maya area. The central area relapsed into obscurity. Only in the Puuc region of Yucatan did the Classic styles persist somewhat longer. This is noticeable in the architecture, in which Classic Maya elements and others from central Veracruz were combined with Toltec influences from the Mexican highlands.

Signs of a gradual breakdown of priestly power appear in the lowlands about 800, well before Toltec times. Deliberately defaced monuments recently discovered at Tikal by William R. Coe, an increase in militarism, and the apparently increasing emphasis on human sacrifice signify impending unrest, which the ruling priests were apparently unable to control. The cause of the complete breakdown of Classic culture in the Maya area and in all of southeastern Mesoamerica is not entirely clear. It seems likely that the disintegration was caused by a combination of factors, rather than by one single cause. A plausible explanation was recently advanced by M. D. Coe (1963, p. 39), who pointed out that the pollen profiles from the Valley of Mexico indicate severe desiccation throughout the Classic period. Therefore diminishing rainfall also in southeastern Mexico may have resulted in economic, cultural, and social disruption. Although the reliability of conclusions based on pollen analysis is still debated, the precarious situation that can arise from sustained drought was dramatically demonstrated recently at Tikal. In this center, which once was a religious and intellectual mecca of the lowlands, the lack of water during the dry season severely hampered the explorations. It was only after the ancient water reservoirs were repaired that the situation was relieved. However, it is not certain whether the stored water was made available to the farmers for large-scale irrigation.

Whatever the causes might have been, between 800 and 928 (the date of the latest inscription) building activities ceased in one center after another. The central lowlands were abandoned and the temples and palaces fell into decay.

In the northern Maya area cultural developments were formerly considered to have taken place only after the abandonment of the central area. However, Yucatan was inhabited during the Formative period, and throughout the Classic shared the characteristics of the central lowlands, although regional variations are apparent.

A strong influx of Toltec traits from highland Mexico mark the beginning of a new era in Yucatan—the Postclassic. Chichén Itzá became the government center at this time, as evidenced by architecture and ceramics. The low reliefs and mural paintings show Toltec supremacy and submission on the part of the Maya. Many innovations, originally developed in Tula, were introduced into Chichén Itzá. Sculptures representing prowling jaguars, vultures, and stylized figures composed of human, bird, and jaguar elements, Chac-Mool figures, thrones in the shape of standing jaguars, columns in the form of feathered serpents used as door lintel supports, Atlantean figures upholding benchlike altars and lintels, colonnades composed of square pillars decorated with warriors in polychrome bas-relief, and other elements, show great similarity at both sites.

Pottery, also, indicates foreign intrusion at Chichén Itzá. Brisk trade with central Veracruz brought quantities of vessels of superior technical and artistic quality into Yucatan. It is believed that the maritime ties between the coast of Veracruz and Yucatan accounted for the greater amount of trade that reached Chichén Itzá than the more landlocked Tula.

The Toltec or Mexicanized conquerors gradually assimilated Maya culture and adopted Maya speech and customs. Between 1200 and 1450 political power over northern Yucatan was concentrated at Mayapán, a city surrounded by a great wall, which contained a population of at least ten thousand. In the fifteenth century, revolts against Mayapán led to the breakup of central control, and the succeeding small independent chieftainships were continually engaged in warfare among themselves. Maya civilization ended with the Spanish conquest of Guatemala in 1525 and that of Yucatan in 1541. The last remnant, which had taken refuge in the Petén area, was subdued in 1697.

Art of the Maya Area

Captions and Notes

PLATES 398–502

398. **CYLINDRICAL VASE WITH BAT-GOD AND GLYPHS.** / El Quiché, Guatemala. Late Classic period. Buff clay with black, white, red, and orange paint, polished. Height, 5 1/4"; diameter, 7 1/4". Collection Dr. and Mrs. William F. Kaiser, Berkeley, Calif.

The two bat-gods and two glyph columns, respectively, differ only in minor variations of detail. The anthropomorphic bat is characterized by the upright pointed nose and cloaklike wings. White crescents on the cloak apparently represent eyes, in this case a death symbol. The necklace resembles the type worn by the death-gods in the Maya codices. The male genitals are uncovered. A vase with strikingly similar ornamentation from Chamá was discovered, broken into many pieces, by Dieseldorff (pp. 665–66) and commented upon by Seler (1908, pp. 641–53). The ornament above the eye is identified on the Dieseldorff vase as the glyph *akbal* (night), but it is not clearly rendered on the vase we illustrate. Differences in the upper and middle glyphs may also be noted in both vases. The bat, a cave-dwelling animal, symbolized the night; in Zapotec and Maya art the anthropomorphic rendering represented a deity of the interior of the earth.

399/400. **CYLINDRICAL VASE SHOWING A PRIEST, SERPENT, MONKEY, AND GLYPHS** (*two views*). / Vicinity of Nebaj, El Quiché, Guatemala. Late Classic period. Clay with red, orange, and black paint on buff. Height, 6 1/2"; diameter, 6 1/2". Dayton Art Institute, Dayton, Ohio.

The chevronlike border design is typical of vases from the Chamá Valley, east of Nebaj (cf. Seler, 1908, pp. 652–69). From the headdress of the priest protrudes a long-stemmed otus flower at which a fish is nibbling. Similar representations occur on stone sculptures at Copán (Stela N, Altar T).

401. **CYLINDRICAL VASE WITH FOUR FIGURES.** / Jaina, Campeche. Late Classic period. Clay, painted red, white, and black on orange. Height, 7 1/2"; diameter, 6 1/2". Collection Stendahl.

Two standing and two kneeling persons face in the same direction. The latter have exceptional necklaces with long strands of red and white beads, tipped with a flower at each end. All have complicated and seemingly fragile headdresses that extend far out in front and in back. A series of sixteen hieroglyphs below the rim have essentially similar components with minor variations. Their meaning is perhaps a repetitive magic phrase, if not merely decorative. The lower ornamental frieze represents the earth.

402. **JAR WITH FLARING SIDES AND FOUR MAMMIFORM SUPPORTS.** / El Quetzal, Guatemala. Early Classic period. Reddish-brown clay with black paint and geometrical designs. Height, 11". Collection Stendahl.

403. **CYLINDRICAL VASE WITH GLYPHS IN PANELS.** / Vicinity of Nebaj, El Quiché, Guatemala. Late Classic period. Clay, painted red, orange, and black on cream. Height, 6"; diameter, 5 1/2". Collection Dr. and Mrs. William F. Kaiser, Berkeley, Calif.

The design is repeated on the other side.

404. **CYLINDRICAL VASE WITH A HUMAN FIGURE COMBINED WITH A BIRD DESIGN.** / Ulúa Valley, Honduras. Late Classic period. Clay, painted brown, red, and orange on buff. Height, 6 3/8"; diameter, 5 1/4". Collection Stendahl.

The design is repeated on the other side of the vase.

405. **TRIPOD PLATE WITH BIRD DESIGN.** / Jaina, Campeche. Late Classic period. Clay, painted red, orange, and black on tan. Height, 4 1/2"; diameter, 15 1/4". Collection Stendahl.

The bird (toucan?) shows three, possibly four, glyphs in its headdress. The one on the right appears to be that of the day *imix*, two other glyphs could be read as *ahau*, the first and last days of the twenty-day cycle. The rim design shows two stylized serpents, whose bodies contain variants of the day sign *caban* (relating to the earth) surmounted by feathers (relating to the sky). A similar motif appears on a polychrome tripod plate in the Dumbarton Oaks Collections. According to Lothrop, the bird may be a vulture.

406. TRIPOD PLATE SHOWING A SEATED PRIEST. / Campeche. Late Classic period. Clay, painted red, orange, and black on buff. Diameter, 16". Collection Dr. and Mrs. William F. Kaiser, Berkeley, Calif.

The priest wears a bead-decorated loincloth. The bead necklace, ear ornaments, and wristlets are painted orange as a substitute for green, the color of jade. Black ovals on arms and the leg indicate a tattooed design.

407. TRIPOD PLATE SHOWING A DEER. / Jaina, Campeche. Late Classic period. Clay with red, orange, and brown paint on buff. Height, 3"; diameter, 10 1/2". Collection Stendahl.

The alternating elements surrounding the central motif are derived from symbols which occur in the celestial bands.

408. TRIPOD PLATE SHOWING A WARRIOR. / Jaina, Campeche. Late Classic period. Clay, painted red, orange, and black on buff. Height, 3 1/2"; diameter, 12 1/4". Collection Mr. and Mrs. Francis V. Crane, Marathon, Fla.

The warrior with a mask holds a spear and carries a jaguar. Ornamental glyphlike designs decorate the rim.

409. SHALLOW TRIPOD PLATE SHOWING TWO INDIVIDUALS SEATED ON A DAIS. / Campeche. Late Classic period. Clay, painted red, orange, brown on buff. Height, 3"; diameter, 12 1/2". Collection Mr. and Mrs. Vincent Price, Los Angeles.

The composition is a somewhat simplified version of a representation on a polychrome tripod plate from the same region, now in the Yale University Art Gallery, Olsen Collection (illustrated in Kidder and Samayoa, pl. 91). On the latter an incense pouch characterizes one of the two seated persons as a priest, and beneath the platform are two deer. It is reasonable to assume that both plates were decorated by the same artist, or at least in the same workshop.

410/411/412/413. CARVED DOUBLE-BOTTOMED RATTLE BOWL (*two views and two schematic drawings*). / El Quiché, Guatemala. Late Classic period. Dark-brown burnished clay with residues of red paint in excised spots. Height, 5 1/8"; diameter, 6 1/2"; space between floors, 5/8". The Dumbarton Oaks Collections, Washington, D.C.

The hemispherical body is decorated with a fluted spiral which begins at the center bottom and which is paralleled by a carved and incised pattern containing glyphs and serpent motifs. Four knobs beneath the glyph band point to the four world quarters. Presumably this vessel was used in ceremonies for the rain-gods, for the symbolism is connected with rain (the spiral design, the glyphs, and the serpent motifs, and the rattle allusive of the sound of the rains). The characteristics and distribution of double-bottomed rattle bowls are discussed by Berlin (1956, pp. 118–19); for a detailed description of this bowl, see von Winning, 1965.

414. VASE WITH STAMPED DESIGN IN TWO PANELS SHOWING A SEATED PRIEST WITH ATTENDANTS. / Chiapas. Late Classic period. Fine brown clay, painted dark brown. Height, 6 3/4"; diameter, 4 3/4". Collection Stendahl.

A dignitary seated on a dais wears an elaborate feather headdress with a fish nibbling at the frontal protrusion. He is receiving an object from a person kneeling on a jaguar head to his left. On the right side is another dignitary in plumed headdress, seated on an animal's head. The composition in each panel is essentially the same, but details vary and indicate that two separate molds were used. Burnishing obliterated some portions of the design. Similar vases from Uaxactún and the Amiché region are illustrated in Kidder and Samayoa, figs. 30, 67, 83.

415. CYLINDRICAL VASE WITH TWO CARVED PANELS. / Puuc region, northeastern Campeche. Late Classic period. Brown clay with traces of stuccoed and painted blue color and inlaid stones. Height, 6 5/8"; diameter, 6". Collection Eugene Berman, Rome.

Beneath a glyph band are two panels showing seated priests.

416. EFFIGY JAR WITH GROTESQUE FACE. / Campeche. Postclassic period. Plumbate ware, red-brown and black. Height, 6"; diameter, 6". Collection Dr. and Mrs. William F. Kaiser, Berkeley, Calif.

Two birds' heads project from the neck of the jar, their wings indicated by incised lines.

417. KNEELING BEARDED HUNCHBACK EFFIGY JAR. / Mexico. Early Postclassic period. Plumbate ware. Height, 10 1/4". American Museum of Natural History, New York.

Plumbate was the only glazed ware in Mesoamerica. It originated in the region of southern Chiapas bordering on Guatemala and was traded over wide areas. Relatively high firing temperatures (about 1750° F.) produced the hard lustrous ware in various shades of orange, red, and gray.

418. ARMADILLO EFFIGY JAR. / Uaymil, Campeche. Early Postclassic period. Orange plumbate ware. Height, 6 1/2". Galerie Israel, Tel-Aviv.

The ringtail and grooves on the back, indicating the carapace, characterize the animal as an armadillo.

419. HUMAN EFFIGY *Incensario* WITH BIRD HEADDRESS./ Northeastern Yucatan. Late Postclassic period. Light-gray clay. Height, 16 1/2″; diameter, 14 1/2″. Collection Stendahl.

The effigy is attached to a thick-walled vase and its legs are free-standing. The two tusks which project from the corners of the mouth and the bird headdress are characteristics of the group of *incensarios* from Mayapán that represent the god of merchants and travelers. Thompson (1957, pp. 608–10) pointed out that this deity, or group of deities, was venerated over a large area, and the merchants presumably spread its cult in the Postclassic period. This piece is illustrated in *Prä-kolumbische Kunst*, item 1009, pl. 95.

420. LARGE CYLINDER DECORATED WITH MASKS. / Chiapas. Classic period. Buff clay with residue of stucco. Height, 29 1/2″. Collection Stendahl.

Several fragmented large cylinders of this type were found inside the substructure of the Temple of the Foliated Cross at Palenque, Chiapas. Their function is not clear—they are bottomless and are therefore neither urns nor the conventional incense burners (Ruz, p. 140, pls. 29–33). They were placed at temple entrances, probably for depositing offerings.

421. LARGE CYLINDER DECORATED WITH MASKS. / Chiapas. Classic period. Brown clay with residue of stucco. Height, 21″. Collection Stendahl.

Of the three superimposed heads, the one in the center has large eyes with the supraorbital plaque of the serpent representations and a fleshless lower jaw as a death symbol.

422. HEAD VASE SHOWING AN OLD MAN'S FACE ON THE FRONT AND TWO GLYPHS ON THE BACK. / Puuc region, Campeche. Late Classic period. Brown clay with white and red paint. Height, 5″; diameter, 5″. Seattle Art Museum, Seattle, Wash.

423. CYLINDRICAL VASE WITH CARVED DESIGN. / Puuc region, Campeche, Mexico. Late Classic period. Brown clay, burnished, with residues of stuccoed and painted blue rim decoration. Height, 6 5/8″; diameter, 6″. Collection Mr. and Mrs. Alan E. Schwartz, Detroit, Mich.

The two panels show a priest beneath a glyph band. One priest is seated between the open jaws of a serpent.

424. INCENSE BURNER LID. / Department of Escuintla, Guatemala. Late Classic to Early Postclassic period. Brown clay. Height, 6 3/4″. Collection Morton D. May, St. Louis, Mo.

The figure serves as a chimney, with openings on the top of the headdress. Represented is a bearded old sun-god characterized by his large eyes, wrinkled nose, and open and toothless mouth with two tusks projecting on the sides. He is seated cross-legged, and the lower part of his body is disproportion-

ately small. With his left arm he holds an object that resembles a corncob. Compare this piece with the face of the sun-god on a large cylindrical incense burner from Palenque (Anders, pl. 1) and the humpback effigy vessel with wrinkled nose from Kaminaljuyú (Kidder, Jennings, and Shook, p. 188, figs. 178 e–h).

425. CYLINDRICAL TUBE WITH LATERAL PANELS. / Chiapas. Classic period. Clay. Red paste with red slip and residues of blue paint. Height, 27″. Isaac Delgado Museum of Art, New Orleans.

The cylinder is decorated with an almost life-size human head. Above and below are masks with large eyes, large nose, and protruding upper jaw. The lateral panels have appliqué decorations of stylized serpent heads seen in profile. The back is undecorated and has a perforation in the center. A similar cylinder, from the Temple of the Cross, Palenque, is in the Museum of Anthropology, Mexico City, and is illustrated in Lothrop, 1964, p. 92.

426. CYLINDRICAL VASE WITH CARVED DESIGN OF SEATED PRIEST. / Northeastern Campeche. Late Classic period. Brown clay. Height, 6″; diameter, 6 1/2″. Collection Mr. and Mrs. Ellsworth La Boyteaux, Orinda, Calif.

The back of the vase is decorated just below the rim by a carved band with four glyphlike motifs, each separated by two vertical bars. For the distribution of Classic Maya pottery with carved glyphlike motifs in bands, see Longyear, 1952, p. 30.

427. LARGE CYLINDRICAL JAR WITH LID. / El Quiché, Guatemala. Late Classic period. Unpolished red-brown clay with red, blue, black, and yellow paint and appliqués. Height, 15 1/2″; diameter, 11″. Collection Stendahl.

The front is decorated with a panel showing the crossed-band motif in relief. Spread over the lid is a jaguar whose body is painted yellow with black spots.

428. CYLINDRICAL VASE WITH RAISED BASE. / Ulúa River Valley, Honduras. Postclassic period. Alabaster. Height, 5 7/8″. Museum of the American Indian, Heye Foundation, New York.

The handles represent vultures. The walls depict two human and four animal figures. A similar but taller vase, in the American Museum of Natural History, New York, is described and illustrated in Stone, 1938, pp. 24–26, fig. 9.

429. CARVED CYLINDRICAL VASE WITH BAT DESIGNS. / Ulúa Valley, Honduras. Postclassic period. Alabaster. Height, 3 5/8″; diameter, 4″. Private collection.

The two handles are bats' heads. Their headbands, consisting of overlapping rectangles, are extended over the cylindrical portion of the vase. The main body of the design appears to be composed of scrolls, which are, however, conventional-izations of two faces. Replicas of the profiles from the handles appear on the body of the vase. The pedestal base is decorated with openwork triangles. This piece is illustrated in Stone (1938, pp. 26–28, fig. 10, vase AA).

430. CARVED CYLINDRICAL VASE WITH JAGUAR HAN-DLES. / Ulúa River Valley, Honduras. Alabaster. Height, 5⁷/₈″; diameter, 6″. The Dumbarton Oaks Collections, Washington, D.C.

On either side of the handles is a face in profile with a large curled upper jaw (serpent?). The pedestal base has openwork decoration. Below the rim and at the base is a series of round plaques overlapping one another, with an oval centerpiece. A similar arrangement occurs on the headdress of the seated person on Stele 11, Piedras Negras (Proskouriakoff, 1950, fig. 52 c).

431/432/433/434/435. BOWL WITH RELIEF DECORATION. / Jaina, Campeche. Late Classic period. Alabaster. Height, 4¹/₂″; diameter, 4″. The Dumbarton Oaks Collections, Washington, D.C.

The globular bowl has a convex base. A bearded priest is carved in low relief on one side. He wears a turbanlike head-dress, a long jade necklace, and points with his finger to the ground, apparently giving a command. Related to this figure is the inscription on the other side of the bowl, consisting of the four glyphs shown in the drawings. One of these is the emblem glyph of Palenque. For a description and glyph analy-sis, see von Winning, 1963, and Barthel, 1967.

436. SEATED FIGURE. / El Quiché, Guatemala. Late Classic period. Reddish clay with blue, yellow, and white paint. Height, 14¹/₄″. Museum of the Ameri-can Indian, Heye Foundation, New York.

The figure wears a headdress with human head effigy. His ornaments consist of earplugs, necklace, wristlets, and anklets. In the back, a loop connects the loincloth with the broken flat base on which the figure rests. This fragmented base prob-ably was part of an incense burner lid.

437/438. BEARDED FIGURE MOUNTED ON A SLAB (*two views*). / El Quiché, Guatemala. Late Classic or Early Postclassic period. Buff clay with red, white, and yellow paint. Height, 16″. Collection Morton D. May, St. Louis, Mo.

The edges of the slab to which the figure is attached are fragmented. A large opening in the base and the open mouth relate this figure to the *incensario* figurine complex. The ear ornaments are painted white and represent flowers; the pectoral (white with a red center) is suspended from a cord indicated by incised lines around the neck. The right leg is bent and rests flat on the ground; of the left leg, which is also bent, only the foot touches the ground; the hand is supported by the knee. This peculiar posture is seen in a Late Classic figurine whistle from the Alta Verapaz representing a ball-

player (Kidder and Samayoa, fig. 77) and in a Late Classic anthropomorphic jaguar figurine from Lubaantún (Gann, 1925, facing p. 142).

439. WHISTLE: FEMALE FIGURE HOLDING A BOWL. / Jai-na, Campeche. Late Classic period. Buff clay with red, white, and blue paint. Height, 10″. Collection Mr. and Mrs. Robert A. Rowan, Pasadena, Calif.

The face is decorated with appliqués on the forehead, lower lip, and chin. The frontal-occipital deformation of her head indicates her high rank, which is further emphasized by the elaborate headdress. She wears a wraparound skirt tied above her breasts and holds a small figurine of which only the legs, attached to the rim of the bowl, are preserved.

440. WHISTLE: STANDING MALE WITH YOKE AND *Hacha*. / Jaina, Campeche. Late Classic period. Buff clay with red and blue paint. Height, 8″. Seattle Art Museum, Seattle, Wash.

Around his waist the figure carries a yoke and a *hacha* (flattened stone head) supported by his left hand. These objects and the kneepads characterize the figure as a partici-pant in a ball game. His right arm is reverentially crossed over his chest. Similar figures are illustrated in Ekholm, 1949, fig. 6, and Groth-Kimball, p. 10.

441. WHISTLE: OLD MAN EMBRACING A YOUNG GIRL. / Jaina, Campeche. Late Classic period. Buff clay with red, white, and blue paint. Height, 6″. Private collection.

The girl is apparently very young and wears her hair in a thick braid in the back. Similar representations are illustrated in Lothrop and others, 1957, pl. LXXV, no. 127; Groth-Kimball, p. 28; and the Codex Dresden, pls. XXI c and XXIII c.

442. WHISTLE: SEATED OLD MAN. / Jaina, Campeche. Late Classic period. Buff clay with traces of red, white, yellow, and blue paint. Height, 5³/₈″. Collec-tion Mr. and Mrs. Russell Dymock Smith, Palos Verdes Estates, Calif.

The figure carries a blanket over his left arm; the right hand once held the staff of the fan which is seen at his right knee. The fan, a symbol of authority, is usually held up.

443. WHISTLE: SEATED WOMAN. / Jaina, Campeche. Late Classic period. Buff clay with red, white, and blue paint. Height, 7¹/₄″. Collection Stendahl.

The figure is dressed in a blouse and skirt, and is adorned with circular earplugs, bracelets, and a necklace.

444. WHISTLE: BEARDED AND MUSTACHED MAN. / Jaina, Campeche. Late Classic period. Buff clay with traces of red, white, and blue paint. Height, 6³/₄″. Dallas Museum of Fine Arts, Dallas, Texas.

The figure's headdress consists of a braiding of cords and a band of circular ornaments. He wears a bead necklace, a large shell pendant, and a wide loincloth.

445. **BEARDED DIGNITARY SEATED ON A THRONE.** / Jaina, Campeche. Late Classic period. Buff clay with traces of blue and white paint. Height, 10″. Collection Mr. and Mrs. Francis V. Crane, Marathon, Fla.

The figure wears a feather headdress with a bird in the center. The face is heavily tattooed. He wears a broad loincloth, with a wide flap in front, partly obscured by a long neck pendant. Between his feet is a basin. A similar figure, believed to represent a high priest and dignitary, is illustrated in Groth-Kimball, 1960, p. 21.

446. **BEARDED DIGNITARY SEATED ON A THRONE.** / Jaina, Campeche. Late Classic period. Buff clay with traces of blue and white paint. Height, 10″. Los Angeles County Museum of Natural History.

This is a companion piece to the figure in plate 445. The figure has a beard and a mustache. The right hand is clenched for the insertion of a staff or similar device.

447. **STANDING MALE IN LOINCLOTH.** / Jaina, Campeche. Late Classic period. Buff clay with traces of blue and red paint. Height, 10¼″. The Museum of Primitive Art, New York.

448. **SEATED MALE WITH JAGUAR EFFIGY HEADDRESS.** / Jaina, Campeche. Late Classic period. Buff clay with white paint. Height, 16¼″. Museum Rietberg, Zurich, Switzerland.

The figure wears beads and a pectoral decoration around his neck, and is dressed in a wide loincloth with the frontpiece extending down over his legs. The nose ridge shows beaded scarifications.

449. **STANDING MALE HOLDING A SERPENT SCEPTER.** / Campeche. Late Classic period. Buff clay painted red, blue, and white. Height, 11″. Collection Mr. and Mrs. Walter H. Annenberg, Philadelphia, Penn.

The elaborate insignia include very large ear ornaments, a breast-plaque, a belt frontpiece in the shape of a head with upturned snout (cf. Proskouriakoff, 1950, fig. 55 a), and a shieldlike ornament on the back. Both scepter and back ornament are removable.

450. **WHISTLE: STANDING MALE WITH A WIDE-BRIMMED, REMOVABLE HAT.** / Jaina, Campeche. Late Classic period. Buff clay with red, white, and blue paint. Height, 9½″. Collection Stendahl.

The figure wears earplugs, loincloth, and a large shell attached to a twisted rope. His nose is prolonged to the forehead to achieve the ideal Mayan profile.

451. **WHISTLE: OBESE MALE IN QUILTED DRESS.** / Uaymil, Campeche. Late Classic period. Buff clay with red and blue paint. Height, 11½″. The Museum of Primitive Art, New York.

The serenity of the facial expression is modeled with great skill, portraying a person of authority. He wears a very tall peaked cap, and a quilted, collared garment beneath his loincloth. His left arm is hidden by a rectangular tasseled shield.

452. **WOMAN WITH WATER JAR ON HER HEAD, CARRYING A CHILD-RATTLE.** / Jaina, Campeche. Late Classic period. Reddish-brown clay with traces of white paint. Height, 6½″. Collection Stendahl.

The figure wears a skirt and a cloak and is ornamented with earplugs, bracelets, and a bead necklace.

453. **MAN PEERING THROUGH THE OPEN BEAK OF A LARGE BIRD HEADDRESS.** / Jaina, Campeche. Late Classic period. Buff clay with red and white paint. Height, 7½″. Collection Stendahl.

The bird's tail forms the crown of the headdress and the wings are indicated on the upper arms.

454. **WOMAN WITH ELABORATE HAIR ARRANGEMENT AND FACIAL TATTOO, HOLDING A FAN.** / Jaina, Campeche. Late Classic period. Buff clay with red and white paint. Height, 9½″. Collection Stendahl.

Incised on the front of her capelike garment is a human head in profile, with a disproportionately small, frontally shown body on the skirt. A shield with arrows (?) and volutes are the motifs on the side of the cape. A similar figure is illustrated in Borhegyi, fig. 3.

455. **WHISTLE: BALLPLAYER WITH A YOKE AROUND THE WAIST.** / Jaina, Campeche. Late Classic period. Buff clay with traces of white paint. Height, 7½″. Collection Stendahl.

The figure's headdress consists of a deer's head with a brooch. His face is tattooed around the mouth. In his left hand he holds a handstone with a jaguar's head; his wrist and knees are protected by bandage and pads to create striking surfaces. A similar figure is illustrated in Borhegyi, fig. 3.

456. **WHISTLE: SEATED FIGURE WITH PADDED AND PUNCTUATED CHEEKS, HOLDING A BABY JAGUAR.** / Jaina, Campeche. Late Classic period. Buff clay. Height, 5″. Collection Stendahl.

457. **WHISTLE: STANDING FEMALE WITH DRESS AND FISH HEADDRESS.** / Jaina, Campeche. Late Classic period. Tan clay with traces of white paint. Height, 6″. Collection Stendahl.

458. RATTLE: STANDING FEMALE WITH BIRD HEADDRESS. / Jaina, Campeche. Late Classic period. Tan clay with red and white paint. Height, 5″. Collection Mr. and Mrs. Donald H. McClelland, Pasadena, Calif.

She is dressed in a blouse and skirt and ornamented with ear pendants, bead necklace, and sash.

459. WHISTLE: STANDING MALE FIGURINE WITH DEER HEADDRESS. / Jaina, Campeche. Late Classic period. Tan clay with red, white, and orange paint. Height, 8 1/4″. Collection Stendahl.

The bearded face is tattooed. A series of overlapping disks between the forehead and the headdress are also part of the headdress of the Late Classic Stele 11, Piedras Negras (Proskouriakoff, 1950, fig. 52 c). A large shell is worn as breast ornament, and the object in the right hand is probably a copal incense bag.

460. STANDING MALE. / Uaymil, Campeche. Late Classic period. Buff clay with traces of red, blue, and white paint. Height, 8 1/2″. Collection Dr. and Mrs. William F. Kaiser, Berkeley, Calif.

The bearded and tattooed face is framed by a pleated cotton headdress surmounted by a large knot whose strands hang over the shoulder. The ear ornaments consist of broad ribbons. He wears a breechcloth, and carries a scarf over the left arm.

461. WHISTLE: FIGURINE GROUP. / Jaina, Campeche. Late Classic period. Buff clay with white paint. Height, 7″. Los Angeles County Museum of Natural History.

A warrior with a barbed spear is leading two bound captives. He wears a helmet with five overlapping birds' heads in profile, held by a chin strap. His neck and chest are protected by cotton quilt armor and he wears a richly embroidered mantle. The reverse side of the figure is plain. The whistle mouthpiece is on the lower left side.

462. CARVED WALL PANEL. / Usumacinta River region, Guatemala. Late Classic period. Limestone. Height, 76″. The Minneapolis Institute of Arts, Minneapolis, Minn.

A dignitary with a very elaborate feathered headdress is depicted frontally, but with his head turned to one side. Below the tip of his nose is a typical Late Classic nose bead. His broad belt is decorated with a mask and a superimposed owl's head. His long and broad loincloth and apron are richly embroidered. His sandals have a high ankle guard. In his left hand is a long bag with a crossed-band motif, and, below, with a rattlesnake's-tail motif. On the basis of these stylistic details the panel was probably in the Péten in the Late Classic period (c. A.D. 751–810).

463. CARVED WALL PANEL WITH EIGHT GLYPH PAIRS. / Piedras Negras region, Guatemala. Late Classic period. Limestone. Height, 74″. Collection Mr. and Mrs. Francis V. Crane, Marathon, Fla.

The fragment is part of a lengthy text of which the Initial Series glyph is missing. It is remarkable, nevertheless, for the fine condition of the carvings and for the delicacy of the design. Thomas S. Barthel is inclined to believe that the text is historical-ritualistic in content. Further study of this carving is in progress.

464. CARVED WALL PANEL. / Usumacinta River Region, Chiapas, Mexico. Late Classic period. Limestone. Height, 18″. Museum of the American Indian, Heye Foundation, New York.

A kneeling figure wears an elaborate headdress composed of an animalistic head topped with feathers and plumes. His body is clothed from chest to waist with a thick padded garment, below which hangs the loincloth apron. Two fan-shaped projections at the waist resemble protective hip pads. He wears a knee pad, anklets, wrist bands, ear ornaments, and a beaded necklace. The left hand holds a round shieldlike device decorated with a glyph. Opposite the headdress are two additional glyphs. The carving is one of a group depicting ceremonial scenes connected with the Mesoamerican "ball game," and the type of protective attire worn by the figure identifies him as one of the player participants. His actual playing garb would no doubt have been much simpler.

465. WALL PANEL (PROBABLY FROM A DOOR JAMB). / Usumacinta River, Guatemala. Late Classic period. Limestone. Height, 66″. Private collection.

There are indications that the two slabs were carved separately and then assembled. The headdress consists of a serpent's large upper jaw, decorated with plumes and a lotus flower. The face of the person appears to have been deliberately damaged. The ornament that projects from under the chin occurs also on a jamb at Xcalumkin and may be a vestigial form of a serpent's lower jaw, according to Proskouriakoff (1950, p. 166, fig. 19 V–T, n, and 94 c). The sandals, too, resemble the type encountered at Xcalumkin (ibid., fig. 30 e). The restrained dancing pose is a diagnostic of the Classic Dynamic Phase (9.16.0.0.0–9.19.0.0.0, which equals A.D. 750–810). It would seem that the stylistic characteristics relate this sculpture to the Puuc area of southern Campeche rather than to the Usumacinta drainage.

466. STANDING FIGURE. / Southern Campeche near the Guatemala border. Late Classic period. Limestone. Height, 84″. Metropolitan Museum of Art, New York.

Beneath the animal headdress is a face with large eyes and prominent cheekbones giving the impression of a death's-head. However, the open mouth with sinuous lips is not a mortuary feature. The breast-plaque consists of a bulky knot of braided material. A broad, fringed loincloth with a rectangular flap is tied in the front. Below the knees the figure wears crossed gaiters (cf. Proskouriakoff, 1950, figs. 29 i and 96 g). In his right hand he holds an oblong object with two cavities.

467. CARVED WALL PANEL. / El Cayo, Chiapas. Late Classic period. Limestone. Height, 32″; width, 27″. Isaac Delgado Museum of Art, New Orleans.

A lengthy hieroglyphic inscription frames a priest-ruler holding a shield and receiving homage from a kneeling person. On the other side is an attendant in the characteristic Maya pose of reverence, holding his right hand on his left shoulder. The faces have been deliberately destroyed. The Initial Series inscription, beginning at the upper left side with its large introductory glyph and continuing vertically in two columns, is badly damaged. The stylistic resemblance to Lintel 1, El Cayo (Maler, 1903, pl. 35), is noted. Dr. J. Eric S. Thompson, in a letter dated May 22, 1965, has kindly furnished the following interpretation of the glyphic text:

9.14.18.15. 1	1 Imix, 19 Yaxkin
9.19	an addition leads to
9.14.19. 7. 0	5 Ahau, 18 Kayab (A.D. 731 GMT).

The moon age is correctly given as six days. There are other additions and subscriptions but the dates from or to which these are counted are not given, nor is there a sign of a period ending or dedicatory date.

468. CARVED PANEL. / Usumacinta River region, Guatemala. Late Classic period. Limestone. Height, 53″. Museum Rietberg, Zurich, Switzerland.

The standing figure in a serpent headdress with plumes holds a shield and a staff divided into sections. For a similar staff tipped with a flint knife protruding from an opened serpent's jaw, see Proskouriakoff, 1950, fig. 64 a. We are indebted to Dr. Linton Satterthwaite of the University Museum, University of Pennsylvania, who has determined the chronological date to be A.D. 810.

469. CORNICE DECORATION IN THE FORM OF A SUN-GOD'S HEAD. / Copán, Honduras. Classic period. Limestone. Height, 8 1/2″. American Museum of Natural History, New York.

470. CARVED LINTEL. / Usumacinta region (Piedras Negras or Yaxchilán). Late Classic Maya period (A.D. 795). Limestone. Height, 23 3/4″. Cleveland Museum of Art. Purchase from the J. H. Wade Fund.

The central figure shows a woman in very ornate garments holding a full-figure manikin, the symbol of civil authority. Her face was destroyed in ancient times. She wears a headdress of very long plumes with pointed tassels. Her ankle-length skirt is fringed with tassels and over it she wears a richly embroidered cloaklike *huipil*. The glyph column below her headdress indicates her name and rank. The last three glyphs on the lower right side of the slab indicate the latest of the dates carved (A.D. 795), which records the date of manufacture of the sculpture. The upper part (approximately one-fourth of the slab) was sawed off in modern times. For a full description, see Hawley, pp. 50–55.

471. CARVED PANEL. / Usumacinta region. Late Classic period. Limestone. Height, 51″. Rijksmuseum voor Volkenkunde, Leiden, the Netherlands.

The two dignitaries facing each other wear very elaborate headdresses which are somewhat alike. The higher rank of the person on the left is indicated by a profusion of ornaments, including a life-size mask strapped to his back. The disks on his breast, his wristlets, anklets, and the loincloth apron are composed of representations of a great number of jade beads. The position of his hands shows that he is depositing several strings of jade beads in a square basket. The face of his robed (female?) companion is unfortunately mutilated. We are indebted to J. E. S. Thompson for interpreting the inscription (9.16.15.0.0 7 *ahau*, 18 *pop*) as equivalent to A.D. 766.

472. SEATED WARRIOR WITH CLUB AND SHIELD. / Campeche. Late Classic period. Stuccoed limestone painted red and blue. Height, 13 1/2″. Private collection.

473. *Hacha*. / Tecpán vicinity, Guatemala. Classic period. Polished gray-green stone. Height, 10 1/2″. Collection Stendahl.

Both sides are identical and show a skull, the bones of the breast and of the arms (humerus, ulna, and radius).

474. PROFILE FRAGMENT. / Campeche. Late Classic period. Stuccoed limestone with traces of red and blue paint. Height, 6″. The Dayton Art Institute, Dayton, Ohio.

475. HEAD. / Honduras. Classic period. Limestone. Height, 7 1/2″. American Museum of Natural History, New York.

476. HEAD WITH TENONED SUPPORT IN BACK. / Copán, Honduras. Classic period. Limestone. Height, 15″. American Museum of Natural History, New York.

477. HEAD FRAGMENT WITH INDICATIONS OF MUSTACHE AND BEARD. / Chiapas. Late Classic period. Stucco with traces of red and green color. Height, 8 1/4″. Collection Stendahl.

478. BIRD PENDANT. / Uaymil, Campeche. Late Classic period. Carved shell. Height, 4 1/2″. Collection Stendahl.

479. MAN AND WOMAN IN EMBRACE. / Jaina, Campeche. Late Classic period. Carved shell. Height, 4 7/8″. Collection William P. Palmer.

Similar scenes can be found in clay figurines and in the Codex Dresden.

480. ORNAMENTS MADE TO REPRESENT DEATH'S-HEADS. / Jaina, Campeche. Late Classic period. Shell.

Height of tallest, $2\,^3/_4$". Collection Dr. Carrol C. Mendenhall, Gardena, Calif.

481. HEAD IN PROFILE. / Jaina, Campeche. Late Classic period. Shell with openwork carving. Height, $3\,^1/_2$". Art Institute of Chicago.

482. PENDANT SHOWING PRIEST WITH BOARLIKE ANIMAL. / Uaymil, Campeche. Late Classic period. Carved shell. Height, $2\,^3/_8$". Collection William P. Palmer.

483. PENDANT. / Jaina, Campeche. Late Classic period. Shell with openwork carving. Length, $3\,^3/_4$". Collection Jay C. Leff, Uniontown, Penn.

A serpent's body surrounds a head seen in profile.

484/485. CARVED DEER BONE SHOWING PRIEST WITH TWENTY GLYPHS (*with schematic drawing*). / Jaina, Campeche. Late Classic period. Length, $10\,^3/_4$". Collection Stendahl.

The relief carving shows a priest seated on a jaguar throne that is covered with a mat, and scattering small round objects. Both throne and mat are symbols of authority. Beneath are the twenty day signs of the Maya calendar, arranged like a hieroglyphic text. Barthel has interpreted this composition as a representation of a priest casting lots (probably using beans) for the purpose of prognostication. In his iconographic and epigraphic analysis (in press) he discovered the reason for the unusual arrangement of the day signs, which begin with the last day of the series (*ahau*). The image of the priest and the hieroglyphic text are closely related. A glyphic parallel for the action of the priest exists at Yaxchilán; a counterpart of the text is depicted in the codices. All in all, the inscription is an accomplishment of the utmost sophistication by the ancient Maya priests.

486. STANDING FIGURE HOLDING A FLINT-TIPPED SPEAR AND A POUCH. / Campeche. Late Classic period. Deer bone (?). Height, 5". Collection Stendahl.

487/488. BONE FRAGMENT WITH RELIEF CARVING (*with schematic drawing*). / Jaina, Campeche. Late Classic period. Mandible of a porpoise. Length, 12". Collection Stendahl.

A dignitary is shown with a headdress consisting of two serpent jaws. He holds a spear and wears a trophy head upside down, with the hair hanging beneath a bow tie. Wristlets and gaiters consist of braided bands. The meaning of the glyphic inscription has not been determined.

489. STANDING MALE FIGURE. / Jaina, Campeche. Late Classic period. Bone with traces of red paint. Height, $3\,^3/_8$". Museum of the American Indian, Heye Foundation, New York.

The figure's headdress is missing.

490. PENDANT. / Nebaj region, El Quiché, Guatemala. Late Classic period. Brown jadeite. Height, $3\,^3/_8$". Collection Stendahl.

Full figure of a priest with large ear disks; a loincloth flap between his legs reaches to the ground.

491. PENDANT. / Nebaj region, El Quiché, Guatemala. Late Classic period. Mottled green jadeite. Height, $4\,^1/_4$". Collection The Rev. Carlos Sanches, Baton Rouge, La.

Full figure of a priest with bird headdress, in profile.

492. PENDANT. / Palenque, Chiapas. Classic period. Green jadeite. Height, $2\,^1/_4$". Museum of the American Indian, Heye Foundation, New York.

493. MINIATURE MASK. / El Quetzal, Guatemala. Early Postclassic period. Hard green stone. Height, $2\,^3/_4$". Museum of the American Indian, Heye Foundation, New York.

Similar small masks, showing human faces with prominent or upturned noses, have been found on the Atlantic slope of Guatemala, and are believed to have been tied to ceremonial staffs (Kidder and Samayoa, fig. 89).

494. PENDANT. / Toniná, Chiapas. Late Classic period (A.D. 731). Green jadeite with gray patches. Height, $4\,^1/_8$". American Museum of Natural History, New York. Squier Collection.

The personage wears cufflike wristlets and anklets and a tubular pectoral. He is seated on a throne decorated with a grotesque face similar to those on Copán stone altars (Easby, p. 76, fig. 2 c).

495. PENDANT. / Toniná, Chiapas. Late Classic period. Opaque, medium blue-green jadeite. Height, $2\,^5/_8$". American Museum of Natural History, New York. Squier Collection.

The head is flanked by sprouting maize leaves. For a discussion, see Easby, 1961, pp. 74–75, fig. 2 a.

496. PENDANT. / El Quiché, Guatemala. Late Classic period. Green jade. Height, 2". Collection Stendahl.

497. PENDANT. / Campeche. Late Classic period. Light-green jadeite. Height, $1\,^1/_2$". Museum of the American Indian, Heye Foundation, New York.

498. EAR PLUG. / Yucatan. Classic period. Green jadeite. Diameter, $1\,^5/_8$". Collection Stendahl.

499. PENDANT. / Campeche. Late Classic period. Green jadeite. Height, $1\,^5/_8$". Museum of the American Indian, Heye Foundation, New York.

500. PENDANT. / Found in Veracruz. Late Classic period. Dark-green jadeite. Height, 1 5/8″. Collection Stendahl.

501. PENDANT. / Campeche. Late Classic period. Green jadeite. Height, 1 1/2″. Collection Stendahl.

502. PENDANT. / Southern Veracruz. Late Classic period. Green jadeite. Height, 1 3/4″. Collection Stendahl.

398. Cylindrical vase with bat-god and glyphs. *El Quiché, Guatemala. Late Classic period. Buff clay with black, white, red, and orange paint, polished. Height, 5 1/4"; diameter, 7 1/4".*

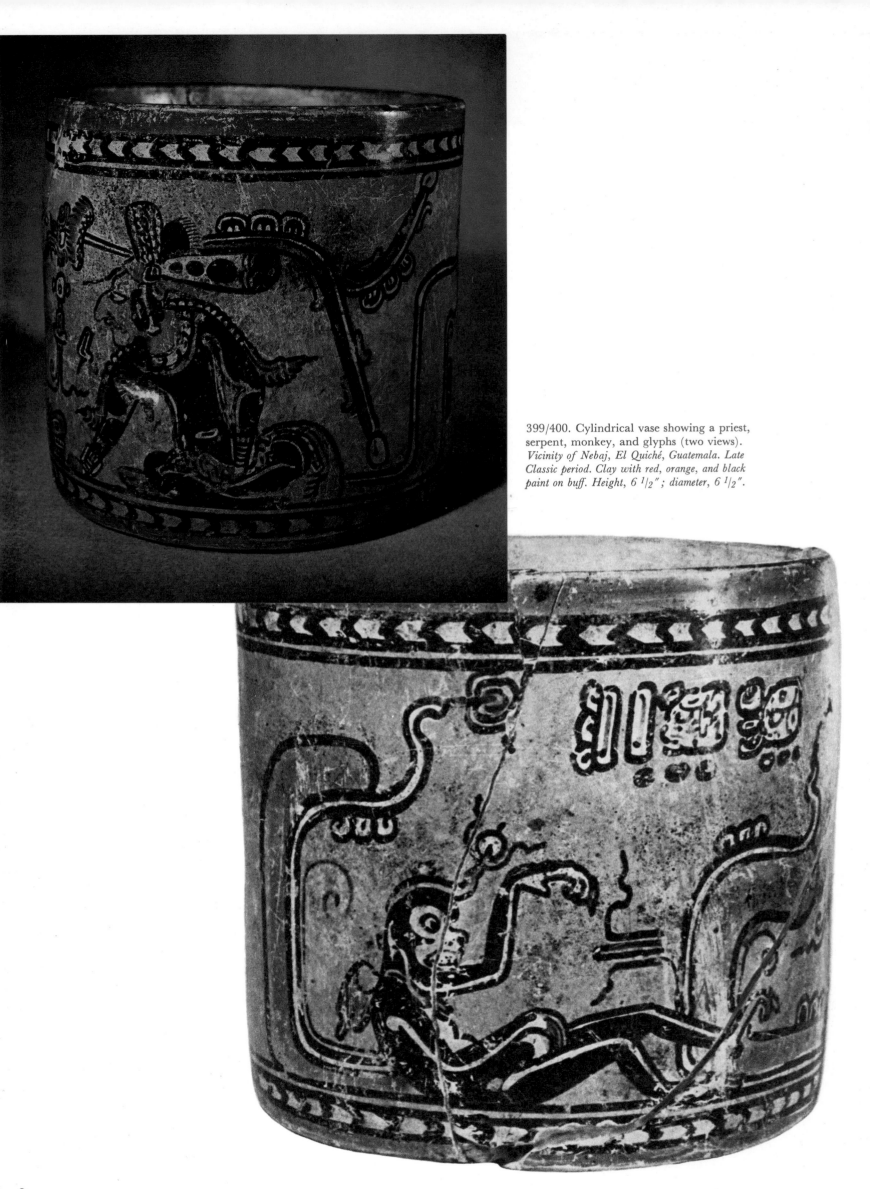

399/400. Cylindrical vase showing a priest, serpent, monkey, and glyphs (two views). *Vicinity of Nebaj, El Quiché, Guatemala. Late Classic period. Clay with red, orange, and black paint on buff. Height, 6 1/2"; diameter, 6 1/2".*

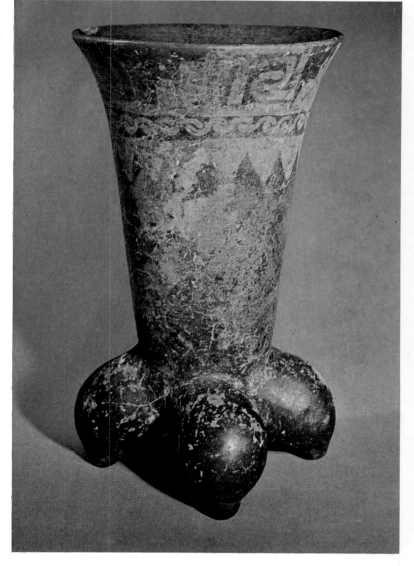

401. Cylindrical vase with four figures.
*Jaina, Campeche. Late Classic period. Clay,
painted red, white, and black on orange. Height,
7 1/2"; diameter, 6 1/2".*

402. Jar with flaring sides and four
mammiform supports. *El Quetzal, Guatemala.
Early Classic period. Reddish-brown clay with
black paint and geometrical designs. Height, 11".*

403. Cylindrical vase with glyphs in panels.
*Vicinity of Nebaj, El Quiché, Guatemala. Late
Classic period. Clay, painted red, orange, and black
on cream. Height, 6"; diameter, 5 1/2".*

404. Cylindrical vase with a human figure
combined with a bird design. *Ulúa Valley,
Honduras. Late Classic period. Clay, painted brown,
red, and orange on buff. Height, 6 3/8"; diameter, 5 1/4".*

405. Tripod plate with bird design. *Jaina, Campeche. Late Classic period. Clay, painted red, orange, and black on tan. Height, 4 1/2″; diameter, 15 1/4″.*

406. Tripod plate showing a seated priest. *Campeche. Late Classic period. Clay, painted red, orange, and black on buff. Diameter, 16″.*

407. Tripod plate showing a deer.
Jaina, Campeche. Late Classic period. Clay with red, orange, and brown paint on buff. Height, 3″; diameter, 10 ¹/₂″.

408. Tripod plate showing a warrior.
Jaina, Campeche. Late Classic period. Clay, painted red, orange, and black on buff. Height, 3 ¹/₂″; diameter, 12 ¹/₄″.

409. Shallow tripod plate showing two individuals seated on a dais. *Campeche. Late Classic period. Clay, painted red, orange, brown on buff. Height, 3″; diameter, 12 ¹/₂″.*

410/411/412/413. Carved double-bottomed rattle bowl (two views and two schematic drawings). *El Quiché, Guatemala. Late Classic period. Dark-brown burnished clay with residues of red paint in excised spots. Height, 5 1/8″; diameter, 6 1/2″; space between floors, 5/8″.*

414. Vase with stamped design in two panels showing a seated priest with attendants. *Chiapas. Late Classic period. Fine brown clay, painted dark brown. Height, 6 ³/₄"; diameter, 4 ³/₄".*

415. Cylindrical vase with two carved panels. *Puuc region, northeastern Campeche. Late Classic period. Brown clay with traces of stuccoed and painted blue color and inlaid stones. Height, 6 ⁵/₈"; diameter, 6".*

416. Effigy jar with grotesque face.
Campeche. Postclassic period. Plumbate ware, red-brown and black. Height, 6″; diameter, 6″.

417. Kneeling bearded hunchback effigy jar.
Mexico. Early Postclassic period. Plumbate ware. Height, 10 1/4″.

418. Armadillo effigy jar.
Uaymil, Campeche. Early Postclassic period. Orange plumbate ware. Height, 6 1/2″.

419. Human effigy *incensario* with bird headdress. *Northeastern Yucatan. Late Postclassic period. Light-gray clay. Height, 16 1/2″; diameter, 14 1/2″.*

420. Large cylinder decorated with masks. *Chiapas. Classic period. Buff clay with residue of stucco. Height, 29 1/2".*

421. Large cylinder decorated with masks. *Chiapas. Classic period. Brown clay with residue of stucco. Height, 21".*

422. Head vase showing an old man's face on the front and two glyphs on the back. *Puuc region, Campeche. Late Classic period. Brown clay with white and red paint. Height, 5"; diameter, 5".*

423. Cylindrical vase with carved design. *Puuc region, Campeche, Mexico. Late Classic period. Brown clay, burnished, with residues of stuccoed and painted blue rim decoration. Height, 6 5/8"; diameter, 6".*

424. Incense burner lid.
Department of Escuintla, Guatemala. Late Classic to Early Postclassic period. Brown clay. Height, 6 3/4".

425. Cylindrical tube with lateral panels.
Chiapas. Classic period. Clay. Red paste with red slip and residues of blue paint, partially covered with a thick lime deposit. Height, 27".

426. Cylindrical vase with carved design of seated priest. *Northeastern Campeche. Late Classic period. Brown clay. Height, 6"; diameter, 6 1/2".*

427. Large cylindrical jar with lid.
El Quiché, Guatemala. Late Classic period.
Unpolished red-brown clay with red, blue, black,
and yellow paint and appliqués. Height, 15 1/2";
diameter, 11".

428. Cylindrical vase with raised base.
Ulúa River Valley, Honduras. Postclassic period.
Alabaster. Height, 5 7/8".

429. Carved cylindrical vase with bat designs.
Ulúa Valley, Honduras. Postclassic period.
Alabaster. Height, 3 5/8"; diameter, 4".

430. Carved cylindrical vase with jaguar
handles. *Ulúa River Valley, Honduras. Alabaster.*
Height, 5 7/8"; diameter, 6".

431/432/433/434/435. Bowl with relief decoration. *Jaina, Campeche. Late Classic period. Alabaster. Height, 4 1/2″; diameter, 4″.*

436. Seated figure.
El Quiché, Guatemala. Late Classic period.
Reddish clay with blue, yellow, and white paint.
Height, 14 1/4″.

437/438. Bearded figure mounted on a slab
(two views). *El Quiché, Guatemala. Late Classic
or Early Postclassic period. Buff clay with red,
white, and yellow paint. Height, 16".*

439. Whistle: female figure holding a bowl. *Jaina, Campeche. Late Classic period. Buff clay with red, white, and blue paint. Height, 10″.*

440. Whistle: standing male with yoke and *hacha. Jaina, Campeche. Late Classic period. Buff clay with red and blue paint. Height, 8″.*

441. Whistle: old man embracing a young girl. *Jaina, Campeche. Late Classic period. Buff clay with red, white, and blue paint. Height, 6".*

443. Whistle: seated woman. *Jaina, Campeche. Late Classic period. Buff clay with red, white, and blue paint. Height, 7 1/4".*

442. Whistle: seated old man. *Jaina, Campeche. Late Classic period. Buff clay with traces of red, white, yellow, and blue paint. Height, 5 3/8".*

444. Whistle: bearded and mustached man. *Jaina, Campeche. Late Classic period. Buff clay with traces of red, white, and blue paint. Height, 6 3/4".*

447. Standing male in loincloth.
*Jaina, Campeche. Late Classic period. Buff clay
with traces of blue and red paint. Height, 10 1/4".*

448. Seated male with jaguar effigy headdress.
*Jaina, Campeche. Late Classic period. Buff clay
with white paint. Height, 16 1/4".*

445. Bearded dignitary seated on a throne.
*Jaina, Campeche. Late Classic period. Buff clay
with traces of blue and white paint. Height, 10".*

446. Bearded dignitary seated on a throne.
*Jaina, Campeche. Late Classic period. Buff clay
with traces of blue and white paint. Height, 10".*

449. Standing male holding a serpent scepter.
*Campeche. Late Classic period. Buff clay painted red,
blue, and white. Height, 11″.*

450. Whistle: standing male with a wide-brimmed, removable hat. *Jaina, Campeche. Late Classic period. Buff clay with red, white, and blue paint. Height, 9 1/2".*

451. Whistle: obese male in quilted dress. *Uaymil, Campeche. Late Classic period. Buff clay with red and blue paint. Height, 11 1/2".*

319

452. Woman with water jar on her head, carrying a child-rattle. *Jaina, Campeche. Late Classic period. Reddish-brown clay with traces of white paint. Height, 6 1/2".*

453. Man peering through the open beak of a large bird headdress. *Jaina, Campeche. Late Classic period. Buff clay with red and white paint. Height, 7 1/2".*

454. Woman with elaborate hair arrangement and facial tattoo, holding a fan. *Jaina, Campeche. Late Classic period. Buff clay with red and white paint. Height, 9 1/2".*

455. Whistle: ballplayer with a yoke around the waist. *Jaina, Campeche. Late Classic period. Buff clay with traces of white paint. Height, 7 1/2".*

456. Whistle: seated figure with padded and punctuated cheeks, holding a baby jaguar. *Jaina, Campeche. Late Classic period. Buff clay. Height, 5″.*

457. Whistle: standing female with dress and fish headdress. *Jaina, Campeche. Late Classic period. Tan clay with traces of white paint. Height, 6″.*

458. Rattle: standing female with bird headdress. *Jaina, Campeche. Late Classic period. Tan clay with red and white paint. Height, 5″.*

459. Whistle: standing male figurine with deer headdress. *Jaina, Campeche. Late Classic period. Tan clay with red, white, and orange paint. Height, 8 1/4″.*

460. Standing male.
Uaymil, Campeche. Late Classic period. Buff clay with traces of red, blue, and white paint. Height, 8 1/2".

461. Whistle: figurine group.
Jaina, Campeche. Late Classic period. Buff clay with white paint. Height, 7".

464. Carved wall panel.
Usumacinta River Region, Chiapas, Mexico. Late Classic period. Limestone. Height, 18".

462. Carved wall panel.
Usumacinta River region, Guatemala. Late Classic period. Limestone. Height, 76".

463. Carved wall panel with eight glyph pairs. *Piedras Negras region, Guatemala. Late Classic period. Limestone. Height, 74".*

323

465. Wall panel (probably from a door jamb). *Usumacinta River, Guatemala. Late Classic period. Limestone. Height, 66″.*

466. Standing figure.
Southern Campeche near the Guatemala border. Late Classic period. Limestone. Height, 84″.

324

467. Carved wall panel.
El Cayo, Chiapas. Late Classic period. Limestone.
Height, 32″; width, 27″.

468. Carved panel.
Usumacinta River region, Guatemala. Late
Classic period. Limestone. Height, 53″.

469. Cornice decoration in the form of a
sun-god's head. *Copán, Honduras. Classic period.
Limestone. Height, 8 1/2".*

470. Carved lintel.
*Usumacinta region (Piedras Negras or Yaxchilán).
Late Classic Maya period (A.D. 795). Limestone.
Height, 23 3/4".*

471. Carved panel.
*Usumacinta region. Late Classic period. Limestone.
Height, 51".*

472. Seated warrior with club and shield.
*Campeche. Late Classic period. Stuccoed limestone
painted red and blue. Height, 13 1/2".*

473. *Hacha.*
*Tecpán vicinity, Guatemala. Classic period.
Polished gray-green stone. Height, 10 1/2".*

474. Profile fragment.
*Campeche. Late Classic period. Stuccoed limestone
with traces of red and blue paint. Height, 6".*

475. Head.
Honduras. Classic period. Limestone. Height, 7 1/2".

476. Head with tenoned support in back.
Copán, Honduras. Classic period. Limestone.
Height, 15".

477. Head fragment with indications of
mustache and beard. *Chiapas. Late Classic*
period. Stucco with traces of red and green color.
Height, ·8 1/4".

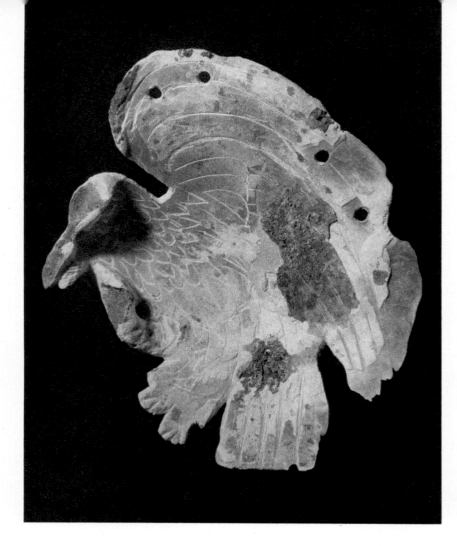

478. Bird pendant.
Uaymil, Campeche. Late Classic period. Carved shell. Height, 4 1/2".

479. Man and woman in embrace.
Jaina, Campeche. Late Classic period. Carved shell. Height, 4 7/8".

480. Ornaments made to represent death's-heads. *Jaina, Campeche. Late Classic period. Shell. Height of tallest, 2 3/4".*

481. Head in profile.
Jaina, Campeche. Late Classic period. Shell with openwork carving. Height, 3 1/2".

482. Pendant showing priest with boarlike animal. *Uaymil, Campeche. Late Classic period. Carved shell. Height, 2 3/8".*

483. Pendant.
Jaina, Campeche. Late Classic period. Shell with openwork carving. Length, 3 3/4".

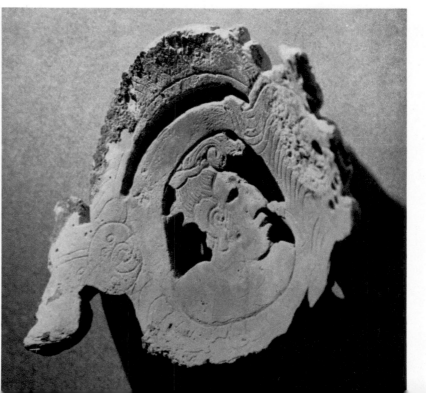

484/485. Carved deer bone showing priest with twenty glyphs (with schematic drawing). *Jaina, Campeche. Late Classic period. Length, 10 3/4".*

486. Standing figure holding a flint-tipped spear and a pouch. *Campeche. Late Classic period. Deer bone (?). Height, 5".*

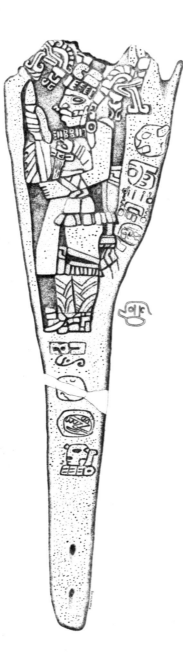

487/488. Bone fragment with relief carving (with schematic drawing). *Jaina, Campeche. Late Classic period. Mandible of a porpoise. Length, 12″.*

489. Standing male figure. *Jaina, Campeche. Late Classic period. Bone with traces of red paint. Height, 3 ³/₈″.*

333

AT RIGHT: CLOCKWISE

496. Pendant.
El Quiché, Guatemala. Late Classic period. Green jade. Height, 2".

497. Pendant.
Campeche. Late Classic period. Light-green jadeite. Height, 1 1/2".

498. Ear plug.
Yucatan. Classic period. Green jadeite. Diameter, 1 5/8".

499. Pendant.
Campeche. Late Classic period. Green jadeite. Height, 1 5/8".

490. Pendant.
Nebaj region, El Quiché, Guatemala. Late Classic period. Brown jadeite. Height, 3 3/8".

491. Pendant.
Nebaj region, El Quiché, Guatemala. Late Classic period. Mottled green jadeite. Height, 4 1/4".

492. Pendant.
Palenque, Chiapas. Classic period. Green jadeite. Height, 2 1/4".

493. Miniature mask.
El Quetzal, Guatemala. Early Postclassic period. Hard green stone. Height, 2 3/4".

494. Pendant.
Toniná, Chiapas. Late Classic period (A.D. 731). Green jadeite with gray patches. Height, 4 1/8".

500. Pendant.
Found in Veracruz. Late Classic period. Dark-green jadeite. Height, 1 5/8".

501. Pendant.
Campeche. Late Classic period. Green jadeite. Height, 1 1/2".

502. Pendant.
Southern Veracruz. Late Classic period. Green jadeite. Height, 1 3/4".

495. Pendant.
Tonina, Chiapas. Late Classic period. Opaque, medium blue-green jadeite. Height, 2 5/8".

335

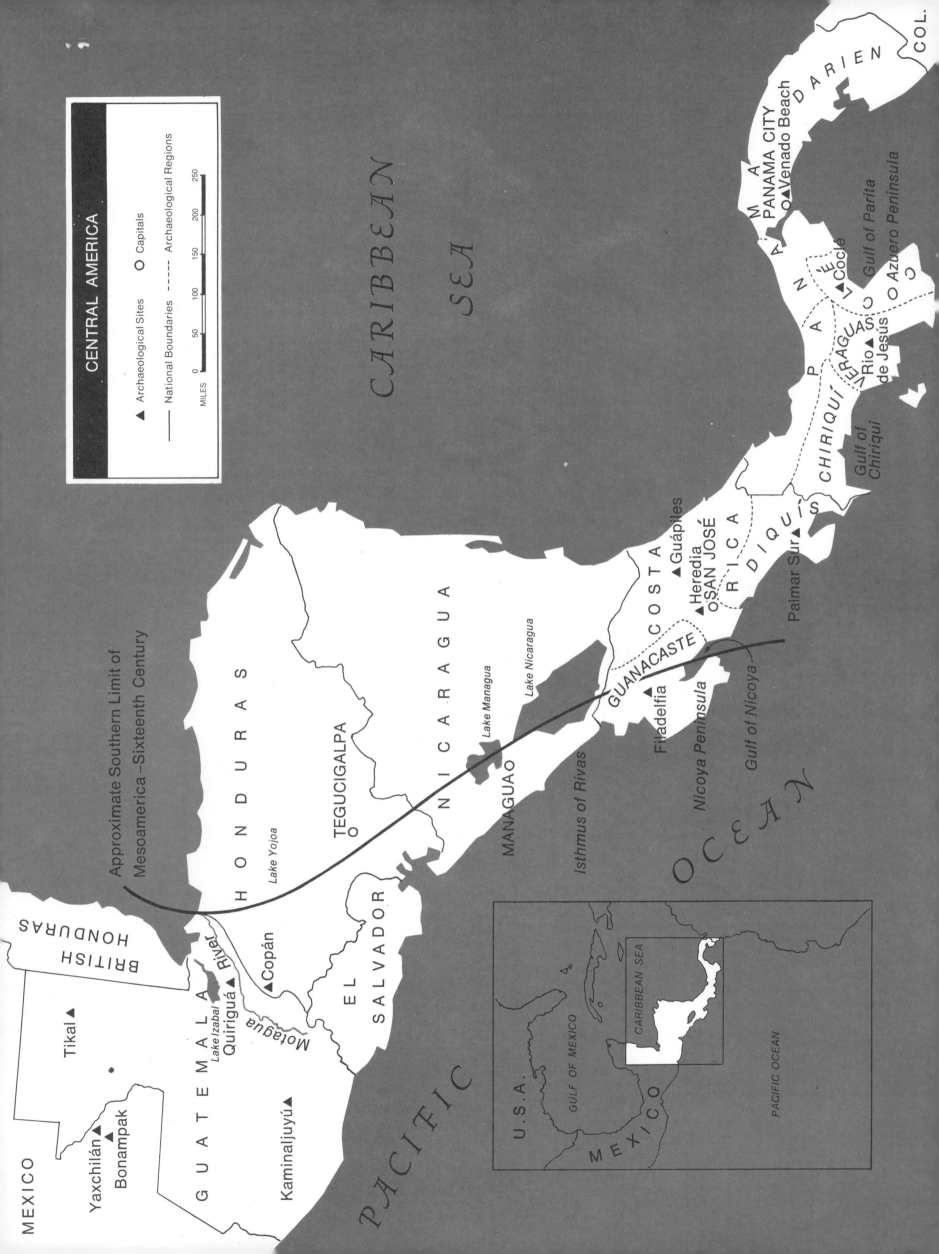

CENTRAL AMERICA

▲ Archaeological Sites   ○ Capitals
— National Boundaries   ---- Archaeological Regions

MILES
0   50   100   150   200   250

MEXICO

CARIBBEAN SEA

PACIFIC OCEAN

GUATEMALA

Tikal ▲

Yaxchilán ▲
Bonampak ▲

Kaminaljuyú ▲

BRITISH HONDURAS

Lake Izabal
Quiriguá ▲   Motagua River
▲ Copán

HONDURAS

Lake Yojoa

TEGUCIGALPA ○

EL SALVADOR

NICARAGUA

Lake Managua

Lake Nicaragua

MANAGUAO

Isthmus of Rivas

Approximate Southern Limit of
Mesoamerica—Sixteenth Century

COSTA RICA

GUANACASTE

Filadelfia ▲

Nicoya Peninsula

Gulf of Nicoya

▲ Guápiles
Heredia ▲
○ SAN JOSÉ

DIQUIS

Palmar Sur ▲

PANAMA

CHIRIQUI

Gulf of Chiriqui

VERAGUAS

Rio ▲
de Jesús

Coclé ▲

Gulf of Parita

Azuero Peninsula

PANAMA CITY ▲
Venado Beach ○

DARIEN

COL.

U.S.A.

GULF OF MEXICO

MEXICO

CARIBBEAN SEA

PACIFIC OCEAN

V I

ART OF LOWER
CENTRAL AMERICA

Art of Lower Central America

Nicaragua, Costa Rica, and Panama

THE CENTRAL AMERICAN LAND BRIDGE between Mexico and Colombia has an ancient culture, tempered by Mexican, Mayan, and South American influences. The area was a well-traveled trade route. Gold figurines from Panama and Colombia have been discovered in Chichén Itzá. Maya pottery was traded to Nicaragua. Nicoya pottery of Costa Rica betrays Toltec-Mixtec characteristics. The people of Panama traded with Ecuador.

The relations between the various regions within lower Central America are as yet uncertain, partly because of the lack of excavations and partly because of insufficient knowledge concerning the prehistoric natural environment. Heavily forested regions that are now considered natural barriers between Central and South America, as for instance the Darien Province, may not have been obstacles to overland traffic in earlier times. Maritime contacts along the Pacific coast which, due to their nature, are difficult to verify archaeologically, must have existed.

Pottery, ornate stone sculpture, and gold jewelry are the more conspicuous representatives of Central American art. Of the three countries in lower Central America—Panama, Costa Rica, and Nicaragua—more than half is unknown archaeologically. In Nicaragua only the Isthmus of Rivas, in the southwestern part, has been excavated. Northwestern and southwestern Costa Rica have been studied more intensively during recent years. Panama is best known of the three.

From present knowledge a tentative developmental sequence has been proposed by Claude Baudez and M. D. Coe (Baudez and Coe, 1961; Baudez, 1963). In view of the fact that the three countries seem to be culturally homogeneous, they are treated as one archaeological area. Surprisingly, the sequence does not parallel the pattern of Mesoamerica, where all cultures developed to a certain level, from which some followed individual trends to reach peaks not attained by others. In the Central American area a slower pace is observed, and cultural increments appear to be of lesser qualitative significance.

Of the six developmental stages, the first three can be summarized very briefly. Evidence of fluted projectile points is indicative of a Paleo-Indian population with no agriculture. The second period is typified by the emergence of thin monochrome pottery dated about 1000 B.C. In Period III (300 B.C. to A.D. 300), distinctive decorative techniques in pottery occur (zoned bichroming), and simple three-legged grinding slabs (metates) indicate that agriculture has become a main food source. In Veraguas some elaborate metates have been found. Monumental sculpture, jade, metal, and figurines do not appear in this period, and no social stratification or important ceremonialism seem to have existed. An exception is seen in the Barriles culture of Panama, with different burial forms, structures, and remarkable monumental sculpture, but relatively simple pottery.

Period IV (A.D. 300–500) shows no striking changes from the preceding one. Polychrome pottery with simple linear motifs occurs, and figurine-whistles are common in northwestern Costa Rica. Indications of incipient social stratification and of the increasing importance of ceremonialism are seen in the construction of earth mounds for burial purposes.

Drastic changes in all regions took place during Period V (A.D. 500–800). Manufacture and distribution of highly specialized artifacts suggest the existence of a stratified society and increased population. Elaborately carved maceheads and metates, full development of metallurgy, and polychrome pottery with geometric designs appear in different regions.

The final period, which lasted from A.D. 800 to the Conquest, is characterized by diversification of elaborate polychrome pottery in geometric and naturalistic designs in Costa Rica and Panama. In all regions there is seen a climax compared with the preceding periods. Burials become more complex and the growing importance of religion is indicated by the spread of monumental sculpture. Beautifully carved metates with three and four legs occur in certain regions but are absent in others. Gold ornaments are abundant in Panama and central Costa Rica.

It would be difficult to attempt to cover in a single volume all phases of the prolific and checkered cultural history of Mexico and Central America. Our brief review and the selection of outstanding examples of pre-Hispanic art illustrated in this volume bring into focus some of the milestones along the course of cultural development and pay tribute to the wisdom of the ancient priest-rulers and to the skill and patience of their craftsmen.

Gold Ornaments from Costa Rica and Panama

OF THE GOLD ORNAMENTS that the conquistadors looted, and of those which were sent to Spain in the decades following the Conquest, practically nothing remains. Much was melted down before leaving the New World. It must have been a bitter task for the ancient goldsmiths of Mexico, who, on the order of Moctezuma II, spent several days reducing heaps of delicately wrought ornaments into bars, which were to be stamped with the royal seal of Spain. Peruvian goldsmiths labored even longer in this ruthless destruction of artistic creation. A large number of gold ornaments which were accidentally discovered in graves in Costa Rica and Panama were also tossed into the crucibles to be transformed into bullion, a procedure that was systematically carried out as late as the middle of the last century.

It is a testimonial to the enormous productivity of the ancient goldsmiths, as well as sheer good luck, that a still sizeable number of superb masterworks of gold has been rescued by museums and private collectors. With the exception of a few discoveries by archaeological excavations, such as those by Caso at Monte Albán and by Lothrop in Coclé and Veraguas, for example, most of these objects bear no indication of their precise provenance. Such pieces are often somewhat vaguely attributed to one ancient site or another on the basis of stylistic characteristics.

Detailed first-hand information on the art of metalworking in Mexico is contained in the sixteenth-century accounts of Sahagún (Codex Florentine, pp. 69–85). Garcilaso de la Vega and a few others reported on the methods used in Peru (Lothrop, 1938). For the Intermediate area, including Costa Rica and Panama, no early historical data are available. Among modern investigators Lothrop in particular described and illustrated a large body of material, and Easby thoroughly analyzed the metalworking techniques. Recently, Emmerich summarized the data of the artistic and technical aspects of metal ornaments from Mexico to Peru, drawing on a large array of sources.

In Central America, Pre-Columbian gold jewelry was far more abundant in the province of Veraguas than in any other region. These objects were widely traded to the south, and to the north as far as Yucatan. Lothrop (1963, p. 95) even cites an instance of a gold pendant having been copied in jade. Many of the Veraguas gold specimens are not of high-grade gold but of a copper-gold alloy. Nevertheless, they were made as skillfully and in the same technique as those of pure gold. Often, after a long period of interment, the copper has corroded and the pieces have become brittle.

The ornaments, shaped as eagles, alligators, bats, and other creatures, were commonly used as pendants. The term eagle, although not entirely accurate, has been used since the days of the first contact by the Spaniards. These bird representations are very stylized and show much variation in detail. They predominate numerically in southern Veraguas and in the Diquís Delta of Costa Rica, where Veraguas influence was strong. The eagle pendants often have attributes of other animals, implying a symbolic connotation rather than a merely ornamental one. A characteristic of Veraguas eagle pendants is the portrayal of the eyes in the shape of small protruding bells.

Alligator pendants, mainly known from Coclé, are solid or hollow-cast in the round. Characteristic of the pendants of the Diquís region are flat square pieces of metal suspended from projecting wires. These danglers were either cut out of hammered sheet metal or individually cast in open molds and polished to remove the mold marks. The suspension wires were cast simultaneously with the entire ornament, a procedure which required remarkable skill in the creation of the preliminary wax model.

Frog pendants of cast gold are commonly found in Colombia, Panama, and Costa Rica. Those of Veraguas are larger and more elaborate, those of Chiriquí are smaller and simpler.

Another class of pendants consists of human bodies with animal heads, customarily called "gods," although it cannot be ascertained that they actually represent deities. In Veraguas, Diquís, and Chiriquí, eagle pendants are male or sexless. Jaguar-god pendants occur with wings or with serpents in these regions. Bat-gods are rare and are confined to Coclé and Colombia (Lothrop, 1963, pp. 95–102).

Among the "acquisitions" of the conquistadors and later explorers, which were carefully recorded in inventories sent to Spain in the sixteenth and early seventeenth centuries, are large numbers of gold disks used as pectorals. Those from Coclé are outstanding for their elaborate workmanship. Such disks are also known from northern Costa Rica to Colombia. Those from Veraguas and Venado Beach (Canal Zone) were traded from Coclé. The disks usually have embossed cones, sometimes referred to as "breasts," and have a dotted embossed edge. They were hammered to shape and annealed to soften the metal and to prevent cracking. Disks of smaller size were usually cast.

Casting of flat objects was done in open molds. Most ornaments, however, are in the round and had to be cast in closed molds by the lost-wax (*cire-perdue*) process, which apparently was invented in Colombia. This process called for a high degree of technical skill and artistry. The object was first modeled of wax mixed with resin, or, if the ornament was to be hollow, the wax model was made over a core of clay mixed with charcoal. This then was encased in clay, which, upon hardening, served as a mold. A funnel was provided for pouring the liquid metal. After a drying period, the mold was preheated to eliminate the wax (hence the term lost-wax process), and the gold or gold-copper alloy was poured. The formation of air and gas bubbles that might obstruct the even flow of the metal presented a hazard that could be checked by providing narrow escape channels. These had to be formed with the aid of wax threads attached to the model in the proper places. After cooling, the mold was broken to extract the ornament. The wirelike protrusions caused by the metal in the vents were clipped and the traces of the stumps polished. In hollow objects the clay-charcoal core was removed, but there are a few pieces known in which this core is still present. Sometimes uneven edges on the wings or on the double crossbars betray the fact that the mold was not completely filled.

In southern Costa Rica and in the Guianas, the only regions where the goldsmiths were unable to melt pure gold or copper, a powdered alloy having a lower melting point than the pure metals was used. This alloy, known as *tumbaga,* was probably invented in Colombia, where most cast objects are made of it and from where this technique spread to Peru, Mexico, and the West Indies, together with the lost-wax process.

In order to give *tumbaga* ornaments the characteristic luster of gold, the surfaces were treated with a process known as *mise en couleur.* This was achieved by prolonged submerging of the object in acid ("pickling") and by annealing, which had the effect of oxidizing and removing the copper on the surface. The resulting rough gold surface was then polished. Such a treatment can be applied effectively only on flat and easily accessible surfaces. The other parts remain rough and have the color of curry powder, as Lothrop has pointed out (1963, p. 97).

Annealing, or tempering, is a process used to prevent metal from becoming too brittle under prolonged hammering. The metal is heated to a dull red, to allow for a readjustment of the microstructure, before hammering is continued. This process has to be repeated at proper intervals. Strangely enough, annealing hardens *tumbaga* and bronze, but softens copper and silver. Gold presents problems in annealing because the object has to be removed from the heat at the right moment before reaching the melting point, a stage which is difficult to detect solely from a change of color.

Soldering was not a highly developed technique and required the use of powdered alloys of gold placed on the edges to be joined. Heat by means of a blowpipe was then directed to the spot to fuse the parts together.

The comparatively few gold ornaments that were discovered in controlled excavations, and under conditions which provided a relevant ceramic stratigraphy, are dated mainly on the basis of polychrome pottery brought in by trade from Coclé. It is generally assumed that metalworking emerged in Lower Central America about A.D. 500, and classic Veraguas, Chiriquí, and Costa Rica ornaments are believed to date from the ninth century onward.

Art of Lower Central America

Captions and Notes

PLATES 503–595

503. HUMAN EFFIGY VASE. / Filadelfia, Guanacaste, Costa Rica. Middle Polychrome period. Cream slip on red clay with black and red paint. Height, 12 1/2″; diameter, 9″. The May Department Stores Company, St. Louis, Mo.

The grotesque human face has long ear pendants. The neck of the vase is decorated with plumed serpent motifs, the limbs and breast-plaque with stylized jaguar heads. This piece is illustrated in Lines, fig. 31.

504. JAGUAR EFFIGY *Incensario.* / Filadelfia, Guanacaste, Costa Rica. Late Polychrome period. Light-brown and grayish clay with white paint. Height, 13 1/2″. The Museum of Primitive Art, New York.

This *incensario* is illustrated in Lines, fig. 32.

505. WIDE-LIPPED BOWL WITH FIGURE WEARING ALLIGATOR MASK. / Filadelfia, Guanacaste, Costa Rica. Late Polychrome period. Red-brown clay, incised. Height, 8 1/2″; diameter, 13″. Collection Stendahl.

The lip of the bowl is shaped like the wings and tail of a bird. This bowl is illustrated in *Präkolumbische Kunst*, pl. 100.

506. CYLINDRICAL BOWL. / Buenos Aires region of Costa Rica. Late Polychrome period. Reddish-brown and dark brown on buff clay. Height, 8 1/4″; diameter, 9 3/4″. Museum Rietberg, Zurich, Switzerland.

The design shows the alligator motif in panels in two rows. It is characteristic of the neighboring Chiriquí region, where it occurs abundantly and in great variation. The alligator has open jaws, an upturned snout, and a long crest on the back of the head, edged with triangular scales. Lothrop's description (1926, p. 172) of the motif is applicable to this bowl, which is illustrated in *Präkolumbische Kunst*, item 1116, pl. 99.

507. PLATE WITH FLARING SIDES AND THREE HOLLOW CYLINDRICAL RATTLE SUPPORTS. / Filadelfia, Guanacaste, Costa Rica. Middle Polychrome period (A.D. 750–1000). Black and red on cream slip. Height, 6 1/4″; diameter, 5 5/8″. Collection Stendahl.

The highly conventionalized decoration combines jaguar and feathered serpent elements.

508. EFFIGY VASE. / Filadelfia, Guanacaste, Costa Rica. Middle Polychrome period. Cream slip on red clay with black and red paint. Height, 12 1/2″; diameter, 9″. Private collection.

The figure on the front with the monkey pectoral may be a monkey-god. On the back is a squirrel modeled in relief. The neck of the vase and the limbs show combined plumed serpent and jaguar-head motifs. This piece is illustrated in Lines, fig. 28.

509. JAGUAR EFFIGY VASE. / Filadelfia, Guanacaste, Costa Rica. Middle Polychrome period. Cream slip on red clay with black and red paint. Height, 14 1/2″; diameter, 10 1/2″. Collection Mr. and Mrs. Peter M. Jenkyn, Austin, Texas.

The neck of the vase is decorated with plumed serpent motifs and the limbs and collar with stylized jaguar heads.

510. GLOBULAR PEDESTAL BOWL. / Filadelfia, Guanacaste, Costa Rica. Late Polychrome period. Red, blue, and black on cream slip. Height, 7 1/4″; diameter, 8″. The Museum of Primitive Art, New York.

Lothrop (1926, p. 191) classifies this "under-slip incised ware" as a subgroup of Nicoya Polychrome Ware. The decoration of stylized plumed serpents shows strong Mexican influence.

511. ANIMAL EFFIGY JAR. / Guanacaste, Costa Rica. Middle Polychrome period. Red, black, and purple on cream slip. Height, 11 1/2″; diameter, 11″. The May Department Stores Company, St. Louis, Mo.

The rim decoration consists of conventionalized plumed serpent designs.

512. HUMAN EFFIGY VASE. / Guanacaste, Costa Rica. Late Polychrome period. Red clay with cream slip and red, black, and brown paint. Height, 13″; diameter, 9″. The May Department Stores Company, St. Louis, Mo.

The features are modeled and painted. The rim of the vase is decorated with conventionalized plumed serpent motifs.

513. VASE WITH ANNULAR BASE. / Filadelfia, Guanacaste, Costa Rica. Middle Polychrome period. Cream slip on red clay with black, red, and purple-brown paint. Height, 14″; diameter, 9 1/2″. Los Angeles County Museum of Natural History.

The zoned decoration represents stylized jaguars and plumed serpents.

514. MAN WITH A JAGUAR MASK HOLDING AN ALLIGATOR. / Diquís region, southwestern Costa Rica. 1000–1500 (?). Brown sandstone. Height, 13″. Collection Mr. and Mrs. James Grant, San Francisco.

515. SEATED MEDICINE MAN BLOWING A FLUTE. / Guápiles region, Costa Rica. 1000–1500 (?). Volcanic stone. Height, 12″. Collection Ulfert Wilke, New York.

The Misquito Indian term *sukia* (medicine man) has been applied to this class of seated male figures, who are shown seated in a thoughtful attitude or blowing a flute (Stone, 1961, p. 197).

516. STANDING FIGURE OF MAN ON PEG BASE. / Cerro Gordo, Diquís region, southwestern Costa Rica. 1000–1500 (?). Volcanic stone. Height, 34 3/4″. The Museum of Primitive Art, New York.

The figure holds a trophy head in one hand and a hand ax or knife in the other. The pendant hanging from a cord around his neck (probably four joined animals) is similar to cast gold ornaments of the region. He wears a beltlike loincloth. His legs are separated and the arms are set off by oval openings, an unusual feature in New World sculpture (Lothrop, 1963, p. 27).

517. MALE FIGURE WITH JAGUAR HEAD AND DOUBLE SERPENT TONGUES. / Diquís region, southwestern Costa Rica. 700–1550(?). Sandstone. Height, 15 1/2″. Collection Morton D. May, St. Louis, Mo.

This statue probably represents a jaguar-god. From the large mouth protrude overlapping canine teeth that are linked to form the letter N. Lothrop (1963, p. 36) observed that this characteristic may have an early (before A.D. 700) Andean origin. The tongues end in serpent heads on the shoulders.

518. STANDING WOMAN WITH CONICAL CAP OR HEADDRESS AND TATTOO MARKS ON ARMS AND CHEST. / Guápiles region, Costa Rica. 1000–1500 (?). Volcanic stone. Height, 17″. Collection Mr. and Mrs. Dübi-Müller, Solothurn, Switzerland.

This figure is illustrated in *Präkolumbische Kunst*, item 1068, pl. 98.

519. ARMADILLO SITTING UPRIGHT. / Guápiles region, Costa Rica. 1000–1500 (?). Granitic rock. Height, 17″. Collection Mrs. Edith Hafter, Zurich, Switzerland.

520/521. SEATED FIGURES WITH JAGUAR HEADS ON PEG BASE. / Northern Panama. 1000–1500 (?). Volcanic stone. Height: left, 23 7/8″; right, 18 7/8″. Brooklyn Museum, New York.

Peg-base figures, some life-size, are found from the Diquís region of Costa Rica south to Coclé province, Panama. They have been found in cemeteries, sometimes in an upright position with the undecorated base stuck in the ground, and probably served as grave markers. A similar figure is illustrated in Dockstader, fig. 188.

522. STANDING MALE HOLDING TROPHY HEAD AND KNIFE OR AX. / Guápiles region, Costa Rica. 1000–1500 (?). Volcanic stone. Height, 33″. Collection Josef Müller, Solothurn, Switzerland.

The figure wears a woven belt.

523. THREE NICOYA POLYCHROME FIGURINES. / Guanacaste, Costa Rica. Middle Polychrome period. Red clay with cream slip and black and red paint. Height, 6″ 1/2 to 8 3/4″. Collection Jay C. Leff, Uniontown, Penn.

The decoration on the figurines indicates colorful clothing, body paint, and tattooing. The central ornament on the headdress of the middle figure is derived from the alligator motif.

524. MACE-HEAD REPRESENTING A JAGUAR. / Nicoya Peninsula, Costa Rica. Early Polychrome period. Stone. Height, 3″. Museum of the American Indian, Heye Foundation, New York.

The head is perforated vertically for insertion of a wooden shaft.

525. MACE-HEAD REPRESENTING AN ANIMAL. / Nicoya, Costa Rica. Early Polychrome period (?). Light-

green stone. Length, 7″. Museum of the American Indian, Heye Foundation, New York.

526. SEATED MAN. / Filadelfia, Guanacaste, Costa Rica. Middle Polychrome period. Red clay with cream slip and red and black paint. Height, 7³/₄″. Collection Mr. and Mrs. Richard G. Sussman, New York.

527. SEATED WOMAN. / Filadelfia, Guanacaste, Costa Rica. Middle Polychrome period (?). Red clay with ocher and red paint. Height, 5¹/₄″. Galerie Israel, Tel-Aviv.

Similar figurines with a load of some kind slung diagonally across the back were reported associated with Nandaime ware (Nicaragua) by Lothrop (1926, p. 263). The figure reproduced here is illustrated in *Präkolumbische Kunst*, item 1102, pl. 102.

528. ANTIPODAL FIGURES. / Guanacaste, Costa Rica. Early Polychrome period (?). Hard light-green stone. Height, 5″. American Museum of Natural History, New York.

529. AX-SHAPED HUMAN EFFIGY PENDANTS. / Guanacaste, Costa Rica. 700–1500 (?). Hard light-green stone. Height, 5¹/₄″ to 6″. Collection Stendahl.

The stones, once highly polished, are now partially eroded. A suspension hole penetrates the figures' neck from side to side.

530. MACE-HEAD IN THE FORM OF A BIRD'S HEAD. / Guanacaste, Costa Rica. Early Polychrome period. Hard gray stone. Length, 3¹/₂″. Collection Stendahl.

The wooden shaft is a later addition.

531. TWO AX-SHAPED PENDANTS. / Guanacaste, Costa Rica. Early Polychrome period (?). Hard greenish stone. Height: 4³/₄″ and 4¹/₂″ respectively. Left: Collection Stendahl; right: Collection Mr. and Mrs. Henry Clifford, Pasadena, Calif.

These stylized human figures have animal characteristics.

532. MACE-HEAD REPRESENTING A HUMAN HEAD. / Filadelfia, Guanacaste, Costa Rica. Early Polychrome period (?). Onyx marble (alabaster). Height, 3¹/₂″. Collection Mr. and Mrs. Vincent Price, Los Angeles.

533. JAGUAR EFFIGY GRINDSTONE. / Guápiles region, Costa Rica. 800–1500 (?). Volcanic stone. Height, 12¹/₂″. Collection Stendahl.

534. JAGUAR EFFIGY GRINDSTONE WITH RAISED RIM. / Guápiles region, Costa Rica. 800–1500 (?). Volcanic stone. Height, 5¹/₂″. Seattle Art Museum, Seattle, Wash.

The tail of the jaguar is joined to the hind leg. A monkey figure appears on either side between foreleg and hind leg.

535. GRINDSTONE WITH FLYING PANEL. / San Isidro de Heredia, Costa Rica. 800–1500 (?). Volcanic stone. Height, 18¹/₂″. The Museum of Primitive Art, New York.

The tablelike grinding surface has a raised edge and stands on three legs. Between them is a "flying panel" adorned with four pelicans. Such elaborately sculptured metates were undoubtedly reserved for ceremonial purposes.

536. JAGUAR EFFIGY GRINDSTONE. / Guanacaste, Costa Rica. 800–1500 (?). Volcanic stone. Height, 15¹/₄″. Collection Mrs. Edith Hafter, Zurich, Switzerland.

537. FOUR-LEGGED GRINDSTONE. / Veraguas, Panama. 800–1200 (?). Volcanic stone. Height, 20″. Collection Mrs. Edith Hafter, Zurich, Switzerland.

538. MULLER WITH BIRD HANDLE. / Veraguas, Panama. 800–1200 (?). Basalt. Height, 5¹/₂″. Collection Stendahl.

The characteristic mullers were stirrup-shaped to permit the rocking movement and at the same time to protect the fingers from the raised edge of the grinding table.

539. GRINDSTONE WITH FLYING PANEL REPRESENTING SERPENTS. / Veraguas, Panama. 800–1200 (?). Volcanic stone. Height, 14″. Thomas Gilcrease Institute of American History and Art, Tulsa, Okla.

540. GRINDSTONE WITH FLYING PANEL. / Central Costa Rica. 800–1500. Volcanic stone. Height, 24″. Isaac Delgado Museum of Art, New Orleans.

The adornments consist of three large beaked birds holding human heads in their claws and standing on alligators. The central monkey figure stands on a land crab and holds a staff representing a human figure standing on the head of a kneeling figure.

541. OFFERING TABLE FRINGED WITH SMALL HUMAN HEADS. / Chiriquí, Panama. 800–1200 (?). Volcanic stone. Height, 8″; diameter, 13¹/₂″. Collection Eugene Berman, Rome, Italy.

542. OFFERING TABLE SUPPORTED BY FOUR MONKEYS. / Veraguas, Panama. 800–1200 (?). Volcanic stone. Height, 8″; diameter, 13¹/₂″. Portland Art Museum, Portland, Ore.

543. JAGUAR EFFIGY. / Coclé, Panama. Late Coclé period (A.D. 1000–1200). Red clay with cream slip and black paint. Height, 9″. Thomas Gilcrease Institute of American History and Art, Tulsa, Okla.

The tail serves as a spout. A similar effigy vessel in Coclé style from Veraguas is illustrated in Lothrop, 1942, fig. 476 b.

544. PISOTE (BADGER) EFFIGY. / Coclé, Panama. Late Coclé period (A.D. 1000–1200). Clay with cream slip and red, purple, and black paint. Height, 11″. Thomas Gilcrease Institute of American History and Art, Tulsa. Okla.

545. PISOTE (BADGER) EFFIGY. / Coclé, Panama. Late Coclé period (A.D. 1000–1200). Clay with cream slip and red, purple, and black paint. Height, 12 1/2″. Thomas Gilcrease Institute of American History and Art, Tulsa, Okla.

546. PEDESTAL PLATE. / Rio de Jesús, Veraguas, Panama. Late Coclé period (A.D. 1000–1200). Red clay with red, purple, buff, and black paint. Height, 6 1/4″; diameter, 10 1/4″. Collection Mr. and Mrs. Francis V. Crane, Marathon, Fla.

Dancing crocodile-god with enlarged feet and claws. Barbed streamers, painted red and purple, are believed to represent plumes (cf. Lothrop, 1942, p. 83 and pl. II a).

547. PLATE WITH RING BASE. / Coclé, Panama. Early Coclé period (A.D. 500–1000). Tan clay with orange slip and red and black paint. Diameter, 12 1/2″. Collection Philip L. Dade, Laguna Beach, Calif.

Each segment of the decoration portrays what Lothrop (1942, p. 31) recognized as "birds with crocodile jaws," because a two-legged animal incorporates the scales and toothed jaw of the crocodile. Two opposing segments also depict the motif "bird-which-looks-forward," alternating with "bird-which-looks-back," a characteristic of the Early Coclé period. In the center is a crab.

548. PEDESTAL PLATE WITH FOUR FISH. / Parita, Azuero Peninsula, Panama. Late Coclé period (A.D. 1000–1200). Red clay with buff slip and red, purple, and black paint. Height, 4″; diameter, 11″. Collection Philip L. Dade, Laguna Beach, Calif.

549. PEDESTAL PLATE. / Rio de Jesús, Veraguas, Panama. Late Coclé period (A.D. 1000–1200). Red clay with buff slip and red, purple, blue, and black paint. Height, 7 1/2″. Collection Stanley R. Grant, New York.

The pattern of circles is intersected by the recurved body of a serpent with forked tail. The rim decoration, consisting of small panels in red, white, and purple, is a diagnostic trait of the Late Coclé Polychrome style. The alternating color pattern is similar to that of the coral snake (Lothrop, 1942, p. 75).

550. CYLINDRICAL BOWL WITH PEDESTAL BASE. / Coclé, Panama. Late Coclé period (A.D. 1000–1200). Red clay with red, purple, black, and buff paint. Height,

5 1/2″; diameter, 7 1/2″. Collection Stendahl.

Two circular crocodiles in juxtaposition are represented three times. The head is indicated only by an eye and jaws. The body is curved and has a pointed tail.

551. DISH WITH RING BASE. / Rio de Jesús, Veraguas, Panama. Late Coclé period (A.D. 1000–1200). Red clay with buff slip and red, black, and purple paint. Height, 2″; diameter, 11 3/4″. Collection Mr. and Mrs. Irwin Hersey, New York.

The design motif is a curled plumed serpent in fine-line style.

552. BIRD EFFIGY PEDESTAL BOWL. / Parita, Azuero Peninsula, Panama. Late Coclé period (A.D. 1000–1200). Red clay with buff slip and red and black paint. Height, 7 1/2″; diameter, 10 1/2″. Collection Philip L. Dade, Laguna Beach, Calif.

Broad protruding flanges represent the wings and tail (cf. Lothrop, 1942, fig. 449).

553. COLLARED GLOBULAR JAR WITH THREE BIRDS. / Rio de Jesús, Veraguas, Panama. Late Coclé period (A.D. 1000–1200). Reddish clay with buff slip and red, purple, and black paint. Height, 9 1/2″; diameter, 10 3/4″. Los Angeles County Museum of Natural History.

554. BREAST-PLAQUE REPRESENTING TWO DANCING ALLIGATORS BACK TO BACK. / Coclé, Panama. Beaten gold with repoussé design. Height, 8 1/4″. Thomas Gilcrease Institute of American History and Art, Tulsa, Okla.

The rim is decorated with alligator scales. There are tiny perforations on the upper and lower parts of the plaque for sewing the ornament onto a garment.

555/556. PLAQUES EACH REPRESENTING AN ALLIGATOR-GOD WITH SIX ALLIGATOR HEADS. / Parita, Azuero Peninsula, Panama. Beaten gold with embossed design. Above, 6″ square; below, 5 7/8″ square. Above: Los Angeles County Museum of Natural History; below: Collection Mr. and Mrs. Francis V. Crane, Marathon, Fla.

The figures are shown full face, arms extended and feet turned outward. The bodies are clearly human, but the hands and feet have claws. The perforations are for attachment to fabric. For a full discussion, see Lothrop, 1937, pp. 112–27. Columbus, on his fourth voyage, saw the caciques in Panama wearing similar ornaments as breast-plaques.

557. PLAQUE WITH TRIANGULAR FACE AND FIVE CONICAL PROJECTIONS. / Veraguas, Panama. Beaten gold with embossed design. Diameter, 7 3/8″. Thomas

Gilcrease Institute of American History and Art, Tulsa, Okla.

558. CIRCULAR PLAQUE WITH MYTHOLOGICAL FIGURE. / Coclé, Panama. Hammered gold with repoussé design. Diameter, 7″. Collection Stendahl.

Depicted is a standing male with his head bent backward. Three feathers form the headdress. A multiple volute emerges from his mouth, reminiscent of the Mesoamerican speech scroll. Both hands are similarly extended, showing the index finger and thumb in grip position. Attached to the front of the belt is a trophy head. Disks of this type were worn by warriors in battle to attract attention to their bravery. The decoration is similar to that on a gilded copper disk from the Sacred Cenote in Chichén Itzá, believed to be stylistically related to the frescoes in Santa Rita Corozal, northern British Honduras (Lothrop, 1952, fig. 60).

559–566. EIGHT PENDANTS. / Diquís region, Costa Rica. Cast gold. Height, 2 1/8″ to 4 1/4″. The Dumbarton Oaks Collections, Washington, D.C.

Top row: left, two bat-gods framed by two bars and vertical ropes; details are partially obscured by twelve danglers. Right, double-headed eagle, its heads partially obscured by two danglers and flanked by two jaguar heads. *Middle row:* left, twin alligators in Veragua style. Center, an anthropomorphic figure with a bird mask; the headdress consists of alligator bodies whose heads rest on the man's shoulders, and the hands are shaped like alligator heads. Right, alligator with four disks attached to its back. *Bottom row:* left, two bat-gods in a frame, tied with ropes around their hips and across their mouths. Center, an eagle with an alligator head and an oval opening in its body. Right, anthropomorphic deity with a small animal in its mouth.

567. HUMAN-BODIED FIGURE WITH DEER HEAD. / La Vaca, Punta Burica, Costa Rica. Cast gold. Height, 4 1/4″. Collection Jan Mitchell, New York.

568. PENDANT WITH TWO MALES IN CORD FRAME. / Chiriquí, Panama. Cast gold. Height, 2″. Collection Jan Mitchell, New York.

One of the men is blowing a twin flute, the other holds a staff. Alligator heads project from heads and knees.

569. JAGUAR PENDANT WITH SERPENT-HEADED TAIL. / Chiriquí, Panama. Cast gold. Length, 3 5/8″. Collection Jan Mitchell, New York.

570. PENDANT DEPICTING FIGURE WITH BIRDLIKE TAIL. / Palmar, Costa Rica. Cast gold. Height, 2 7/8″. Collection Jan Mitchell, New York.

The headdress consists of an ax-shaped ornament with lateral extensions containing alligator scales. The figure holds two axes with unusually accentuated V-shaped notches.

571. ALLIGATOR PENDANT. / Southern Costa Rica. Cast gold. Length, 5 1/4″. Collection Stendahl.

572/573/574. CAST GOLD PENDANTS. / *Above:* Eagle. Diquís region, Costa Rica. Height, 5 3/4″. *Below:* Anthropomorphic jaguar-gods. Chiriquí, Panama. Height: left, 4 7/8″; right, 3 3/4″. The Dumbarton Oaks Collections, Washington, D.C.

This eagle has a long beak which curves down to its body. The extremities and headdress of the god on the left terminate in alligator heads; such heads flank the figure and cap the knees of the god on the right.

Although the term eagle, applied because of the characteristic long beak, may not be an accurate term for the bird portrayed, it is used here since it is well established in the literature. These pendants were suspended from the wearer's neck by means of a string inserted in the loops on the back of the ornament.

575. PENDANT OF A WINGED ANTHROPOMORPHIC DEITY WITH FOUR DANGLERS. / Coclé, Panama. Cast gold. Height, 2″. Cleveland Museum of Art.

576. PENDANT REPRESENTING THE ALLIGATOR-GOD. / Coclé, Panama. Cast gold. Height, 2 7/8″. Cleveland Museum of Art.

Alligator heads project from the head and the base of the standing figure.

577. FROG PENDANT. / Veraguas, Panama. Cast gold. Height, 2 3/4″. Collection Stendahl.

578. DOUBLE-HEADED EAGLE PENDANT. / Veraguas, Panama. Cast gold. Height, 3 1/8″. Collection Amalia de Schulthess, Florence, Italy.

579. THREE ALLIGATORS. / Azuero Peninsula, Panama. Cast and soldered gold. Height, 2 3/4″. Collection Philip L. Dade, Laguna Beach, Calif.

The three pieces were attached by soldering to gold bars connecting the tails and feet.

580. PENDANT REPRESENTING A CRAYFISH. / Veraguas, Panama. Cast gold. Height, 3 1/4″. Cleveland Museum of Art.

581. ANTHROPOMORPHIC JAGUAR PENDANT. / Coclé, Panama. Cast gold. Height, 3 1/4″. Cleveland Museum of Art.

582. JOINED FIGURES HOLDING AXES AND CLUBLIKE OBJECTS. / Parita, Azuero Peninsula, Panama. Cast gold. Height, 5 5/8″. Denver Art Museum.

The inserts which composed the lower half of the figures are missing, as are the bangles which were at one time attached to six hook appendages.

583/584. TWO RINGS WITH FROG EFFIGIES ON EACH. / Parita, Azuero Peninsula, Panama. Cast gold. Finger size. Collection Philip L. Dade, Laguna Beach, Calif.

585. STANDING FIGURE. / Coclé style, Panama. Cast gold. Height, $2\,^1/_8$″. Collection Jan Mitchell, New York.

586/587/588. SEAHORSE AND TWO TUSK-SHAPED ORNAMENTS. / Venado Beach, Canal Zone. Cast gold. Height of seahorse, $2\,^1/_2$″; height of ornaments, $3\,^3/_4$″. Thomas Gilcrease Institute of American History and Art, Tulsa, Okla.

The seahorse is hollow, finished on all sides, and has two danglers suspended from the nose and two from the tail.

589. ANIMAL PENDANT. / Coclé style, Panama. Hollow cast gold. Height, 1″. Collection Jan Mitchell, New York.

590. ANIMAL PENDANT. / Coclé style, Panama. Hollow cast gold. Height, $1\,^1/_4$″. Collection Jan Mitchell, New York.

591/592. ANIMAL PENDANT. / Parita, Azuero Peninsula, Panama. Carved copal with sheet gold overlay. Height: left, $2\,^3/_4$″; right, 2″ standing as shown. Museum of the American Indian, Heye Foundation, New York.

The monkey on the left has gold overlay on his arms, tail, and one leg. The other leg is missing. The monkey on the right has gold overlay on his mouth, tail, and feet.

593. PENDANT. / Parita, Azuero Peninsula, Panama. Cast gold with bone insert. Height of gold portion, $2\,^1/_2$″; height of bone insert, $3\,^1/_2$″. Height assembled, $4\,^1/_2$″. Private collection.

The upper section represents the head of a zoomorphic deity, decorated with danglers. The hands hold rods which attach to the face mask. A carved bone alligator can be inserted half way, its body and tail forming the lower section of the pendant.

594/595. FISH PENDANTS. / *Left:* Veraguas, Panama. Cast gold and copper alloy. Length, $4\,^1/_2$″. *Right:* Venado Beach, Canal Zone. Cast gold with remnants of the clay and charcoal core still inside. Length, $3\,^1/_8$″. Collection Mr. and Mrs. Felix Guggenheim, Beverly Hills, Calif.

503. Human effigy vase.
*Filadelfia, Guanacaste, Costa Rica. Middle
Polychrome period. Cream slip on red clay with
black and red paint. Height, 12 $^1/_2$"; diameter, 9".*

504. Jaguar effigy *incensario.*
Filadelfia, Guanacaste, Costa Rica. Late Polychrome period. Light-brown and grayish clay with white paint. Height, 13 1/2".

505. Wide-lipped bowl with figure wearing alligator mask. *Filadelfia, Guanacaste, Costa Rica. Late Polychrome period. Red-brown clay, incised. Height, 8 1/2″; diameter, 13″.*

506. Cylindrical bowl.
Buenos Aires region of Costa Rica. Late Polychrome period. Reddish-brown and dark brown on buff clay. Height, 8 1/4″; diameter, 9 3/4″.

507. Plate with flaring sides and three hollow cylindrical rattle supports. *Filadelfia, Guanacaste, Costa Rica. Middle Polychrome period (A.D. 750–1000). Black and red on cream slip. Height, 6 1/4″; diameter, 5 5/8″.*

508. Effigy vase.
Filadelfia, Guanacaste, Costa Rica. Middle Polychrome period. Cream slip on red clay with black and red paint. Height, 12 1/2"; diameter, 9".

509. Jaguar effigy vase.
Filadelfia, Guanacaste, Costa Rica. Middle Polychrome period. Cream slip on red clay with black and red paint. Height, 14 1/2"; diameter, 10 1/2".

510. Globular pedestal bowl.
Filadelfia, Guanacaste, Costa Rica. Late Polychrome period. Red, blue, and black on cream slip. Height, 7 1/4"; diameter, 8".

511. Animal effigy jar.
Guanacaste, Costa Rica. Middle Polychrome period. Red, black, and purple on cream slip. Height, 11 1/2"; diameter, 11".

512. Human effigy vase.
Guanacaste, Costa Rica. Late Polychrome period.
Red clay with cream slip and red, black, and
brown paint. Height, 13"; diameter, 9".

513. Vase with annular base.
Filadelfia, Guanacaste, Costa Rica. Middle
Polychrome period. Cream slip on red clay with
black, red, and purple-brown paint. Height, 14";
diameter, 9 1/2".

514. Man with a jaguar mask holding an
alligator. *Diquís region, southwestern Costa Rica.
1000–1500(?). Brown sandstone. Height, 13".*

515. Seated medicine man blowing a flute.
*Guápiles region, Costa Rica. 1000–1500 (?).
Volcanic stone. Height, 12".*

516. Standing figure of man on peg base. *Cerro Gordo, Diquís region, southwestern Costa Rica. 1000–1500(?). Volcanic stone. Height, 34 3/4".*

517. Male figure with jaguar head and double serpent tongues. *Diquís region, southwestern Costa Rica. 700–1550(?). Sandstone. Height, 15 1/2".*

518. Standing woman with conical cap or headdress and tattoo marks on arms and chest. *Guápiles region, Costa Rica. 1000–1500(?). Volcanic stone. Height, 17".*

519. Armadillo sitting upright. *Guápiles region, Costa Rica. 1000–1500(?). Granitic rock. Height, 17".*

520/521. Seated figures with jaguar heads on peg base. *Northern Panama. 1000–1500(?).* *Volcanic stone. Height: left, 23 7/8″; right, 18 7/8″.*

522. Standing male holding trophy head and knife or ax. *Guápiles region, Costa Rica. 1000–1500(?). Volcanic stone. Height, 33″.*

523. Three Nicoya polychrome figurines.
Guanacaste, Costa Rica. Middle Polychrome period.
Red clay with cream slip and black and red paint.
Height, 6 1/2" to 8 3/4".

524. Mace-head representing a jaguar.
Nicoya Peninsula, Costa Rica. Early Polychrome
period. Stone. Height, 3".

525. Mace-head representing an animal.
Nicoya, Costa Rica. Early Polychrome period (?).
Light-green stone. Length, 7".

526. Seated man.
Filadelfia, Guanacaste, Costa Rica. Middle Polychrome period. Red clay with cream slip and red and black paint. Height, 7 3/4".

527. Seated woman.
Filadelfia, Guanacaste, Costa Rica. Middle Polychrome period(?). Red clay with ocher and red paint. Height, 5 1/4".

528. Antipodal figures.
Guanacaste, Costa Rica. Early Polychrome period(?). Hard light-green stone. Height, 5".

529. Ax-shaped human effigy pendants.
Guanacaste, Costa Rica. 700–1500(?). Hard light-green stone. Height, 5 1/4" to 6".

530. Mace-head in the form of a bird's head.
Guanacaste, Costa Rica. Early Polychrome period. Hard gray stone. Length, 3 1/2".

364

531. Two ax-shaped pendants.
*Guanacaste, Costa Rica. Early Polychrome
period (?). Hard greenish stone. Height: 4 3/4"
and 4 1/2" respectively.*

532. Mace-head representing a human head.
*Filadelfia, Guanacaste, Costa Rica. Early Polychrome
period (?). Onyx marble (alabaster). Height, 3 1/2".*

365

533. Jaguar effigy grindstone.
Guápiles region, Costa Rica. 800–1500(?).
Volcanic stone. Height, 12 1/2".

534. Jaguar effigy grindstone with raised rim.
Guápiles region, Costa Rica. 800–1500(?).
Volcanic stone. Height, 5 1/2".

535. Grindstone with flying panel.
San Isidro de Heredia, Costa Rica. 800–1500(?).
Volcanic stone. Height, 18 1/2".

536. Jaguar effigy grindstone.
Guanacaste, Costa Rica. 800–1500(?). Volcanic
stone. Height, 15 1/4".

537. Four-legged grindstone.
Veraguas, Panama. 800–1200(?). Volcanic stone.
Height, 20".

538. Muller with bird handle.
Veraguas, Panama. 800–1200(?). Basalt. Height,
5 1/2".

539. Grindstone with flying panel representing
serpents. *Veraguas, Panama. 800–1200(?).*
Volcanic stone. Height, 14".

540. Grindstone with Flying Panel.
Central Costa Rica. 800–1500. Volcanic stone.
Height, 24″.

541. Offering table fringed with small
human heads. *Chiriquí, Panama. 800–1200(?).*
Volcanic stone. Height, 8″; diameter, 13 1/2″.

542. Offering table supported by four
monkeys. *Veraguas, Panama. 800–1200(?).*
Volcanic stone. Height, 8″; diameter, 13 1/2″.

543. Jaguar effigy.
Coclé, Panama. Late Coclé period (A.D. 1000–1200). Red clay with cream slip and black paint. Height, 9".

544. Pisote (badger) effigy.
Coclé, Panama. Late Coclé period (A.D. 1000–1200). Clay with cream slip and red, purple, and black paint. Height, 11".

545. Pisote (badger) effigy.
Coclé, Panama. Late Coclé period (A.D. 1000–1200). Clay with cream slip and red, purple, and black paint. Height, 12 1/2".

546. Pedestal plate.
*Rio de Jesús, Veraguas, Panama. Late Coclé
period (A.D. 1000–1200). Red clay with red,
purple, buff, and black paint. Height, 6 1/4";
diameter, 10 1/4".*

547. Plate with ring base.
*Coclé, Panama. Early Coclé period (A.D. 500–
1000). Tan clay with orange slip and red and
black paint. Diameter, 12 1/2".*

548. Pedestal plate with four fish.
*Parita, Azuero Peninsula, Panama. Late Coclé
period (A.D. 1000–1200). Red clay with buff slip
and red, purple, and black paint. Height, 4";
diameter, 11".*

549. Pedestal plate.
*Rio de Jesús, Veraguas, Panama. Late Coclé
period (A.D. 1000–1200). Red clay with buff slip
and red, purple, blue, and black paint. Height,
7 1/2".*

550. Cylindrical bowl with pedestal base.
*Coclé, Panama. Late Coclé period (A.D. 1000–
1200). Red clay with red, purple, black, and buff
paint. Height, 5 ¹/₂"; diameter, 7 ¹/₂".*

551. Dish with ring base.
*Rio de Jesús, Veraguas, Panama. Late Coclé
period (A.D. 1000–1200). Red clay with buff slip
and red, black, and purple paint. Height, 2";
diameter, 11 ³/₄".*

552. Bird effigy pedestal bowl.
*Parita, Azuero Peninsula, Panama. Late Coclé
period (A.D. 1000–1200). Red clay with buff slip
and red and black paint. Height, 7 ¹/₂"; diameter,
10 ¹/₂".*

553. Collared globular jar with three birds.
*Rio de Jesús, Veraguas, Panama. Late Coclé period
(A.D. 1000–1200). Reddish clay with buff slip
and red, purple, and black paint. Height, 9 ¹/₂";
diameter, 10 ³/₄".*

554. Breast-plaque representing two dancing alligators back to back. *Coclé, Panama. Beaten gold with repoussé design. Height, 8 1/4".*

555/556. Plaques each representing an alligator-god with six alligator heads. *Parita, Azuero Peninsula, Panama. Beaten gold with embossed design. Above, 6" square; below, 5 7/8" square.*

567. Human-bodied figure with deer head.
La Vaca, Punta Burica, Costa Rica. Cast gold.
Height, 4 1/4".

568. Pendant with two males in cord frame.
Chiriquí, Panama. Cast gold. Height, 2".

569. Jaguar pendant with serpent-headed
tail. *Chiriquí, Panama. Cast gold. Length, 3 5/8".*

570. Pendant depicting figure with birdlike tail. *Palmar, Costa Rica. Cast gold. Height, 2 7/8".*

571 Alligator pendant.
Southern Costa Rica. Cast gold. Length, 5 1/4".

572/573/574. Cast gold pendants.
Above: Eagle. Diquís region, Costa Rica. Height,
5 ³/₄". Below: Anthropomorphic jaguar-gods.
Chiriquí, Panama. Height: left, 4 ⁷/₈"; right,
3 ³/₄".

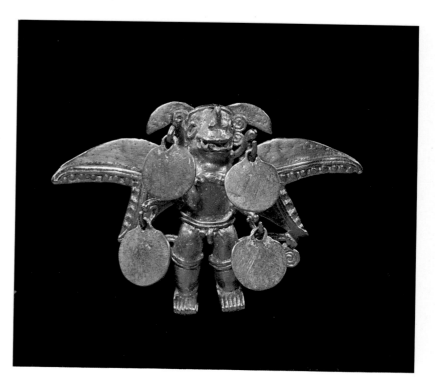

575. Pendant of a winged anthropomorphic
deity with four danglers. *Coclé, Panama. Cast*
gold. Height, 2".

576. Pendant representing the alligator-god.
Coclé, Panama. Cast gold. Height, 2 ⁷/₈".

577. Frog pendant.
Veraguas, Panama. Cast gold. Height, 2 ³/₄″.

578. Double-headed eagle pendant.
Veraguas, Panama. Cast gold. Height, 3 ¹/₈″.

579. Three alligators.
Azuero Peninsula, Panama. Cast and soldered gold. Height, 2 ³/₄″.

580. Pendant representing a crayfish.
Veraguas, Panama. Cast gold. Height, 3 ¹/₄″.

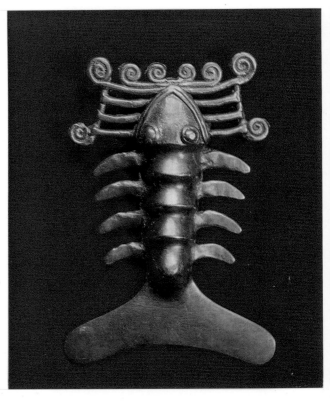

583/584. Two rings with frog effigies on each.
Parita, Azuero Peninsula, Panama. Cast gold.
Finger size.

585. Standing figure.
Coclé style, Panama. Cast gold.
Height, 2 1/8".

581. Anthropomorphic jaguar pendant.
Coclé, Panama. Cast gold. Height, 3 1/4".

582. Joined figures holding axes and clublike
objects. *Parita, Azuero Peninsula, Panama. Cast*
gold. Height, 5 5/8".

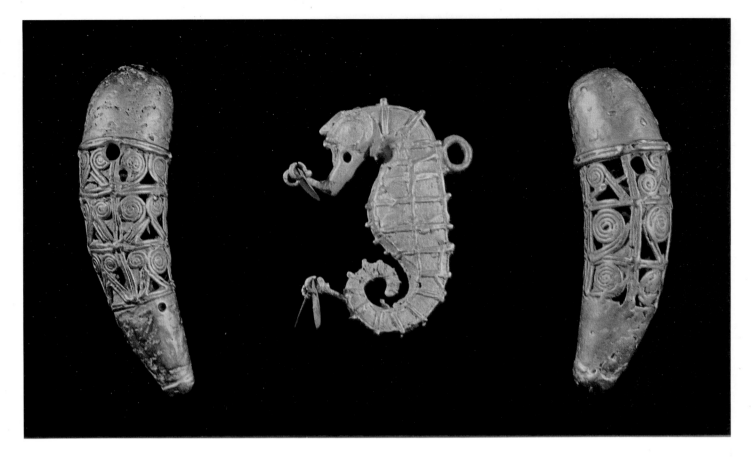

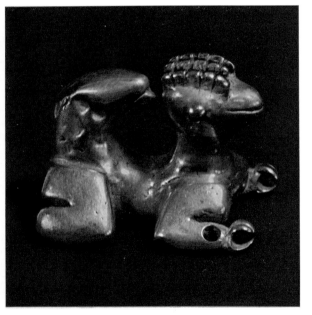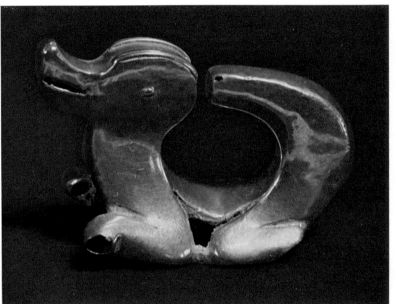

586/587/588. Seahorse and two tusk-shaped
ornaments. *Venado Beach, Canal Zone. Cast gold.
Height of seahorse, 2 1/2″; height of ornaments,
3 3/4″.*

589. Baby chick.
Coclé style, Panama. Hollow cast gold. Height, 1″.

590. Duck.
*Coclé style, Panama. Hollow cast gold. Height,
1 1/4″.*

591/592. Monkey pendants.
*Parita, Azuero Peninsula, Panama. Carved copal
with sheet gold overlay. Height: left, 2 3/4″;
right, 2″ standing as shown.*

593. Pendant.
*Parita, Azuero Peninsula, Panama. Cast gold with
bone insert. Height of gold portion, 2 1/2″;
height of bone insert, 3 1/2″. Height assembled,
4 1/2″.*

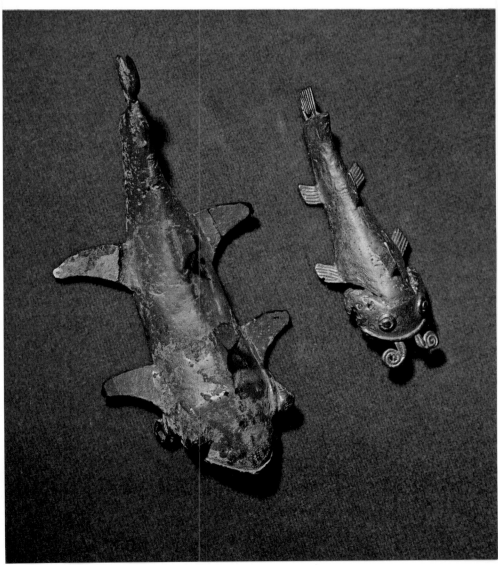

594/595. Fish pendants.
*Left: Veraguas, Panama. Cast gold and copper
alloy. Length, 4 1/2″. Right: Venado Beach, Canal
Zone. Cast gold with remnants of the clay and
charcoal core still inside. Length, 3 1/8″.*

BIBLIOGRAPHY

ACOSTA, JORGE R. 1958–59. "Exploraciones arqueológicas en Monte Albán," *Revista Mexicana de Estúdios Antropológicos* (Mexico), XV, pp. 7–49.

ALCINA, FRANCH, JOSE. 1961. "Pequeñas esculturas antropomorfas de Guerrero (Méjico)," *Revista de Indias* (Madrid), XXI, no. 84, pp. 295–349.

ANDERS, FERDINAND. 1963. *Das Pantheon der Maya.* Akademische Druck- und Verlagsanstalt, Graz.

Arte precolombino del occidente de México. 1946. Secretaría de Educación Pública, Mexico D.F.

BARTHEL, THOMAS S. 1964. "Epigraphische Marginalien" in: *Estúdios de Cultura Maya,* V. Mexico D.F.

———— 1967. "Notes on the Inscription on a Carved Bone from Yucatan" in: *Estúdios de Cultura Maya,* VI. Mexico D.F., pp. 223–41.

BAUDEZ, CLAUDE F. 1963. "Cultural Development in Lower Central America" in: *Aboriginal Cultural Development in Latin America* (Smithsonian Miscellaneous Collections, CXLVI, no. 1, pp. 45–54), Smithsonian Institution, Washington, D.C.

———— and MICHAEL D. COE. 1961. "Archaeological Sequences in Northwestern Costa Rica" in: *Akten des 34. Internationalen Amerikanistenkongresses,* pp. 366–73. Horn, Austria.

BERLIN, HEINRICH. 1956. "Late Pottery Horizons of Tabasco, Mexico," *Contributions to American Archaeology and History,* no. 59 (Carnegie Institution of Washington Publication 606). Washington, D.C.

BLISS COLLECTION. *See* LOTHROP, S. K. and others.

BOOS, FRANK H. 1966. *The Ceramic Sculpture of Ancient Oaxaca.* A. S. Barnes, New York.

BORHEGYI, STEPHAN F. DE. 1961. "Ball-game Handstones and Ball-game Gloves" in: *Essays in Pre-Columbian Art and Archaeology,* pp. 126–51. Harvard University Press, Cambridge, Mass.

CASO, ALFONSO. 1927. *El teocalli de la guerra sagrada* (Monografías del Museo Nacional de Arqueología, Historia y Etnografía). Mexico D.F.

———— 1933. "Idolos huecos de barro de tipo arcáico," *Anales del Museo Nacional de Arqueología, Historia y Etnografía* (Mexico D.F.), VIII, pp. 577–81.

———— 1938. *Thirteen Masterpieces of Mexican Archaeology.* Editoriales Cultura y Polis, Mexico D.F.

———— 1949. "Una urna con el dios mariposa," *El México Antiguo* (Mexico D.F.), VII, pp. 78–95.

———— and IGNACIO BERNAL. 1952. *Urnas de Oaxaca* (Memorias del Instituto Nacional de Antropología e Historia, II). Mexico D.F.

CODEX BORGIA. *Eine altmexikanische Bilderschrift der Bibliothek der Congregatio de Propaganda Fide.* Commentary by Eduard Seler. 3 vols. Berlin, 1904–9.

CODEX DRESDEN. *Die Maya-Handschrift der Sächsischen Landesbibliothek Dresden.* Dresden, 1962.

CODEX FLORENTINE. Illustrations for BERNARDINO DE SAHAGUN, *General History of the Things of New Spain.* Trans. from the Aztec by Charles E. Dibble and Arthur J. O. Anderson. Book 9: *The Merchants* (Monographs of the School of American Research and the Museum of New Mexico, no. 14, part X). The School of American Research and the University of Utah. Santa Fe, New Mexico, 1959.

CODEX LAUD. *Códice Laud.* Introduction and notes by Carlos Martínez Marín. *Instituto Nacional de Antropología e Historia, Serie Investigaciones 5.* Mexico D.F., 1961.

CODEX MENDOZA. Ed. and trans. by James Cooper Clark. 3 vols. London, 1938.

CODEX NUTTALL. *Ancient Mexican Codex Belonging to Lord Zouche of Haryngworth.* Introduction by Zelia Nuttall. Peabody Museum of American Archaeology and Ethnology. Cambridge, Mass., 1901.

COE, MICHAEL D. 1962. "Preliminary Report on Archaeological Investigations in Coastal Guanacaste, Costa Rica" in: *Akten des 34. Internationalen Amerikanistenkongresses,* pp. 358–65. Horn, Austria.

———— 1962. "Costa Rican Archaeology and Mesoamerica," *Southwestern Journal of Anthropology* (Albuquerque), XVIII, no. 2, pp. 170–83.

———— 1963. "Cultural Development in Southeastern Mesoamerica" in: *Aboriginal Cultural Development in Latin America* (Smithsonian Miscellaneous Collections, CXLVI, no. 1, pp. 27–44). Smithsonian Institution, Washington, D.C.

COE, WILLIAM R. 1962. "A Summary of Excavation and Research at Tikal, Guatemala: 1956–61," *American Antiquity* (Salt Lake City), XXVII, no. 4, pp. 479–507.

COVARRUBIAS, MIGUEL. 1957. *Indian Art of Mexico and Central America.* Alfred A. Knopf, New York.

DIESELDORFF, E. P. 1904. "A Clay Vessel with a Picture of a Vampire-headed Deity," *Bureau of American Ethnology Bulletin* 28, pp. 665–66. Washington, D.C.

DOCKSTADER, FREDERICK J. 1964. *Indian Art in Middle America.* New York Graphic Society, Greenwich, Conn.

DRUCKER, PHILIP. 1943. "Ceramic Sequences at Tres Zapotes, Veracruz, Mexico," *Bureau of American Ethnology Bulletin* 140. Washington, D.C.

———— 1943. "Ceramic Stratigraphy at Cerro de las Mesas, Veracruz, Mexico," *Bureau of American Ethnology Bulletin* 141. Washington, D.C.

EASBY, DUDLEY T., JR. 1956. "Ancient American Goldsmiths," *Natural History* (New York), LXV, pp. 401–9.

———— 1956. "Orfebrería y orfebres precolombinos," *Anales del Instituto de Arte Americano* (Buenos Aires), IX, pp. 21–35.

———— 1961. "Fine Metalwork in Pre-Conquest Mexico" in: *Essays in Pre-Columbian Art and Archaeology* by S. K. LOTHROP and others. Harvard University Press, Cambridge, Mass.

EISLEB, DIETER. 1961. "Steinplastiken im Mezcala-Stil aus den Sammlungen des Berliner Museums für Völkerkunde," *Baessler-Archiv* (Berlin), n.s. 9 (34), pp. 217–32.

EKHOLM, GORDON F. 1942. "Excavations at Guasave, Sinaloa, Mexico," *American Museum of Natural History Anthropological Papers,* XXXVIII, part 2. New York.

———— 1944. "Excavations at Tampico and Panuco in the Huasteca, Mexico," *American Museum of Natural History Anthropological Papers,* XXXVIII, part 5. New York.

———— 1949. "Palmate Stones and Thin Stone Heads: Suggestions on Their Possible Use," *American Antiquity* (Menasha, Wis.), XV, no. 1, pp. 1–9.

EMMERICH, ANDRE. 1965. *Sweat of the Sun and Tears of the Moon: Gold and Silver in Pre-Columbian Art.* University of Washington Press, Seattle.

Escultura precolombina de Guerrero. 1964. Universidad Nacional Autónoma de México, Mexico D.F.

Esplendor del México Antiguo. 1959. 2 vols. Centro de Investigaciones Antropológicas de México, Mexico D.F.

FIORESCANO, ENRIQUE. 1964. "La serpiente emplumada, Tlaloc y Quetzalcoatl," *Cuadernos Americanos* (Mexico D.F.), CXXXIII, no. 2, pp. 121–66.

FLORENTINE CODEX. *See* CODEX FLORENTINE.

FRANCO, JOSE LUIS. 1960. "Mezcala Gro.: Modelos planos de templos," *Centro de Investigaciones Antropológicas de México Bulletin* 7, pp. 3–6. Mexico D.F.

—— 1961. "Representaciones de la mariposa en Mesoamérica," *El México Antiguo* (Mexico D.F.), IX, pp. 195–244.

GANN, THOMAS. 1900. "Mounds in Northern Honduras," *Bureau of American Ethnology Annual Report* for 1897–1898, part 2, pp. 661–92. Washington, D.C.

—— 1925. *Mystery Cities: Exploration and Adventure in Lubaantun.* Duckworth, London.

GARCIA PAYON, JOSE. 1955. "La ofrenda del altar de la Gran Pirámide, Zempoala, Veracrúz," *El México Antiguo* (Mexico D.F.), VIII, pp. 57–65.

GROTH-KIMBALL, IRMGARD. 1960. *Maya Terrakotten.* Verlag Ernst Wasmuth, Tübingen. English ed.: *Mayan Terracottas.* Praeger, New York, 1961.

Guía Oficial, Sala de las Culturas del Golfo. 1957. Instituto Nacional de Antropología e Historia. Mexico D.F.

Handbook of the Robert Woods Bliss Collection of Pre-Columbian Art. 1963. The Dumbarton Oaks Collections, Washington, D.C.

HAWLEY, HENRY H. 1963. "A Maya Relief," *Bulletin of The Cleveland Museum of Art* (Cleveland), March, 1963, pp. 50–55.

Indigenous Art of the Americas, Collection of Robert Woods Bliss. 1947. National Gallery of Art, Smithsonian Institution, Washington, D.C.

KAPLAN, FLORA. 1961. "A Shell from Mexico," *El México Antiguo* (Mexico D.F.), IX, pp. 289–96.

KELEMEN, PAL. 1956. *Medieval American Art.* Macmillan, New York.

KELLY, ISABEL. 1949. "The Archaeology of the Autlan-Tuxcacuesco Area of Jalisco," *Ibero-Americana* (Berkeley), XXVII.

KIDDER, ALFRED V.; JESSE D. JENNINGS; EDWIN M. SHOOK. 1946. *Excavations at Kaminaljuyú, Guatemala* (Carnegie Institution of Washington Publication 561). Washington, D.C.

—— and CARLOS SAMAYOA CHINCHILLA. 1959. *The Art of Ancient Maya.* Thomas Y. Crowell, New York.

KIRCHHOFF, PAUL. 1946. "La cultura del occidente de México a través de su arte" in: *Arte Precolombino del Occidente de México,* pp. 49–69. Secretaría de Educación Pública, Mexico D.F.

KRICKEBERG, WALTER. 1948. "Das mittelamerikanische Ballspiel und seine religiöse Symbolik," *Paideuma* (Frankfort), III, no. 3–5, pp. 118–90.

—— 1956. *Altmexikanische Kulturen.* Safari-Verlag, Berlin.

KUBLER, GEORGE. 1954. *The Louise and Walter Arensberg Collection.* II: *Pre-Columbian Sculpture.* Philadelphia Museum of Art, Philadelphia.

—— 1962. *The Art and Architecture of Ancient America; the Mexican, Maya, and Andean Peoples* (Pelican History of Art). Penguin Books, Harmondsworth.

LEIGH, HOWARD. 1961. "Head Shrinking in Ancient Mexico," *Science of Man* (Garden Grove, Calif.), II, no. 1, pp. 4–7.

LINES, JORGE A. 1942. "Esbozo arqueológico de Costa Rica" in: *Actas, 27° Congreso Internacional de Americanistas, México, 1939,* pp. 217–22. Reprint with 40 illustrations not included in the *Actas* is cited in the present volume. Instituto Nacional de Antropología e Historia, Mexico D.F.

LINNE, SIGVALD. 1934. *Archaeological Researches at Teotihuacán, Mexico* (Ethnographic Museum of Sweden n.s. Publication 1), Stockholm.

—— 1938. *Zapotecan Antiquities and the Paulson Collection in the Ethnographic Museum in Stockholm* (Ethnographic Museum of Sweden n.s. Publication 4), Stockholm.

—— 1941. "Teotihuacan Symbols," *Ethnos* (Stockholm), VI, pp. 174–86.

—— 1942. *Mexican Highland Cultures: Archaeological Researches at Teotihuacan, Calpulalpan and Chalchicomula in 1934–35* (Ethnographic Museum of Sweden n.s. Publication 7), Stockholm.

—— 1943. "Humpbacks in Ancient America," *Ethnos* (Stockholm), VIII, pp. 161–86.

LONGYEAR, JOHN M. 1944. "Archaeological Investigations in El Salvador," *Memoirs of the Peabody Museum of Archaeology and Ethnology,* IX, no. 2. Cambridge, Mass.

—— 1952. *Copan Ceramics* (Carnegie Institution of Washington Publication 597). Washington, D.C.

LOTHROP, S.K. 1926. *Pottery of Costa Rica and Nicaragua.* 2 vols. Museum of the American Indian, Heye Foundation, New York.

—— 1937. "Coclé, an Archaeological Study of Central Panama," part 1. *Memoirs of the Peabody Museum of Archaeology and Ethnology,* VII. Cambridge, Mass.

—— 1938. *Inca Treasure as Depicted by Spanish Historians.* Publication 2, The Southwest Museum, Los Angeles.

—— 1942. "Coclé, an Archaeological Study of Central Panama," part 2. *Memoirs of the Peabody Museum of Archaeology and Ethnology,* VIII. Cambridge, Mass.

—— 1950. "Archaeology of Southern Veraguas, Panama," *Memoirs of the Peabody Museum of Archaeology and Ethnology,* IX, no. 3. Cambridge, Mass.

—— 1952. "Metals from the Cenote of Sacrifice, Chichén Itzá, Yucatan," *Memoirs of the Peabody Museum of Archaeology and Ethnology,* X, no. 2. Cambridge, Mass.

—— 1956. "Jewelry from the Panama Canal Zone," *Archaeology* (New York), IX, March, pp. 34–40.

—— 1963. "Archaeology of the Diquís Delta, Costa Rica," *Papers of the Peabody Museum of Archaeology and Ethnology,* LI. Cambridge, Mass.

—— 1964. *Treasures of Ancient America: the Arts of the Pre-Columbian Civilizations from Mexico to Peru.* Skira, Geneva.

LOTHROP, S. K. and others. 1957. *Pre-Columbian Art: Robert Woods Bliss Collection.* Phaidon, London.

—— 1961. *Essays in Pre-Columbian Art and Archaeology.* Harvard University Press, Cambridge, Mass.

LUMHOLTZ, CARL. 1904. "Decorative Art of the Huichol Indians," *Memoirs of the American Museum of Natural History,* III, part 3, pp. 281–327.

MALER, TEOBERT. 1903. "Researches in the Central Portion of the Usumatsintla Valley," part 2, chapter 13. *Memoirs of the Peabody Museum of Archaeology and Ethnology,* II, no. 2. Cambridge, Mass.

MARQUINA, IGNACIO. 1951. "Arquitectura prehispánica," *Memorias del Instituto Nacional de Antropología e Historia,* 1. Mexico D.F.

MASON, J. ALDEN. 1945. "Costa Rican Stonework; the Minor C. Keith Collection," *Anthropological Papers of the American Museum of Natural History,* XXXIX, part 3. New York.

MEDELLIN ZENIL, ALFONSO. 1960. *Cerámicas del Totonacapan; exploraciones arqueológicas en el centro de Veracrúz.* Universidád Veracruzana, Xalapa.

NICHOLSON, H. B. 1962. "Pre-Hispanic Central Mexico: Major Sculpture." Mimeographed. Submitted for publication in *Handbook of Middle American Indians.* University of Texas Press, Austin. (in press)

NOGUERA, EDUARDO. 1962. "Nueva clasificación de figurillas del horizonte clásico," *Cuadernos Americanos* (Mexico D.F.), CXXIV, no. 5, pp. 127–36.

PADDOCK, JOHN (ed.). 1966. *Ancient Oaxaca: Discoveries in Mexican Archaeology and History.* Stanford University Press, Stanford, Calif.

PAZ, OCTAVIO and A. MEDELLIN ZENIL. 1962. *Magia de la risa.* Universidád Veracruzana, Xalapa.

PORTER, MURIEL N. 1956. "Excavations at Chupícuaro, Guanajuato, Mexico," *Transactions of the American Philosophical Society* (Philadelphia), n.s. XLVI, part 5.

Präkolumbische Kunst aus Mexiko und Mittelamerika. Catalogue of the first showing, October-December, 1958, in the Haus der Kunst, Munich, of a traveling exhibition. Successive showings, with respective catalogues, were held in Zurich, Paris, The Hague, Berlin, and Vienna in 1959, and in Frankfort and Rome in 1960.

PROSKOURIAKOFF, TATIANA. 1950. *A Study of Classic Maya Sculpture* (Carnegie Institution of Washington Publication 593). Washington, D.C.

—— 1954. "Varieties of Classic Central Veracruz Sculpture," *Contributions to American Archaeology and History,* XII, no. 58 (Carnegie

Institution of Washington Publication 606: 2). Washington, D.C.

RUZ LHUILLIER, ALBERTO. 1958. "Exploraciones arqueológicas en Palenque: 1954," *Anales del Instituto Nacional de Antropología e Historia* (Mexico D.F.), X, pp. 117–84.

SAENZ, CESAR A. 1961. "Tres estelas en Xochicalco," *Revista Mexicana de Estudios Antropológicos* (Mexico D.F.), XVII, pp. 39–66.

———— 1962. "Xochicalco; temporada 1960," *Informes del Instituto Nacional de Antropología e Historia* (Mexico D.F.), no. 11.

SAHAGUN, FRAY BERNARDINO DE. *See* CODEX FLORENTINE.

SELER, EDUARD. 1908. *Gesammelte Abhandlungen zur amerikanischen Sprach- und Altertumskunde*, III. Berend & Co., Berlin.

———— 1915. *Gesammelte Abhandlungen zur amerikanischen Sprach- und Altertumskunde*, V. Berend & Co., Berlin.

SHEPARD, ANNA O. 1956. *Ceramics for the Archaeologist* (Carnegie Institution Publication 609). Washington, D.C.

STONE, DORIS Z. 1938. "Masters in Marble," *Middle American Research Series* 8, part 1. Tulane University, New Orleans.

———— 1941. "Archaeology of the North Coast of Honduras," *Memoirs of the Peabody Museum of Archaeology and Ethnology*, IX, no. 1. Cambridge, Mass.

———— 1961. "The Stone Sculpture of Costa Rica" in: *Essays in Pre-Columbian Art and Archaeology*, pp. 192–209. Harvard University Press, Cambridge, Mass.

Tenayuca: estudio arqueológico de la pirámide de este lugar. 1935. Secretaría de Educación Pública, Mexico D.F.

The Olmec Tradition. 1963. Catalogue of an exhibition shown from June 18 to August 25, 1963. The Museum of Fine Arts, Houston.

THOMPSON, J. ERIC S. 1956. *The Rise and Fall of Maya Civilization*. University of Oklahoma Press, Norman.

———— 1957. "Deities Portrayed in Censers at Mayapan," *Carnegie Institution of Washington Current Reports* no. 40, pp. 599–632. Washington, D.C.

TOZZER, ALFRED M. 1957. "Chichen Itzá and Its Cenote of Sacrifice: A Comparative Study of Contemporaneous Maya and Toltec," *Memoirs of the Peabody Museum of Archaeology and Ethnology* XI, XII. Cambridge, Mass.

VAILLANT, GEORGE C. 1931. "Excavations at Ticoman," *Anthropological Papers of the American Museum of Natural History* XXXII, part 2. New York.

———— 1962. *Aztecs of Mexico*. Revised by Suzannah B. Vaillant. Doubleday, Garden City.

VON WINNING, HASSO. 1947. "Certain Types of Stamped Decoration on Pottery from the Valley of Mexico," *Notes of the Carnegie Institution of Washington* no. 86, pp. 202–13. Washington, D.C.

———— 1947. "A Symbol for Dripping Water in the Teotihuacan Culture," *El México Antiguo* (Mexico D.F.), VI, pp. 333–41.

———— 1948. "The Teotihuacan Owl–and–Weapon Symbol and Its Association with 'Serpent Head X' at Kaminaljuyú," *American Antiquity* (Menasha, Wis.), XIV, no. 2, pp. 129–32.

———— 1958. "Figures with Movable Limbs from Ancient Mexico," *Ethnos* (Stockholm), XXIII, no. 1, pp. 1–60.

———— 1958. "An Unusual Incense Burner from Colima," *Masterkey* (Los Angeles), XXXII, no. 2, pp. 40–42.

———— 1959. "Eine keramische Dorfgruppe aus dem alten Nayarit im westlichen Mexico" in: *Amerikanistische Miszellen* (Festband Franz Termer). *Mitteilungen aus dem Museum für Völkerkunde* (Hamburg), XXV, pp. 138–43.

———— 1959. "A Decorated Bone Rattle from Culhuacan, Mexico," *American Antiquity* (Salt Lake City), XXV, no. 1, pp. 86–93.

———— 1959. "An Incised Bone Artifact from Cholula, Mexico," *Masterkey* (Los Angeles), XXXIII, no. 2, pp. 67–70.

———— 1959. "El Sacerdocio" in: *Esplendor del México Antiguo*, I, pp. 141–48. Centro de Investigaciones Antropológicas de México, Mexico D.F.

———— 1959. "The Montgomery Collection of Early Meso-American Pottery and Figurines," *Masterkey* (Los Angeles), XXXIII, no. 3, p. 94–102.

———— 1960. "Further Examples of Figurines on Wheels from Mexico," *Ethnos* (Stockholm), XXV, no. 1–2, pp. 63–72.

———— 1961. "Teotihuacan Symbols: the Reptile's Eye Glyph," *Ethnos* (Stockholm), XXVI, no. 3, pp. 121–66.

———— 1961. "Two Figurines with Movable Limbs from Veracruz, Mexico," *Masterkey* (Los Angeles), XXXV, no. 4, 140–46.

———— 1961. "A Relief-decorated Aztec Stone Block," *El México Antiguo* (Mexico D.F.), IX, pp. 461–72.

———— 1962. "Two Pottery Molds in Maya-Toltec Style," *Masterkey* (Los Angeles), XXXVI, no. 3, pp. 87–96.

———— 1963. "Una vasija de alabastro con decoración en relieve" in: *Estudios de Cultura Maya*, III, pp. 113–18. Mexico D.F.

———— 1967. "Una vasija-sonaja Maya de doble fondo" in: *Estudios de Cultura Maya*. Mexico D.F., pp. 243–50.

WASSEN, S. HENRY. 1960. "A Find of Coclé-style Pottery in a Single Veraguas Grave, Panama," *Annual Reports of the Etnografiska Museet, 1957–1958*, pp. 62–81. Gothenburg.

WILLEY, GORDON R. 1966. *An Introduction to American Archaeology*. I: *North and Middle America*. Prentice Hall, Englewood Cliffs, N.J.

WRIGHT, NORMAN P. *El enigma de xoloitzcuintli*. Instituto Nacional de Antropología e Historia, Mexico D.F.

PHOTO CREDITS

Ferdinand Anton, Munich 440; Sid Avery and Associates, Los Angeles 68; Floyd Faxon, Los Angeles 52, 142, 147, 160, 185, 197, 216, 298, 331, 339, 358, 359, 368, 369, 388, 539, 542; Peter Furst, Los Angeles 237; Carmelo Guadagno, New York 428, 492, 524, 591, 592; Wolfgang R. Hartmann, New York 49; Herz, Tel Aviv 327; Hickey and Robertson, Houston 42, 43; Joseph Klima, Jr., Detroit 423; L. W. Love, Atlanta 106; Stuart Lynn, New Orleans 540; Nickolas Muray, New York 431, 449, 572–74, 559–66; Parade Studios, Cleveland 51, 429, 593; William Reagh, Los Angeles 20, 228, 340; Armand Solis, Los Angeles 253, 259; Bob J. Shultz, Los Angeles 270, 271; Julius Shulman, Los Angeles 2, 4, 59, 62, 64, 77, 79, 90, 93, 99, 112, 118, 151, 170, 181, 189, 218, 219, 240, 257, 258, 285, 378, 414, 416, 505; Soichi Sunami, New York 186; Charles Uht, New York 10, 56, 205, 292, 330, 516, 535; Wettstein & Kauf, Zurich 191.